Aubrey Beardsley

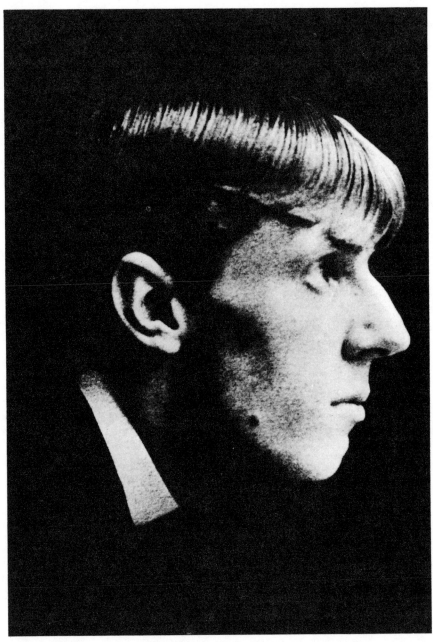

Aubrey Beardsley *(Courtesy of The Bodley Head Ltd.)*

Title page art *(Courtesy of Fogg Art Museum, Harvard University, Grenville L. Winthrop Bequest)*

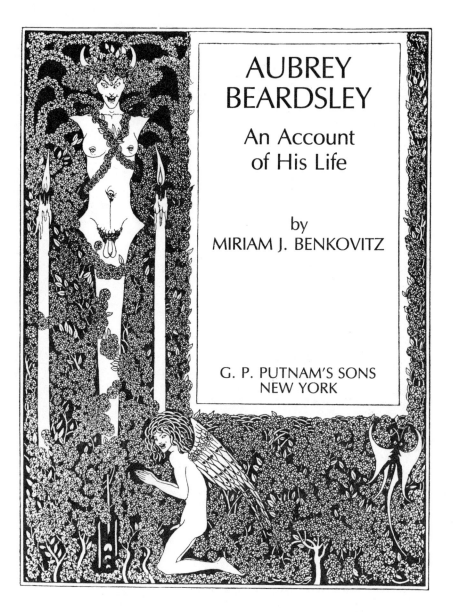

AUBREY BEARDSLEY

An Account of His Life

by
MIRIAM J. BENKOVITZ

G. P. PUTNAM'S SONS
NEW YORK

*To the memory of
my Mother*

Library of Congress Cataloging in Publication Data

Benkovitz, Miriam J.
  Aubrey Beardsley, an account of his life.

  Bibliography: p.
  Includes index.
  1. Beardsley, Aubrey Vincent, 1872-1898.
2. Artists—Great Britain-Biography. I. Title.
NC242.B3B38 1980   741'.092'4 [B] 80-13356
ISBN 0-399-12408-X

PRINTED IN THE UNITED STATES OF AMERICA

FOREWORD

Material about Aubrey Beardsley is abundant. He and his work were discussed often in newspapers and journals during his lifetime, and numerous acquaintances began to record their versions of him almost as soon as he was laid to rest. As the years passed, interest in Beardsley was unflagging, with A. E. Gallatin and R. A. Walker in particular contributing much to its vitality. Since the great exhibition of Beardsleyana mounted under the direction of Brian Reade at the Victoria and Albert Museum in 1966, writers on life and design have produced valuable comments. These include books and articles by Brigid Brophy, Kenneth Clark, W. G. Good, Mr. Reade, and Stanley Weintraub.

Beardsley's ability as an artist explains much of that continuing interest. His association with the best that was known and thought in his day—despite the scandal and gossip often attached to it—is responsible as well. At the same time, the question of Beardsley's character still provokes considerable discussion. Part of the problem is that a man who lives less than twenty-six years has little time to fix his character. Besides, as Mr. Good put it, Beardsley usually "kept to himself". As a result, Aubrey Beardsley has been credited with great evil and great saintliness.

In an attempt to evaluate Beardsley's character more precisely, I have depended first of all on his letters, so ably edited by Henry Maas, J. L. Duncan, and W. G. Good. Occasionally, I have corrected a date or supplemented incomplete letters by means of autograph letters to or about Beardsley or other autograph material in the collection of the Princeton University Library. Further corrections or additions have come from Catalogue 165 of Dulau & Co., *Books from the Library of John Lane and other Books of the Eighteen-Nineties*, compiled by Percy Muir in 1930 and lent to me by George F. Sims. Additional sources for valuable material have been Mr. Good and Mr. Reade.

Other manuscript material has been made available to me by Suzanne Bolan, Director of the Phililp H. & A. S. W. Rosenbach Foundation; J. A. Edwards, Archivist of Reading University Library; Kenneth A. Lohf, Librarian for Rare Books and Manuscripts, Columbia University Libraries; Richard M. Ludwig, Assistant University Librarian for Rare Books & Special Collections, and Alfred A. Bush, Curator, both of the Princeton University Library; and Lola Szladits, Curator of the Henry W. and Albert A. Berg Collection, The New York Public Library.

The Reference Department of Scribner Library, Skidmore College, has been tireless in providing material already published. I have also had help with published material from the Wilburs of the Grammercy Bookshop, Robert Mueller of J. Stephan Lawrence, and Anthony Rota, John Byrne, and Arthur Uphill of Bertram Rota Ltd.

Alan Clodd and Timothy d'Arch Smith have helped in many ways. Jean Lambert made a motor trip to Dieppe both pleasant and informative. Eunice and Earl Pardon tried to teach me not only to look at Beardsley's drawings but to see them as well. In addition I wish to acknowledge assistance of various kinds from Karl Beckson, the Newspaper Library of The British Library, Columbia University Libraries, Bernard R. Crystal, Elaine Davis, Ian Fleming, Alvin Gammage, Lynn Gelber, Laurence Josephs, Philip Kaplan, T. G. Kay, Frank Kermode, Gwen Kerr, T. S. Kraweic, Malcolm S. Lawrence, Patricia-Ann Lee, Phyllis and L. S. Marchand, Ben Meiselman, Gloria Moore, Winifred Myers, The New York Public Library, Astor, Lenox and Tilden Foundations, Princeton University Library, Reading University Library, R. T. Risk, The Philip H. and A. S. W. Rosenbach Foundation, John Ryder, Carl Schwartzman, Beryl Sims, Barbara Smith, The Humanities Research Center of the University of Texas at Austin, Patricia A. Weller, Julia K. Williams and the porters' desk of various hotels in Brighton, Dieppe, Paris, and especially that of the Westbury Hotel, London.

Miriam J. Benkovitz

July 1979

I had in his presence a greater sense of power than has come to me from any young man of his age.

William Butler Yeats

C'est très grave ce que vous pensez faire, très grave, mais si enfin vous tenez quand même à être artiste, un bon artiste, eh bien, monsieur, faites de lignes, rien que des lignes.

Jean Ingres to Edgar Degas

PROLOGUE

F OR Aubrey Beardsley, the year from mid-April 1894 to the same time in 1895 was a miraculous period. The year before it and the one after were rewarding, but in no way did they equal that period 1894–1895 in gratification and enjoyment. The poet John Keats had a similar year. Perhaps life gives it as compensation to the very gifted who will die in the youthful flowering of their promise. But for Beardsley, as for Keats, the year proved to be fragile; it bloomed and it was gone. Still, it might be called Beardsley's *annus mirabilis;* and, while it lasted, it was glorious.

On a practical level, Beardsley had security for that brief time. He lived and worked in a house in Cambridge Street, Pimlico, which he and Mabel, his sister, had recently purchased. The house was an ordinary one, very like its neighbors. But it was precious to the Beardsleys; it was the first and only home of their own. During most of 1894 and early 1895, Aubrey Beardsley seemed well. His tubercular lungs appeared to be healing. He suffered no hemorrhages until November and then he improved rapidly. Furthermore, for once in his life, Beardsley's financial position was stable. He owed a few bills—his tailor's, as usual, and a book bill for which he could pay with a drawing—but his income was reasonable and steady and it seemed safe.

That apparent security came from Beardsley's association with *The Yellow Book*. It made its first appearance on April 16, 1894, with six of Beardsley's drawings, including those for both upper and lower covers and the title-page; and for the next year, *The Yellow Book* and Aubrey Beardsley were almost synonymous. In March 1894, he had attracted considerable comment with his illustrations for the English-language edition of Oscar Wilde's *Salome*. They were called extravagant, "audacious," a "piquant maddening potion." And now, in the public mind, the "yellow nineties" and Beardsley were inseparable. Certainly many of his drawings for *The Yellow Book* warranted notice. Significant examples of Beardsley's picture-making powers in that first issue are drawings for the title-page, the one called *Night Piece*, and a portrait of the actress Mrs. Patrick Campbell. All are subtly influenced by the Japanese print, all show enormous economy of line. Perhaps the portrait of Mrs. Campbell is most representative. In it, without articulating perspective, without reproducing factual space, Beardsley created the illusion of space. His typically left-curving, upward diagonal line, which sets the drawing on the page, leads to a focal point, the black blot of his subject's hair and headdress, emphasized by a single white flower. And all his lines, whether white on black or black on white, produce a spatial and very subtle ambiguity, a tension between black and white which developed later, in other artists, as abstraction.

Because of *The Yellow Book*, Beardsley was sought after and gazed at and imitated. Between naughty swirls of their skirts and naughtier dance-steps which exposed their knees, music hall soubrettes sang out his name from the stage of the Gaiety. He was invited to teas, to garden parties, to at-homes on every day of the week. He was often at the Café Royal, sprawled on a red plush banquette before a marble table; or at Jimmy's for kidneys or oysters; or the Crown, a pub in Charing Cross Road, where endless talk was washed down with hot gin and water. He knew Edward Burne-Jones and Sir Frederick Leighton, George Moore and William Butler Yeats and Henry James and Edmund Gosse, Herbert Beerbohm Tree and Mrs. Campbell and Réjane. His associates, each successful and each well known in his way, included Oscar Wilde, briefly, and Wilde's "Sphinx," Ada Leverson, and her husband. It included, too, William Rothenstein, Max Beerbohm, the Joseph Pennells, and the entire *Yellow Book* set. That meant John Lane, its publisher, and Henry Harland, its editor, and his wife Aline and the contributors to the periodical, both writers and artists—Netta Syrett, Ella D'Arcy, Pearl Craigie (who called herself John Oliver Hobbes), Walter Sickert, Richard Le Gallienne, Kenneth Grahame, Victoria Cross and many more. These were not fashionable nor were they of high birth and noble lineage. They were, or so they said of themselves, intellectuals, artists. And as such were they not something superior? Were they not, as they declared, the very "salt of the earth"? And Aubrey Beardsley was prominent among them.

CHAPTER I

AUBREY Vincent Beardsley was born at Brighton on August 21, 1872, the son of Ellen Agnus Pitt and Vincent Beardsley. Aubrey was the second of their two children. Mabel, the first, was a year less three days older, her birth date being August 24, 1871. She, too, was born at Brighton at 12 (now 31) Buckingham Road. The house at 12 Buckingham Road was the home of Surgeon-Major William Pitt, Retired, who had returned to Brighton, the place of his boyhood, after service with the East India Company at Bengal and after a brief stay on the island of Jersey. At Brighton, with his wife and three daughters, Pitt had settled into the three-story house at the corner of Buckingham Road and West Hill Place, a quiet location well away from the Front. His household was an expansive one with the easy comfort of servants, overly sump-tuous meals, and much coming and going of family members. To that household Ellen had come to have both her children and to recover after their births.

Ellen, William Pitt's middle daughter, had allowed herself to be approached by Vincent Beardsley, a visitor come from London in search of pleasure or health or both (he was tubercular), on Brighton Pier. It was hardly a conventional thing to do; but to Ellen, Vincent implied real adventure with his city ways, his free spending from a small inheritance left him by an inn-keeping grandfather, his sad eyes and luxuriant moustache. She failed to notice that it covered a surly mouth and that at thirty-one he was already getting bald. Despite the fact that they were never formally introduced, they courted each other in the "trite lawns" of the Pavilion. And eventually Ellen led him to the house in Buckingham Road for approval from the Surgeon-Major and the rest of her family, and then to the altar. On October 12, 1870, less than two months after her twenty-fourth birthday, Ellen and Vincent Beardsley were married in the Church of Saint Nicholas of Myra at the height of a violent storm.

The storm might have predicted the quality of their marriage, but in fact it lacked even the fire of clashing temperaments to explain its character. It merely languished into indifference. It disintegrated. Immediately after their wedding the bride and groom went to London, where they took lodgings with Henry Russell, a music hall performer, and Mrs. Russell. There Vincent fathered Mabel and Aubrey. After that he recedes into the background of the Beardsleys' family life. His little money vanished. Some of it went within a year after his marriage to pay off a widow who maintained that he had promised to marry her. He sold his London property, a house in Euston Road, and what was left of his inheritance, if anything was, dwindled away with the expenses of a wife and children. For the rest of her life Ellen was separated from the plenty she had known in her father's home, and the question of money or the lack of it plagued the Beardsleys without let-up.

Both Vincent and Ellen were eventually forced to find jobs. Her employment was suitable to a lady of genteel background; from time to time she worked as a governess or a music teacher or both when family circumstances demanded it. Vincent was employed by the New Westminster Brewery Co. of Earl Street as early as 1873, and he was still with them in late 1887. At some point in the seventies, he worked with the West India and Panama Telegraph Co., possibly interrupting his job with the Westminster Brewery for a brief time. His next employer was Crawley & Co.'s Alton Ale Stores, 45 Wandsworth Road, Vauxhall. That job continued at least until January 23, 1883, but it very likely ended shortly thereafter. Occasionally, Vincent worked as a clerk for various wine merchants.[1] As the years went by, his eyes grew angry and his mouth, still under a moustache, tight and bitter. The insignificance of his appearance went unchanged.

Except for the fact that he was present at Mabel's wedding in late September 1903, Vincent Beardsley's participation in family life was negligible, and he is seldom mentioned. Certainly Aubrey Beardsley's references to his father are infrequent. In 1878, when he was six, Aubrey sent a note to his father, expressing love. Several times, as a small boy, in letters to his mother or sister, Aubrey sent love to Vincent. Thereafter, in all his surviving letters, Aubrey alluded only twice more to his father.[2]

Ellen dominated the Beardsleys' life both in day-to-day practices and in aspirations. After Aubrey was born, she was ill a long while with puerperal fever; but when she took her son to London, Ellen returned to an established pattern. Both the children had been born in her father's home. Any of their needs which she could not meet were met by her family or friends according to her decisions. She and not her husband solved their financial problems. She gave an impermanent aura to their entire existence by the fact that the family had no home of its own. With or without Vincent, in London or elsewhere, the Beardsleys were either in lodgings or a flat made from someone's home. In other ways, too, she set the tone of their life. Ellen Beardsley later told how, each evening, she played six pieces on the piano for the edification of her husband and two children, willing captives or not. In that way, she said, she gave them variety and "the best music." She supervised their reading, too, so that at least the children had their minds unsullied by "rubbish." One result was that at an early age Mabel had read Scott and Dickens, although at six she refused to read Carlyle.[3]

Mabel, at six, may have set her foot down, but Ellen Beardsley was still "one" with her "dearest boy," Aubrey—or so she said. Later he, too, demonstrated a mind of his own, and his mother could do no more than lament "his little tempers & naughtinesses." But as a small boy, Aubrey was "gentle, affectionate, whimsical."[4] He was also, even from birth, a frail child. His sister spoke of his "extreme fragility" and compared him to a "delicate little piece of Dresden china." She said that once "he helped himself . . . by a fern up a high flight of steps."[5] If any of that worried his mother, she gave no evidence of it, saying only that he was "Pucklike." But she stressed his instinctive awareness of music. Before Aubrey had reached his first birthday, he "was accustomed to crawl to the piano and sit down close beside it," waiting for his mother to play. When she did, he kept time with a toy. In an effort "to try and put him out—from four time to six," she changed the beat, but Aubrey was not confused. As soon as he was old enough, she began to teach him music.

Of course, all her efforts were not spent on Aubrey. Ellen taught Mabel "recitations, the expressions and so on." At times they both "got so worked up over something sad" that they paused to "cry in each other's arms, and then dry" their eyes and "go on again." They went on long enough for Mabel to learn material from a number of writers, but she relied especially on Dickens. She was able to "recite from *Pickwick* for two hours on end," doing the "skating scene too wonderfully."[6]

But Ellen Beardsley took greater pride in her son's very early ability to play Chopin and the fact that, at the age of four, he "listened intently" and with enjoyment to a symphony concert at the Crystal Palace.[7] She made sure that Aubrey's musical interests were fostered whether he was at home or at school. When his music teacher at his first school failed to allow him a "tune," Ellen sent him

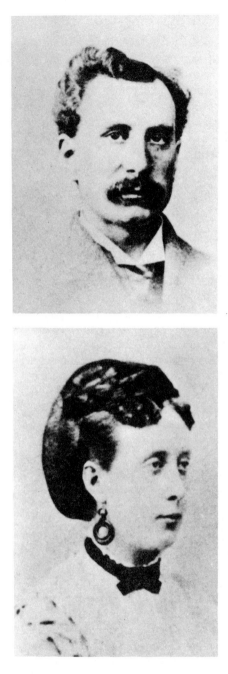

Left, Vincent Paul Beardsley, Aubrey's father. Below, Aubrey Beardsley at the age of two *(Courtesy of The Bodley Head Ltd.)*

Left, Ellen Agnus Beardsley, Aubrey's mother *(Courtesy of The Bodley Head Ltd.)*

a sonata (although by that time he was learning to play "Fading Away"), and she inquired over and over in letters about his progress.[8]

ii

Aubrey Beardsley's first school was Hamilton Lodge in Hurstpierpoint, a village mildly notable for the application of its name to one of Ronald Firbank's characters and for its magnificent oaks. It is located some eight miles over the South Downs from Brighton. The school was operated by a Miss Wise and a Miss Barnett, one or both of whom may have been friends of Ellen Beardsley. But the chief reason she chose the school for her son was its presumably healthful situation. Aubrey, aged seven, showed signs of tuberculosis.

Aubrey went to Hamilton Lodge reluctantly. He was a timid little boy who suffered in his imagination[9] and who anticipated every possible difficulty. But the school proved to be more endurable than he had thought possible. The entire school was taken to circuses, to fêtes, and for long walks. The boys were fed pudding daily, they had a dog named Fido, and they did not tease young Beardsley. After Christmas, he started music lessons with Miss Barnett, who, he declared, was "nearly bald" with teaching him.

When he returned for his second year at Hamilton Lodge, Aubrey had adjusted to school life. He was enough at ease to add to his pastimes the composition of verses in pseudo-Chaucerian language, which he recorded in a decorative script. He also began to draw. At first he copied drawings of cathedrals and then he began work on a carnival, "a long series of grotesque figures in colour."[10] But the most convincing testimony to Aubrey's acceptance of school life occurred when he violated a rule of Hamilton Lodge and Miss Wise, the headmistress, punished him with a whipping. She was determined to make him cry. He was determined to be as stoic as schoolboy myth required and not to utter so much as a whimper. As his mother might well have said, he was resolved to "shine" with his schoolmates. That word "shine" as Ellen Beardsley applied it to her son is slang, of course; but it is delineative slang, since it suggests both an origin of behavior and a consequence. On this simple level, the consequence is implicit in the word itself, to exhibit brilliance. In the matter of origin, psychiatrists might talk not of vanity, as Mrs. Beardsley did, but of fantasy and role-playing. For psychiatrists, fantasy of this sort, common among the gifted, is derived from an unsatisfactory reality. For Beardsley, each instance of role-playing was determined by the

21

person or persons whose role he played and, hopefully, outplayed. And each role was momentary. As he grew older and both his situation and his emotions grew more complex, naturally his roles and his reasons for them became more complex too. Now and then, they persisted over a period of time. Fantasy, role-playing, was a practice which was to serve him and which he was to serve all his life. Only in his last weeks or even days did he abandon it. This time Beardsley was eminently successful. He refused to cry and Miss Wise had to "give in."[11]

Aubrey Beardsley did not return to Hamilton Lodge after the end of the school year 1881. Despite constant assurance in his letters that he was "quite well," that he needed no medicine, that he was happy, Aubrey could not convince his mother. In the autumn of 1881 she took him to Epsom for a stay of about two years so that he might "get strong." There they lodged with Mrs. Mary Anne Clarke at 2 Ashley Villas in Ashley Road. Mabel was with them, but whether Vincent was is uncertain. He was employed at that time by Crawley's Brewery at Vauxhall, and he may have gone daily to London by train or he may have spent the work days in London and Sundays with his family.[12]

Indeed little is certain about the Beardsleys' stay in Epsom or about the next few years of Aubrey's life. Possibly in Epsom Aubrey earned his first fee from drawings, £30 paid him by Lady Henrietta Pelham. He wrote to her from Epsom about drawings copied from books she had given him and offered to make more drawings for a bazaar.[13] But the payment was for a set of menu and guest cards decorated with figures copied from Kate Greenaway. Besides, if Lady Henrietta, who was one of Ellen's acquaintances, commissioned Aubrey out of pity for the Beardsleys' desperate poverty, as some accounts say, then his first earnings came after the family returned to London in 1883. Mabel stated that he earned the £30 then.[14]

In either case, the fee was extremely welcome, and Aubrey knew it. He knew that he had helped his parents and especially his mother when she badly needed help. In fact the return to London early in 1883 and the events of 1884 turn at least in part on a shortage of money. Life in Epsom while Vincent worked in London was expensive. Once back in London, both Ellen and Vincent found that jobs available to them were inadequate. More than likely Vincent was unemployed; at about this time, Crawley's Brewery supplied him with letters of recommendation. From necessity, Ellen decided to capitalize on her children. Thereupon, as Mabel put it, she and Aubrey "entered into public and social life." They performed occasionally in concert and frequently at "private entertainments." They were especially popular with Mrs. Kemyss Betty, who was at home in St. James' Square.

Mabel and Aubrey Beardsley were a remarkable pair of children, both thin, both tall; while not identical in features or colouring, they were very similar. Even then Aubrey wore his red-brown hair in a fringe over his forehead, and he was pale, as Mabel was not. Aubrey, touted as a "musical genius," a prodigy, a boy not yet eleven who composed nocturnes, played the piano alone or in duets with his sister. Mabel also recited those excerpts from Dickens.

But none of this was enough. The total Beardsley income could not support a family. Furthermore Ellen was ill. And so in August 1884, Mabel and Aubrey went to live with Sarah Pitt, Ellen's maiden aunt, at 21 Lower Rock Gardens, Brighton. Miss Pitt was a woman of some means and decided opinions. She saw to it that the children were in bed at dark and up with the first light. She disapproved of playthings and so allowed none. The only amusement which she tolerated was a history book, Green's *Short History of England*. From it, to fill his days, Aubrey began to compile a history of the Spanish Armada. But the two children were forced into an unnatural reliance on each other and on the only activity, apparently, which their aunt sanctioned, church-going. In fact, she encouraged them to go often to church, and the children toiled up the hill to the Church of the Annunciation of Our Lady.[15]

Obviously by this time, 1884, young Beardsley had developed firm interests and attitudes. He enoyed writing, he was acutely aware of the power of money, and his religious devotion and his capacity for affection were strong. Despite his aunt's severity, Aubrey and his sister had a real regard for Miss Pitt, an affection which she evidently reciprocated. She left each £500 at her death in 1891, and during his stay at Brighton Grammar School, Aubrey visited her often. Of course he may have done so as much out of gratitude as affection, since she paid his fees at Brighton Grammar School.

iii

Aubrey Beardsley apparently commenced as a day student at Brighton Grammar School, 80 Buckingham Road, in November. When the January 1885 term began, he became a boarder,[16] living in the school boarding house next door to the school. On his first day as a boarder, Aubrey was dressed in a middy blouse and knickerbockers which exposed his painfully thin legs. Later he took to Eton suits which hung on him "as clothes would hang on sticks without any suggestion of a calf." He grew at an alarming rate, so that early in each term his trousers parted company with his Eton jacket, socks showed above his boots, and his long thin hands were "some four or five inches below his cuffs." Even to schoolboys, Beardsley's hands and his "beautifully shaped nails" were apparent.[17] One contemporary described him on that first day as "sitting in a corner of the 'day room' looking the picture of misery and showing very evident signs of home-sickness. His figure, straight and slender, gave an impression, at first sight, of a sprightly well-groomed boy, and the curious red-brown colour of his hair claimed . . . attention instantaneously. His hair was brushed smoothly and flatly on his forehead and over part of his immensely high and narrow brow. . . ."[18]

Very likely Beardsley's first encounter with A. W. King, science master as well as Aubrey's house master, was more typical. When King first saw Beardsley, he was giving a disquisition on the qualities of Shakespeare's plays, "contrasting in grand style the histories, the comedies, and the tragedies."[19] But the stature of the expert on Shakespeare was soon reduced. Aubrey proved to be unsatisfactory in spelling and deficient in arithmetic, since he did not know the multiplication tables. Although he spoke as a true Beardsley when he contemptuously described the multiplication tables as a waste of time so long as he "could count money" and "had it to count," he was sent to the Lower School. The next day after tea, in a "drawing-room entertainment," he protested loudly against a "man of his years and experience being put with babies to learn tables and spelling." King found him in the covered playground giving a "graphic delineation" of his hardships and at once sent him off to "tidy up" the bookcases in King's study.[20]

Nothing could have been more fortunate for Beardsley. He found a long-time friend in King, who proved to be a wise and generous counselor and a perceptive schoolmaster. King eased Beardsley's way through school so that instead of the lonely, frustrating experience it might have been, his stay at Brighton Grammar School was happy and valuable in the free expression of his gifts. Thanks to King, Beardsley actually found his way as an illustrator during those years, although, as so often happens with young people, he did not realize that fact at the time.

Beardsley was not the usual schoolboy and he competed in none of the usual ways of boyhood. He cared nothing for games and he was a poor swimmer. Examinations were a necessity, not a challenge. He hardly studied at all until time for the examinations, and then "a little hard work at the end" got him through. His musical gifts, he indulged privately. As soon as anyone entered a room where he was playing the piano, he stopped and moved to a chair where he began to read.

Beardsley was feverishly hungry for books, especially in his first year. His playbox, which Mabel had helped pack, contained a number of volumes from the Mermaid Series. Once or twice, he went with J. Thurston Hopkins, a classmate, to his home in Worthing, a coastal town near Brighton, and from there carried away a wide selection of books, everything from Chatterton and the *Decameron* to Edgar Allan Poe to *Lives of All the Notorious Pirates*. For a time after that, his talk was filled with supposed piratical expressions, "hark 'e" and "hanging look" and one or two others. But as a rule the books, like the piano, were a constant and private pleasure. Every moment he had to spare he sat lost in some book, his "long hands drawn up on one side like the paws of a squirrel."[21] Hopkins said that once Beardsley took up a book, he became so immersed in it and in some personal world where his mind could "adventure in space and eternity" that the retreat of awareness from his eyes was visible. Sometimes, to the dismay of his schoolmasters, he even deserted the classroom for the private world where he and his imagination lived.

That Beardsley was not a "force in the ordinary sense of school-life" is hardly surprising. Yet King managed, as Beardsley said, to keep him "in some sort of conceit" with himself.[22] This King did usually by walks and long talks. Afterwards, Aubrey declared he would "*never*" forget their "evenings together in the old room."[23] But King also found ways for Beardsley to demonstrate his talents, though naturally King steered them towards his own enthusiasm, the school's frequent theatrical entertainments. He wrote or arranged most of them unless they were operettas. In that case, King's colleagues Fred Edmonds and C. T. West were the creators.[24] Beardsley participated in both with the encouragement of King as well as that of a classmate, Charles B. Cochran, later Sir Charles Cochran, impresario.

In November 1884, young Cochran had been removed from a school at Eastbourne at the reqeust of its headmaster. He objected to the fact that the boy had climbed the school wall and gone to see the Guy Fawkes celebration in the town. Cochran was promptly taken to Brighton Grammar School, where he was allowed to enter owing to the unusual sympathy and ability of E. J. Marshall, its headmaster, with "wild irresponsible boys" or merely difficult ones such as Cochran.[25] Thus he was a new boy, as Beardsley was, in the January 1885 term. At his first dinner at the school, Cochran sat next to "a delicate-looking boy, thin, red-haired, and with a slight stoop. He was a particularly quick talker, used his hands to gesticulate, and altogether had an un-English air about him."[26] That boy, of course, was Aubrey Beardsley. The two were soon allowed to share a private study, and thereafter much of what they did with their school years they did together. Needless to say their studies played little part. The bond between them was a feeling for the stage, and as often as they could manage the money—sometimes got by selling personal possessions—and the free time, they went to Mrs. Nye Chart's Brighton Theater. Cochran remembered in particular Olga Nethersole and "Lal" Brough in *Modern Wives*. Beardsley was entranced by both the music and the wordless, impressionistic story-telling of the French pantomime *L'Enfant Prodigue;* he went three times to see it.

Cochran and Beardsley also had friends in common, especially G. F. Scotson-Clark, son of the Reverend Frederick Scotson-Clark, organist and composer. Young Scotson-Clark was a "strange impressive youth" with a mind of his own about music, literature, food, and drawing (in which he had some proficiency).[27] Scotson-Clark and Beardsley first met owing to their interest in drawing. Both took their work for criticism in after-school hours to "Johnny" Godfrey, one of the masters. At that time Beardsley was enthusiastic over Fred Barnard, who made drawings of Henry Irving, and Beardsley—or Beale, as he was called—copied Barnard's work as well as making numerous sketches on his own of Irving. Scotson-Clark, as a small boy, had once sat on the knee of that "most beautiful goddess" Ellen Terry and he longed to be an actor. Love of the theater, then, was another bond between these two boys, a bond which made young Cochran a welcome third. They began to organize house concerts; and although Scotson-Clark, as a day-boy, could take no part in them, he could help with rehearsals.

The first school entertainment in which these boys participated was a "sort of discussion between English rulers and their Courtiers." The various characters—Henry II, Bishop Langton, Oliver Cromwell, and others—were introduced to the audience by "'Minerva' a sort of Greek Chorus." Beardsley, "tastefully attired in one of the matron's night dresses, a flaxen flowing wig and a Roman Gladiator's helmet," played the part, giving a long dull speech in rhyming couplets.[28]

Then they began to take part in other "little weekly" presentations at the school, farces, songs, recitations, in which, according to Cochran, Beardsley was remarkable. He recited most impressively Thomas Hood's two pieces, *Eugene Aram* and "Mary's Ghost," and in 1887 he read the skating scene from *Pickwick Papers*, taking over both the material and the manner which his mother had taught Mabel. He played the Frenchman Victor in *Ici On Parle Français;* he performed in *The Spitalfields Weaver*. But Beardsley was more effective dramatically in two School Prologues, a part of the Brighton Grammar School's annual Christmas performance at the Dome. King wrote these each year, long rhymed summaries of national and local events. Beardsley appeared first as "Schoolboy" in a prologue in 1886. The next year, while Cochran played Henry VII, Beardsley acted as The Spirit of Progress, repeating his triumph of the year before when he had drawn the "loud applause of three thousand not uncritical people," [29] parents, old boys, and locals.

To learn his lines, Beardsley took himself alone to the old Chain Pier, in the 1880s a decaying relic of former fashion. There, where the sun shone bright and clear and a breeze blew fresh from the sea, he paced back and forth while he committed his speeches to memory. The Chain Pier was Beardsley's favorite retreat, anyway. However glib his talk with his fellows and however convivial his associations with them, he was extremely self-contained and many of his pleasures were solitary ones. From the beginning of his stay at the school, he went often to visit his aunt Sarah Pitt. Beardsley kept on with his reading (Cochran called it a "leaning toward literature"), and he enjoyed his music. He began to be "prolific with original verse," a pastime which afforded him his first publication of any kind when "The Valiant" appeared in *Past and Present*, the school magazine, in June 1885. An offshoot of his addiction to pirates, "The Valiant" ends with these two stanzas,

> "Come on!" the *Valiant*'s captain cried,
>   "Come on, my comrades brave,
> And if we die we shall not sink
>   Inglorious 'neath the wave."
>
> When the morning came, and the men arose,
>   The pirates where were they?
> The ship had sunk and all its crew;
>   Dead 'neath the sea they lay. [30]

Beardsley liked being published, but the school magazine seemed limited; so he started sending verses to a local paper called *Brighton Society*. Eventually they published a poem called "A Ride in an Omnibus" with the signature W. V. Beardsley, and almost a year later, "A Very Free (Library) Reading with apologies to W. S. Gilbert," a set of comic verses on a librarian, with no signature. [31]

Although Henry Earp, the instructor, urged Beardsley, with Scotson-Clark, to remove himself from the class in painting, both King and H. A. Paine, Beardsley's form master, encouraged him to draw. He began by making caricatures of the headmaster and his schoolfellows. These were sometimes offensive to their subjects, so King urged Beardsley to put his ability to more pleasing use. He proceeded then to illustrate the second book of Virgil's *Aeneid*, adding an episode or two of his own. Then, as Queen Victoria's first Jubilee approached in 1887, he produced a clever drawing which exemplified puns on cricket terms. King had him re-draw it with lithographer's ink, and the sketch duly appeared in the Jubilee number of *Past and Present*.[32] Here was the first publication of a drawing by Beardsley. Still, caricature was irresistible. He drew six sketches of scenes from the Brighton Grammar School's presentation of the farce *Ici On Parle Français*, enacted early in 1888. Four contained drawings of Cochran as Spriggins, the leading character. In September or October 1888, Beardsley made pictures depicting his headmaster's misadventures of the previous summer in the Selkirk Mountains of British Columbia. He drew them on glass so that they served as lantern slides for a part of Marshall's lectures about his travels.[33]

Then in December 1888, Beardsley's interests and gifts came together in the Christmas program when *The Pay of the Pied Piper*, a comic operetta, was presented at the Dome. Beardsley participated in nearly every aspect of the production. He helped design costumes; he helped make up the actors, using water colors instead of grease paint; he took part in both the Prologue and *The Pay of the Pied Piper;* and he drew eleven charming illustrations for the program. Beardsley's friendship with Scotson-Clark nearly foundered on these drawings. Scotson-Clark had made twelve drawings for Browning's *Pied Piper*, so he secured a copy of the script of the school's operetta and illustrated it. He left the pictures with Marshall, the headmaster, who eventually sent Beardsley to return them. Beardsley examined the designs, took Scotson-Clark's idea, and made drawings of his own. Scotson-Clark admitted that they were superior to his, but he resented Beardsley for a time after his work was printed (with apologies for his inexperience in preparing drawings for reproduction).[34]

Aubrey Beardsley at the age of thirteen *(Courtesy of The Bodley Head Ltd.)*

Beardsley's sketch of Charles B. Cochran as Sprig in the Brighton Grammar School's production of *Ici on Parle Français (From Charles B. Cochran*, Secrets of a Showman, *London, 1925)*

CHAPTER II

i

BEARDSLEY'S participation in *The Pay of the Pied Piper* marked his last official association with Brighton Grammar School and the end of his school days. He withdrew from school at the end of the Michaelmas Term, 1888, that is, at Christmas, 1888,[1] and went to London. There he lived with his parents in a lodging house kept by Thomas Gardner at 32 Cambridge Street, Pimlico. Almost at once, he began work as a clerk in the surveyor's office of the District of Clerkenwell and a part of Islington. The job was temporary; he planned to leave it as soon as the formalities of employment and an opening at the Guardian Life and Fire Insurance Company in Lombard Street could be arranged. That came sooner than he had anticipated, so that on January 1, 1889, Beardsley went as a clerk with the Guardian Insurance Company.[2]

Doubtless, Beardsley would have preferred the stage as a career. His theatrical activities at school had given him what recognition, even notability, he had there. Mabel, his sister, was much smitten with play acting. In the days immediately after his leaving school, the two Beardsleys, Mabel and Aubrey, were often at the theater, waiting long hours before curtain time in order to be sure of standing room when the curtain went up. Most memorably, they saw Henry Irving in *Macbeth*, although Beardsley disliked Ellen Terry as Lady Macbeth.[3] Almost at once, too, Mabel and Aubrey set up their own theater which they called The Cambridge Theatre of Varieties, after their London address, and together they gave at least two different performances in 1888 and 1889. Who made up their audiences, outside of the family, is uncertain. For both, Aubrey prepared the programs, with his own lettering and sketches. Once Mabel was listed as "Madame Mâbélè," a *"Costumier,"* and Aubrey as "M. Aubré," a *"Perruquier."* For another program, "The Jolly Masher" was announced as "A Charade in 4 acts" with Mabel and her brother taking at least two parts each. Songs, for which he also drew an announcement, accompanied the charades.

Aubrey, however, had no choice of profession, and he knew he

31

must take a job for the sake of what it would pay. The Beardsleys needed his earnings, which might one day reach as much as £80 a year. And they had decided that he was old enough to start at once. On January 1, 1889, when he announced himself as "in Business," Beardsley was little more than four months past his sixteenth birthday. At that age he was aware of special powers, but he was so uncertain as to their quality and what to make of them that he worked at none. He was restless and unwilling to focus on any one. In fact he was still too immature to know which to develop and too gentle to drive in any one direction.

Fortunately his job was not a burden. "I don't exactly dislike [it] but am not (as yet) frantically attached," he told King. Beardsley admitted that his work was not hard; the greatest difficulty he had to face was sitting in front of a poster "designed by no less a person than Sir Edward Poynter," the extremely prolific Royal Academician who was a constant reminder of another kind of life.[4]

At the same time, Beardsley had many diversions: the theater, acting with Mabel, walks in London, the galleries and museums of London, occasional sketching, and above all, reading. If he knew any young women, they meant nothing to him. At Brighton, he had written letters of undying passion to a Miss Felton, addressing her, "My own love,"[5] but now books seemed more important. He added John Ford's plays to his Mermaid dramatists and at once decorated the book with the date, March 9, 1889, and a number of sketches. Dating and ornamenting his books was an old habit with Beardsley, as it is perennially with many school children. In his volume of Christopher Marlowe's plays, he had written "A. V. Beardsley from his loving self" and the date, May 4, 1887. In it, too, he had practiced writing his name and the date in four different calligraphies and he had made sketches of Marlowe's four heroes, Tamburlaine, Barrabas, Faustus, and Edward II.[6] He continued the same practice in his copies of Goethe's *Faust*, translated by Bayard Taylor, and of Fielding's *Tom Jones*. In each he wrote his name and the date—June 1889 in the *Faust* and August 7, 1889, in the other book—and made appropriate drawings on the loose endpapers.[7] Beardsley's copy of Shakespeare's poems, which he dated March 17, 1889 beneath his signature, carries not only a drawing in pencil of Shakespeare but numerous, thoughtful annotations as well.[8] He commented on the poet's likelihood of eternal youth through poetry, the wealth of his political ideas, and his "art place" as fixed by Lessing. Beardsley had read his book's introductory material to good effect. Above the title for "Venus and Adonis," he noted Shakespeare's fertility and condensation of thought and his "sweet rhythm." Then Beardsley

quoted, "He goes on kindling like a mete[o]r through the dark air."
But his greatest interest was in the sonnets. "They show S's passage
from foreign to national art," he wrote. He thought Pembroke
"refined & a patron of poetry . . . above caste . . . self-willed, the
most logical object of the sonnets." "Its such," Beardsley wrote,
"likely to win S's esteem." He noted, too, the sonnets' emphasis on
making the most of youth, "which advise," he added, "would have
been more applicable to female beauty than masculine as in 2nd
Sonnet 40 would be a mans prime."

Such observations, as well as his sketches, are hardly different
from any intelligent and sensitive boy's. But they are noteworthy in
Beardsley's case because they are the background of his early work.
Beardsley enjoyed the visible world. Going daily to his office, miles
across London, partly on foot and partly by horse-drawn omnibus,
he observed with unabated interest every sight London offered him.
He saw its streets thronging with carriages and drays of every kind,
and he watched the endless passage of people—crossing sweepers,
dustmen, boardmen, newspaper hawkers, fishmongers, bobbies,
flower women and fruit girls, fine ladies and harlots, toughs and
"toffs." Through the rain and fog and the shifting light of the city he
saw it wear "the beauty of the morning," its noble and ignoble
buildings, its parks and trees. But Beardsley had not yet the
draftsman's vocabulary or the technique to make these serve his
drawings. Instead, his habit of thoughtful reading, like his attention
to opera, provided him with the subject for many of his early
drawings and prepared for his unique concept of illustration.

Beardsley was not to reach his prime. The first warning came in
the final quarter of that year 1889, probably in early November.
Beardsley was "so dreadfully ill" that he was forced to leave his post
in the insurance office. He wrote to King, in a letter dated January 4,
1890, that "some weeks ago" he had had a "bad attack of blood
spitting." He had gone to see Dr. Edward Symes Thompson, a
specialist in tuberculosis, who declared that Beardsley was in "a
shocking state of health" and marveled at his existence in "such a
worn-out condition." The doctor, however, had diagnosed
Beardsley's lungs as healthy but his heart as "so weak that the least
exertion" brought on "bad haemorrhage."[9]

Beardsley's Christmas had been kept on slops and over basins, and
he got through his days with almost incessant reading. Recently he
had found Daudet's books especially enjoyable, and he added that he
had come to read French almost as readily as English. Quite possibly
Beardsley's mother would have credited those statements to his
urgency to "shine." Vanity, she said, "made him want to shine &

please the person he wrote to."[10] Whether he hoped to "shine" with his former schoolmaster or not, Beardsley clearly enjoyed Daudet and the new facility with French. Although he was only seventeen, his interests were iridescent. He was enormously interested in every aspect of the world around him.[11] He loved gaiety, he liked the hustle and bustle of London, its noise, its movement,[12] and its dignity. But he also delighted in books and in learning from them. And from all of it he derived material for impressions, ideas, meditation. In other words, Beardsley's first and most enduring pleasures were those of the mind.

Thus the occasion for the letter to A. W. King was neither to complain of his illness nor to "shine." Beardsley wrote to announce his first professional publication, a short piece of fiction called "A Story of a Confession Album," which appeared in *Tit-Bits* on the same day as the letter was written, January 4, 1890.[13] Told in the first person, the story castigates the fashionable "Confession Album." Owing to a fictitious statement which the narrator made in such an album, his fiancée has ended their engagement. It is a simple tale presented in a straightforward manner and thereby has an aura of reality. For this piece, Beardsley received £1.10s.

That payment led Beardsley to a decision. Once again the question of money and the necessity to earn it nagged at him, as it would throughout his life. He had lived his seventeen years between what E. M. Forster termed gentility and poverty. The Beardsleys had gentility, but they lived always at the line which separates a meager living from poverty. Aubrey had heard too much talk about money and he had been too long dependent on his mother's maneuvers or a relative's generosity not to give money importance. Mabel dreamed of going to a university; she even had an opportunity for a scholarship to Cambridge. But she was forced to refuse it and to accept a post at the Polytechnic School for Girls in Langham Place. Aubrey was convinced that he had lost his job with the insurance company. He was ill and without prospects. He concluded, then, that since *Tit-Bits* paid for his writing, writing was the direction he must take. He resolved to end his drawing, to "crush it out" of himself.[14] And so he set to work as diligently as his illness allowed to combine his enthusiasm for the theater with writing. He attempted a three-act play but he could not get beyond the first act. He managed, however, to write a monologue called "A Race for Wealth" and a short farce, "A Brown Study." On November 7, 1890, Beardsley's former schoolmate C. B. Cochran produced the farce at the Royal Pavilion for a meeting of the Brighton Grammar School Old Boys Association; both Cochran and Scotson-Clark had parts in it. Beardsley said that his monologue was also presented, but no record of it survives. Apparently "A Brown Study" was well received; Beardsley remarked on its success, however small, in a letter to King.[15]

ii

Between the two letters to King, the one of January 4, 1890, telling about his illness and his publication in *Tit-Bits* and the one of July 13, 1891, telling about "A Brown Study," Beardsley's goals and the likelihood of realizing them had changed. His whole life had taken a firm direction. His attempts at writing had proved unproductive. More important was a fact which he explained rather apologetically to King. Beardsley had been unable to "crush . . . out" the "drawing faculty" and submitting, as he said, "to the inevitable," he had allowed it "to come uppermost."[16] Thereafter he concentrated on his drawing, working at it with great fervor.

Beardsley's sense of composition was instinctive, but he lacked form. Much of his early drawing had been caricature, comic in its exaggerations. Then, while retaining the comic, he had added another dimension as early as 1888, the grotesque. The programs for The Cambridge Theatre of Varieties and a depiction of Paganini exemplify the combination. Meanwhile, Beardsley had tried other approaches. A drawing of Sarah Bernhardt, also made in 1888, stands halfway between caricature and a realistic portrait-sketch. A scene from Ibsen's *Ghosts*, made some two years later, is another realistic depiction, even though the right arm of the central figure is out of drawing. The picture *Holywell Street, London* is an attempt at Impressionism.

But by 1890, when Beardsley decided on drawing as his *métier*, he had turned his attention first to the Italian artists who preceded Raphael, Mantegna in particular. Mabel reported their frequent visits to the National Gallery, where she and Aubrey lingered over those artists. Beardsley was moved as well by that period's recent exponents the Pre-Raphaelites, currently led by Edward Burne-Jones, an artist whom Beardsley particularly admired. His first enthusiasm for the Pre-Raphaelites derived from Scotson-Clark. He was employed as clerk by a Brighton wine-merchant who owned a fine collection of paintings, including a number by the Pre-Raphaelites. According to Scotson-Clark, his employer first made him aware of Rossetti, and Scotson-Clark "lost no time in acquainting Beardsley" with the "new outlook" Rossetti had induced and with Ford Madox Brown and

35

Burne-Jones.[17] Beardsley's wraith-like *Dante in Exile*, drawn about 1890 and sometimes described as "in the manner" of William Blake,[18] suggests in its detail and in the modeling of the figure of Dante a move toward Pre-Raphaelitism. It is fully developed in the pictures called *Tannhäuser*, *The Litany of Mary Magdalen*, *Hail Mary*, *Hamlet*, and others drawn at about that same time. The subjects are varied, but they have no real consequence in Beardsley's evolving art. Even *Tannhäuser*, an essential part of Beardsley's history, is important only for its form, as was each of the drawings made in 1890 and 1891.[19]

In early 1891, the Beardsley family moved once more, this time to a lodging house kept by a Mrs. Elizabeth Ford, at 59 Charlwood Street, Pimlico.[20] Shortly after the move, Aubrey's health had improved to the point where a visit to his aunt Sarah Pitt at Brighton seemed advisable. He stayed two weeks, a "glorious" time for Scotson-Clark, whose office was only blocks away. He and Beardsley talked, they painted and drew and "built castles in the air." One of their castles was a plan for a small shop in Bond Street or Piccadilly, where "little original drawings in black and white" and "little impressionist landscapes" were to be on sale at ten or fifteen shillings. They discussed Herkomer's School, an art school, at Bushey Heath and once they sat up all night long in Aunt Sarah's dining-room, drawing and "occasionally taking a draught from a flagon of Australian Burgundy à la Balzac." At daybreak, Beardsley walked home with Scotson-Clark, who then showed Beardsley for the first time how to mix paints. While his host took a nap, Beardsley painted a "Burne-Jones head with a green face & blue hair against a purple sun." During that visit he made other drawings, too, such as a ballet girl "à la Chéret" labeled *Ballerina Dissoluta* and a second "Burne-Jones head," which he called "the Frog Lady" but labeled *La Belle Dame sans Merci*, to indicate his devotion to Keats.[21] Even though Beardsley was still playful, still eager and ingratiating, his boyhood had come to an end. Having faced so severe an illness, he could never be a boy again.

When Beardsley left Brighton, he returned to work. Contrary to his expectations, he found that his clerk's post at the Guardian Life and Fire Insurance office awaited him. The winter of 1890–1891 was an unusually damp, dark one, hardly compatible with his health. He might have benefited from another climate, but back he went to the job for which he was so eminently unsuited. At least this time he found a congenial fellow-worker, A. H. Pargeter, whose enthusiasm led Beardsley to read Dante, where, as in much of his reading, he found subjects for his drawings and a confirmation of a developing interest in Italian art.

Beardsley went back to his old habits, too. Chief among them was his use of his lunch-time to visit the bookshop of Jones and Evans in Queen Street, Cheapside. It was the shop from which he had bought his copy of Shakespeare's poems and the other books dated 1889.[22] Frederick H. Evans, who operated the business, maintained a haven for book lovers. They were never pushed to buy, never interrupted in reading a book from the shelves or bins of the shop, and if they wanted to discuss their interests, literary or musical or theatrical, Evans was eager to talk.[23] Evans was an ugly little man with acute sensibilities. He could not fail to notice Beardsley's tall angular frame and his drawn face under its auburn fringe. And at length he began to discuss with Beardsley the things which fired them both. Beardsley confessed that he drew "a little" and began to show his work to Evans. Aware at once that this boy had unusual possibilities, Evans struck a bargain with Beardsley, books in exchange for drawings. One of the first to serve this exchange was the drawing *Dante in Exile.* Furthermore, being a first-rate amateur photographer—George Bernard Shaw called him the best in London—Evans made photographs of Beardsley and platinotypes of Beardsley's drawings, distinguishable from the originals only by Evans' mark on them, for sale from his shop. But most important in 1890 and 1891 was Evans' recognition of Beardsley's ability and an unflagging interest in him.

At the same time, Beardsley had aroused the special interest of the Reverend Alfred Gurney, vicar of St. Barnabas, Pimlico, the most fashionable and ritualistic Anglo-Catholic church in London. Gurney was not only a man of the cloth; he was as well a scholar in church ritual, a spiritualist, the author of short allegorical tales, an occasional poet, a collector of drawings in a small way, a wealthy man with a wide acquaintance. He had once been curate at St. Paul's in Brighton, where Mrs. Beardsley had known him. Now, very likely because of Gurney, the Beardsleys (that term may or may not include Vincent Beardsley) made St. Barnabas their place of worship. After the late Sunday morning service, they often went next door to the College or Clergy House, where Gurney provided a sumptuous lunch for friends and relations. Two of his curates, Father G. H. Palmer, an expert in music, and the Reverend Gerald Sampson with his brother Julian Sampson, a sometime art critic and dilettante, were often present for lunch. So were the Halifaxes with their young son, the vicar's reprobate brother, Willie Gurney, a sister-in-law, Mrs. Russell Gurney, and Helen, a small niece who was the child of Edmund Gurney, and various members of literary or artistic groups.

When the child Helen Gurney composed a long poem, what was more natural than that Beardsley illustrate it? He also began making the vicar's Christmas cards, always pious in design, for which he was properly paid. Gurney and his sister-in-law liked to examine the portfolio which for a time Beardsley took everywhere he went, and the Gurneys bought his early drawings, so that his work, with that of Rossetti and William Morris, decorated Gurney's walls.[24] At the luncheon table where Gurney, with his long forked beard and inscrutable blue eyes, presided, Beardsley heard highly intellectual conversation, much talk of current activities in the creative world and the endless opportunities which London offered for viewing art works not always available to the public. He learned that he might see Frederick Leyland's dining-room in his home at Prince's Gate, where Whistler had created the Peacock Room and where his painting *La Princesse du Pays de la Porcelaine* was hung.

On a Sunday in early July 1891, probably July 5, Mabel and Aubrey visited the Leyland house, much to Aubrey's gratification. He saw Whistler's impudent *tour de force* and Leyland's "glorious collection," works by recent or contemporary English artists (Watts, Rossetti, Millais, Burne-Jones, and Ford Madox Brown) as well as those by more famous earlier artists from Lippo Lippi to Leonardo da Vinci and Rubens.[25] The experience was so inspiriting that the two young Beardsleys determined to visit Edward Burne-Jones' studio the next week and see his collection. They had been told that the presentation of a visiting card would admit them.

On the next Sunday, a warm summer's day, when they left the Gurney luncheon table, Mabel and Aubrey (carrying his portfolio) set off for the "great adventure of Aubrey's life,"[26] a visit to Edward Burne-Jones' studio in his home, The Grange, at 49 North End Road, West Kensington. When they arrived, they learned that the studio had been closed to visitors for some time and they could see Burne-Jones only by appointment. Sorely disappointed, they were walking away when Burne-Jones came after them and insisted that on so warm a day they must not have come so far for nothing.

According to their mother, Burne-Jones was prompted to this kind act by a glimpse of Mabel's "beautiful red-gold" hair. Seeing them from his garden, he may simply have felt sorry for two disconsolate young people. In either case, when they turned he had a full view of this remarkable pair. Mabel, as one impartial friend described her, was "a rather big girl," erect but "scarcely" to be "called pretty," with her "ginger" hair and a "nice pink-and-white, slightly freckled complexion." Perhaps her charm lay in her "courtesy of manner."[27] Aubrey spoke of himself as an eighteen year old with "a sallow face

Going thro' the rooms

Beardsley's sketch of his and Mabel's visit to Frederick Leyland's home in Prince's Gate to see Whistler's Peacock Room *(Courtesy of The Bodley Head Ltd.)*

and sunken eyes, long red hair, a shuffling gait and a stoop."[28] Nevertheless, if George Moore, the novelist, can be trusted, there was a singular similarity between these two both in appearance and in manner. Aubrey was visible in Mabel. She was taller than he; her coloring was more robust, and her eyes were smaller. But in them could be "read" Aubrey. Without identical features, they had a like "cast of countenance." And although Mabel's talk was "less bracing" than his, Aubrey's "pierced through hers." Moore had a simile for these two: "The atmosphere of the valleys compared with that of the hills."[29]

Now Burne-Jones insisted that they come back to The Grange for tea and a sight of the pictures. They were jubilant, and back they went. As Mabel put it, "So behold the two, now radiant with excitement, returning on either side of the Master."[30] They went back to the garden where they found Mrs. Burne-Jones and Mrs. Oscar Wilde with Cyril and Vyvyan, her two sons.[31] The entire group then went into the house and to the studio. Entering Burne-Jones' house, according to one visitor, was like going "into the depth of a shady grove." It was "both rich and remote," filled with "things Italian," Morris furniture, and Burne-Jones' pictures and studies. Once in the studio, the master noticed Beardsley's portfolio and, after inspecting the pictures it held, said to him, "Give up whatever you may be doing—for Art."[32] That was, Beardsley said, "an exciting moment."

His account of the same afternoon is more complete. Beardsley said that Burne-Jones explained everything in the studio. After he was done, Beardsley, who "by chance" had his portfolio with him, asked Burne-Jones to evaluate the drawings in it. He had looked at only two, *Saint Veronica on the Evening of Good Friday* and *Dante at the Court of Don Grande della Scala*, when he declared, "There is *no* doubt about your gift, one day you will most assuredly paint very great and beautiful pictures." Then this man whom Beardsley regarded as "the greatest living artist in Europe" inspected the rest of the portfolio and said, "All are *full* of thought, poetry and imagination. Nature has given you every gift which is necessary to become a great artist. I *seldom* or *never* advise anyone to take up art as a profession, but in *your* case *I can do nothing else.*"[33] They returned to the garden for tea and Burne-Jones began to talk of formal training for Beardsley and offered to find the most suitable school. After Mrs. Burne-Jones congratulated him and remarked on how "very severe" a critic her husband could be, Beardsley left The Grange in a glow of happiness and the illusion of success already achieved.

Ellen Beardsley was prompt to "share" her "pleasure in Edward Burne-Jones' appreciation of Aubrey" with Father Gurney and to keep him informed of each subsequent visit or letter. As for Aubrey, his euphoria was short-lived.[34] He was still chained to his job at the "Fire Office," he was still dependent on the Gurneys for "substantial help" with his art work (Mrs. Russell Gurney was evaluating the "bulk" of his current drawings with a view to purchasing), and in no time at all he was complaining of being most "horribly dull." By early August, Mabel and Mrs. Beardsley were at Woking for a stay of two months while Aubrey and his "pater" were alone in London and "not having a particularly lively time of it."[35]

There was, of course, the immediate question of an art school. Earlier in the summer, Beardsley and his friend Scotson-Clark had applied to the Herkomer School of Art at Bushey, Hertfordshire, and promptly been refused for the current term because the school was filled. They were advised to submit drawings with an application for the next term. Actually neither Scotson-Clark nor Beardsley could afford the Herkomer School, since attendance there meant leaving their regular jobs, Scotson-Clark's in Brighton and Beardsley's in London. In any case, Beardsley was fortunate that he could not go to Herkomer's; it very likely would have curbed his individuality. And soon after his visit to the "immortal E.B.J.," Beardsley had a letter from Burne-Jones suggesting two other schools, the Royal College of Art in South Kensington and the Westminster School of Art headed by Frederick Brown.

To help Beardsley reach a decision, Scotson-Clark came up from Brighton and spent a Sunday with the Beardsleys. He brought with him two songs of his own composition, a musical setting to Christina Rossetti's "When I am dead my dearest" and a song about Robin Hood, for which he had also written the words. Mrs. Beardsley played the accompaniment, and Scotson-Clark sang. Then, as arranged by Scotson-Clark, the two young men and Mabel paid a visit to G. F. Watts and his pictures. Watts was at work on his *Requiescat* and a portrait of Walter Crane. Scotson-Clark sat at Watts' feet while Mrs. Watts took the Beardsleys around the studio. After Aubrey recognized a sketch of Burne-Jones' *Wheel of Fortune*, he spoke of his acquaintance with Burne-Jones, and the matter of an art school arose. Watts promptly urged Beardsley to go to no school. Of course he ignored this advice and later spoke of Watts as a "disagreeable old man" but "nice" to him. When the two young men at last talked about the choice Beardsley must make, he settled on Frederick Brown's Westminster School, partly because the second place suggested by Burne-Jones, the South Kensington School, required Beardsley to draw "scrolls and circles and spirals" for his application, and he felt incompetent. Besides, Brown was fresh from Paris, "a young man with all the traditions of the Parisian Studios."[36] Scotson-Clark advocated night classes, and Beardsley welcomed the suggestion, especially since Burne-Jones had said that Beardsley, with his gifts, needed no more than two hours' work each day to learn the "grammar" of his art.[37]

Burne-Jones had cautioned Beardsley against allowing any schools' discipline to "languor" him, and to King, Beardsley spoke bravely of the years of hard work ahead of him. But the distance between his "present position and Herkomer's Glory Hole" seemed immeasurable. He sent verses filled with doubt and anxiety to Scotson-Clark:

I

The lights are shining dimly round about,
The Path is dark, I cannot see ahead;
And so I go as one perplexed with doubt
Nor guessing where my footsteps may be led.

II

The wind is high, the rain falls heavily,
The strongest heart may well admit a fear,
For there are wrecks on land as well as sea
E'en though the haven may be very near.

III

The night is dark and strength seems failing fast
Though on my journey I but late set out,
And who can tell where the way leads at last?
Would that the lights shone clearer round about.[38]

iv

That Mabel and Mrs. Beardsley—especially Mrs. Beardsley—were away from home during this time of depression was fortunate. His mother always maintained that she and Aubrey "were one," that she knew "every thought of his heart" although he never confided in her.[39] Her attempts to get through the façade which her son erected against her were invariably defeated, and her probing in her misguided effort to help him only made his depression worse. This time, without her, it could run its course.

In any case, although he was suffering from weak and inflamed eyes, Beardsley could hardly be disconsolate in view of the excitement and satisfaction he had in every stroke of his pen. His drawing went well. Even before he began attendance at the Westminster School, he could note "decided headway." In mid-October, he reported that "Mr Fred Brown," head of his school, seemed to have "great hopes" for him. By December, Beardsley had turned into innumerable pictures his reading from Aeschylus to Chaucer to William Morris. He had visited Burne-Jones again with a freshly stocked portfolio, he had made a passionate study of Mantegna, and he had amazed himself by his growth as an artist in only two months' time.[40]

Meanwhile, in early August 1891, King made a visit to London. He and Beardsley sat together at the Covent Garden Hotel while Beardsley exhibited to King what drawings Mrs. Gurney was not holding. He was surprised at Beardsley's progress and very much impressed. He encouraged Beardsley to stick to his clerk's job but to go with his portfolio as often as possible to any publishers who produced illustrated books and to ask for work. King demonstrated his good faith by taking several of Beardsley's drawings away with him. The year before, King had left Brighton to become secretary of Blackburn Technical Institute in Lancashire. He had promptly inaugurated a journal for the Institute, *The Bee*. So, on his return to Blackburn, King sold one or two of Beardsley's drawings to a W. Richard Haworth. The one called *Hamlet Patrem Manis Sequitur*, King offered to Haworth for 10s, but the drawing ended up in *The Bee*. On Christmas morning Beardsley received a copy of *The Bee* with a lithograph after his drawing printed in sanguine as frontispiece.[41]

Beardsley told King that of all the things received that Christmas day, none was more welcome than *The Bee*. Evans, the bookseller, had been reproducing Beardsley's drawings and offering platinotypes of them for sale at his shop, but the reproduction in *The Bee* provided a wider audience and suggested fulfillment of Beardsley's ambition to be an illustrator. He asked to contribute to future issues of *The Bee* from time to time and early in 1892 he prepared a second drawing, but it never appeared. An essay on line and line drawing, written especially for *The Bee*, he withdrew when he discovered a similar article by Walter Crane already in print.[42]

Such setbacks were minor. By then, early 1892, even more serious ones left Beardsley virtually unmoved. Following King's advice to call on publishers who brought out illustrated materials, Beardsley arranged to show his portfolio to W. E. Henley, editor of *The National Observer*. It was a lively journal which published some of the best writers of the time—Stevenson, Kipling, Meredith, Yeats— while maintaining its editor's militant imperialism. According to Beardsley's account, as he mounted the stairs to Henley's Great College Street rooms, he heard a loud, angry voice. When he got to the top, he saw through an open door, an abject young man standing, terrified, and listening to a "large red man" behind a desk. Convinced that the angry man was Henley, Beardsley turned and ran down the stairs and along the street until he was well away. He never went back, he never spoke to Henley.[43]

v

Beardsley told that incident himself. It amused him to recount his adventures, and he could laugh at them and at himself as gaily as his hearers. He told it to Elizabeth Robins Pennell, (Mrs. Joseph Pennell), American author and critic, ostensibly to explain his dodging from room to room to avoid Henley at the Pennells' Thursday evenings at their flat in Buckingham Street.

Beardsley had already met Joseph Pennell, but he first went to the Pennells' flat owing to the wife of another American, Aline Harland. Her husband, Henry, had had some literary success in New York, where he published novels under the name Sidney Luska. In July 1889, Aline and Henry Harland had suddenly decided to settle in England, in or near London, and within two weeks they had given up their flat in Beekman Place, New York, and sailed with Harland's parents for England. After journeying to Chester and into Wales as far north as Bangor, they visited Paris, which they knew and loved even to the "very odours of its streets" from an extended stay three years earlier. In the autumn of 1889, armed with letters of introduc- tion to Henry James and others from Harland's godfather Edmund Stedman, the American stockbroker, poet, and critic, the Harlands settled in London. They lived briefly "at the tender mercies of the keepers of lodging houses." Then in mid-1890 they moved into a flat at 144 Cromwell Road with their possessions, sent from New York, supplemented by "picking up Chippendale for a song" in the "old curiosity shops of London."[44]

Throughout all this coming and going and setting up their flat, the Harlands made numerous acquaintances. Among them was Whistler, gentled by his recent marriage to Beatrix Godwin and for a time the Harlands' best friend. Henry described "Jemmy" as "a most eccentric, kind-hearted, brilliant delightful creature." Others included Edmund Gosse, whom the Harlands feared owing to his "reputation for a *mauvaise langue*" but found to be all kindness; Henry James; Andrew Lang, with "the big head to an alarming degree"; Rudyard Kipling, "amusing"; H. Rider Haggard, "an overgrown school-boy"; Thomas Hardy, "interesting, but not up to his books"; Walter Besant and William Sharp and Mona Caird, Aline's "heart-sister."[45] Meanwhile, Aline practiced "trills" to stay in voice and Henry kept at his "daily stint of fiction," turning out novels and short stories with regularity.

All this went on despite the fact that early in 1890 Henry Harland suffered "bleeding of the lungs." His illness sent him hurrying to Dr. Edward Symes Thompson, the eminent London specialist in the treatment of tuberculosis. It was Thompson who had diagnosed Beardsley a few months earlier as suffering from a weak heart.[46] Harland and Beardsley met in Thompson's office, very likely in 1892, when Harland was once more a "limp rag" and Beardsley recovering from a short severe illness of early 1892. Harland was an enthusiastic talker and Beardsley was a clever, witty one. They got on, and eventually at 144 Cromwell Road Beardsley produced his ubiquitous portfolio for the Harlands. Naturally, Aline at once thought of Joseph Pennell, a fellow American and an artist.

Beardsley was introduced to Mrs. Pennell in the late autumn of 1892. Both the Pennels were Philadelphians. Joseph was tall and handsome, an artist whose etchings and lithographs of landscapes and architectural views were flawless in technique. Elizabeth was not as good to look upon as her husband, but she made up for the fact with energy and enthusiasm. Both were sure of themselves, and they took for granted the advantage to an aspiring young artist of fraternizing with them and with those who came to their flat, among them Phil May, Walter Crane, Whistler and Mrs. Whistler, one or another young Sickert, and Bob Stevenson. Elizabeth Pennell later remembered her first sight of Beardsley in the early dusk of a cold evening, when he appeared boyish (he was then a few months past his twentieth birthday), certain of his worth, natural, eager. He moved easily with her other guests—except Henley—observant, receptive to what he saw and heard.

By that time, Beardsley was a professional artist and, while still faithful to the set which gathered at Gurney's luncheon table, he was very much at home with a certain artistic and literary group in London. At Christmas time, 1891, Aymer Vallance had called at 89

Charlwood Street. He had come with an introduction from the Reverend C. G. Thornton, one of the clergymen at the Church of the Annunciation in Washington Street, Brighton, the church Mabel and Aubrey had attended when they lived with Sarah Pitt, their aunt. Some eighteen months earlier Thornton had told Vallance about Beardsley's gifts and urged him to call; but, thinking the clergyman could be neither a good judge nor a disinterested one, Vallance had put off the visit. Of course in one respect, he was right. A man in his late thirties, Vallance was an admirer of William Morris and an associate for at least two years, that is, since 1890 when Morris established the Kelmscott Press. Thornton was aiming at some sort of relationship with the great Morris for Beardsley.

Vallance may have been dilatory about making the call, but when he finally did he was extremely impressed with Beardsley and with what he found in Beardsley's portfolio. First was the extent of his reading as demonstrated by the literary pieces he chose to illustrate. These included *Manon*, *Madame Bovary*, numerous tales by Balzac, saints galore, *Tartarin*, Shelley's *Cenci*, Racine. Then there was the strength and fluidity of Beardsley's line. "Nothing less than revelation," Vallance said and, as Burne-Jones had done, told Beardsley he must devote himself to his art. "And give up making out insurance policies in Lombard Street?" Beardsley replied. "Impossible."[47] Nevertheless, he was pleased, exhibiting a "child-like delight" at Vallance's admiration. And Vallance persisted. He wanted Londoners in the art world to see Beardsley's work and, in addition, he offered to introduce the young man to William Morris.

It was Beardsley's turn to be impressed. He had recently read Morris' *Earthly Paradise* and found it "simply enchanting." Indeed, Morris seemed to Beardsley almost as worthy of admiration as Burne-Jones. When Vallance reported that Morris was preparing to issue *Sidonia the Sorceress* from Kelmscott House and suggested that Beardsley supply an example of his drawing, he eagerly set to work; and after it was finished, Vallance took him and his drawing to Morris. Later Vallance said that "fearful lest" Aubrey "fall under unworthy influences," he had looked forward to Morris' moral impact on Beardsley. But that statement was well after the fact.[48] In any case, Morris was indifferent to the gifted boy and churlish about his drawing. To wonder what Morris saw when he looked at it is inevitable. He said that he thought the draperies well done but the central figure not pretty enough. Beardsley realized that he could never please the cross-grained Morris; so after a half-hearted effort to alter the face of Sidonia, Beardsley abandoned all thought of Morris.[49]

Vallance did not give up. On February 14, 1892, he invited friends to his rooms to meet Beardsley. Perhaps it was a small gathering; only two guests besides Beardsley can be identified, Robert Ross and More Adey. Adey was Ibsen's translator at least once and an art critic. Vallances' contemporary, he was a close friend of Robbie Ross. The two men later shared a house at 15 Vicarage Gardens, Kensington, and they were associates in the Carfax Gallery. Ross, aged twenty-three in 1892 and thus almost three years older than Beardsley, was a member of a distinguished Canadian family. He had been brought to England to live when he was only two. In October 1888, he had gone up to King's College, Cambridge. There, despite prowess as an oarsman which put him in King's second boat, Ross quickly alienated his fellow students, who thereupon subjected him to merciless "ragging." Ill as a result, he left Cambridge and went to London, where he took rooms in Church Street. He began to work as a literary journalist and art critic. He and Adey were already at Vallance's rooms when the "youthful apparition" who was Aubrey Beardsley "glided in." Ross had expected an "ordinary genius" with hair worn "*ébouriffé*," but Beardsley's "rather long brown hair" was "brushed smoothly and flatly on his head and over part of his immensely high and narrow brow," and as always he had "a most delightful and engaging smile both for friends and strangers." At first he was "shy, nervous, and self-conscious" but endowed with "strange and fascinating originality." Beardsley soon lost his shyness and began to talk gaily and emphatically. His opinions were independent as he spoke of music, Molière, *Manon Lescaut*, and Balzac. Beardsley's admiration of Balzac derived from his exploration of the passions masked by the conventions of a hypocritical society, and his knowledge of Balzac was immense. It astounded More Adey, an authority on the subject, although he shook his head in disbelief when Beardsley called *King Lear* inferior in the subtlety of its perceptions to Balzac's *Le Père Goriot*.[50]

As usual, Beardsley had with him his portfolio of "marvellous drawings" and Ross, after he had subdued his amazement at the young artist, turned his attention to the drawings. One, *The Triumph of Joan of Arc*, Ross wanted to buy. Beardsley had described it as "A 1" when he was at work on it, the previous August. Still pleased with the picture, he now refused to part with it. By mid-May 1892, however, he had made a replica called *The Procession of Joan of Arc*, and he delivered it to Ross in exchange for a check.

When he wrote to thank Ross for the payment, Beardsley asked for information about Paris hotels. Beardsley was preparing to make his first visit to Paris. He had reported to King in December 1892 that Sarah Pitt, "the old aunt" he used to "pay so many visits to when at school," had left him £500. That, plus occasional sales of his drawings, including this one to Ross and several to the bookseller Evans, made it financially possible for him to keep up his share of household expenses—a major share—and still spend the holiday time granted him by the Fire Office in Paris.[51]

Beardsley had had this visit in mind since he learned of the £500, and for it he had made careful plans. As he told King, after recovering from his illness in the first weeks of the year when he could do little or no drawing, Beardsley had "set to work" and "struck out a new style and method of work which was founded on Japanese art but quite original in the main." He explained that his new drawings were "something suggestive of Japan but not really japonesque."[52]

This new style of Beardsley has sometimes been credited to the influence of Whistler and more specifically to his work in Frederick Leyland's home, which Beardsley had seen shortly before the visit to Burne-Jones. It has been ascribed, too, to Beardsley's inventiveness, to mere accident which he recognized as useful and made serve him.[53] Either may be entirely correct. Certainly he can not have escaped an awareness of *Japonisme*. It had come to England no later than the International Exhibition of 1882. Japanese influence was soon apparent in furnishings for the home, and Japanese prints—*Ukiyo-e*, pictures of the "fleeting world" printed by means of blocks of cherry wood cut as planks are—were readily available in both England and France well before they interested Beardsley. A portrait of Zola by Manet, who died in 1883, shows a Japanese print on the writer's wall. By 1883 or soon thereafter, Monet, among French Impressionists, was most obviously concerned with the possibilities in color and composition of the Japanese print. It appealed as well to Whistler and Burne-Jones, although they were at opposing ends of the spectrum on nearly everything else. Beardsley's bookseller friend Evans had Japanese prints in his rooms. Indeed, all around Beardsley were Japanese objects such as furniture, ceramics, porcelains and prints, or European ones made in imitation of the Japanese, or still better, inspired by them. What was more natural than for Beardsley to come to his new style through observation?

Above, Michael de Lisio's bronze sculpture of Beardsley after a photograph by Frederick H. Evans, reproduced below *(Courtesy of Michael de Lisio, the sculptor)* Below, Photograph of Beardsley by Frederick H. Evans *(Courtesy of The Bodley Head Ltd.)*

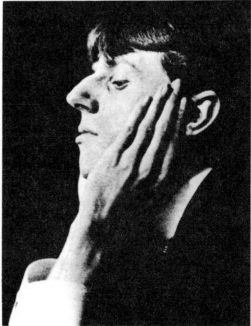

The Japanese print had been determined technically, that is by the limitations of the woodblock. It projected an illusion of depth and form by ambiguity of line. Beardsley's line was his first concern, and he began to refine it so as to render modeling and even texture to a remarkable degree by placement rather than shading. His drawings were increasingly concerned first with line and then with pattern. He began to shift the focal point of his drawing from conventional to diagonal planes, and he balanced blank space against "black blot." His new work, Beardsley said, consisted of "fantastic impressions treated in the finest possible outline with patches of 'black blot.'"[54] Reality in the graphic pattern had no importance. It had none for Burne-Jones either, but his direction was toward some remote valley in a never-never land inhabited by knights and princesses and a strange beast or two. Beardsley, on the other hand, increasingly depicted some version of the world around him. A tree, a column, or the façade of a building occasionally fulfilled a design which emphasized a human figure. Such figures derived from reality, but by the time he got them into black and white they were abstractions, the essence of the reality, which served as elements of a pattern.

All this was not achieved instantaneously. At first, Beardsley had hardly more than the perception of what he wanted to do. Nevertheless, he "forged ahead" with drawings in this new mode in the spring of 1892. Each night at about nine, after a full day at the insurance office, he sat down at his drawing table. King said that it was lighted by two candles because he had demonstrated to Beardsley, while they were both at Brighton Grammar School, the beauty in the play of light and shade in a room where there was no "overall glare of gas and electric light" and not more than two candles. Later, when he was free to choose his work-time, Beardsley adapted to daylight or whatever light was at hand. He began each drawing by sketching in pencil, covering a sheet of paper with "apparent scrawls." These were constantly erased and blacked in again and again until the whole surface of his paper "became raddled from pencil, india rubber, and knife." When he had built up his design to something closely approximating a final form, he inked it in with a gold pen, sometimes disregarding the pencil lines, all carefully rubbed out afterwards. Thus he produced about twenty drawings which he described as "quite mad and a little indecent" in subject. They were filled with "strange hermaphroditic creatures wandering about in Pierrot costumes or modern dress; quite a new world," he said, of his "own creation."[55] Even though some of these monstrous images were derived from Mantegna, Beardsley was nevertheless honest when he said that he allowed himself to see visions only on paper.

The twenty drawings were made to travel in his portfolio to Paris. What he expected from the drawings when he got them there is impossible to say. Much is unclear about Beardsley. In view of the family's finances, he could be castigated as foolhardy or praised as courageous for going to Paris at all. Mabel, in both 1891 and 1892, had passed with highest honors the "Higher Women's Examination," the Cambridge University "Local," so that she ranked fifth in all England. As a result, she had the offer of a scholarship from Newnham College, Cambridge, but she was forced to refuse it. If to do so was a hardship, it was tempered by the fact that her real ambition was for the stage. Since prospects were not very promising there either, she went to a teaching job at the Polytechnic School for Girls in Langham Place.[56] The sister and brother were heavily taxed to keep the household going. Their father's part in these years is almost totally unrecorded. He lived with them at Charlwood Street, but participation in family affairs or in the ambitions of his two children goes unmentioned. Doubtless Mabel fostered Aubrey's determination to make a place for himself as an artist. Such encouragement, whether through love or faith in him, from a loving sister is natural; but that she did urge him to go is only conjecture. That he made up his own mind about Paris and that he very likely would have gone with or without Mabel's encouragement is also conjecture. Beardsley wrote hundreds of letters and notes in his short lifetime, but almost none is intimate; in almost none did he openly and uncompromisingly delineate himself. Many attitudes and emotions are implicit in his letters, but he almost never referred to them. Once or twice Beardsley felt discouragement or despair; once or twice, as in writing to Scotson-Clark, Beardsley was exhilarated, and he could be misleading. But his aims, his affections, his obsessions and hopes must usually be inferred, except for the obvious fact that his drawing was at the very heart of his existence.

Paris was a part of his campaign to enter the world of art. Paris was the international *atelier*. Not to have been to Paris argued simpleness; to have been then implied seriousness of purpose. Beardsley meant to go. He had Robbie Ross' suggestions for a hotel. He had as fine a wardrobe as he could manage. Although he never went as far as Whistler in the dandyism which provoked Degas' rebuke that Whistler often behaved as if he had no talent, Beardsley saw himself as a man of fashion, immaculate, elegant, restrained.[57] He had letters to William Rothenstein, the young English artist living in Paris, and to Puvis de Chavannes, in a sense Burne-Jones' French counterpart. Burne-Jones had given Beardsley the letter. He had stocked his purse and his portfolio, and he went to Paris.

Exactly when he went, except for the fact that it was in the month of June 1892, is uncertain. Indeed, little can be said with certainty about Beardsley's three weeks in Paris. He may have stayed at the Hôtel de Portugal et l'Univers in the rue Croix des Petits Champs. He had many a meal—more than he cared to remember—at one or another Duval. He went to the Rat Mort, considered *outré* in the evening owing to its reputation as a haven for lesbians after dark. When he got back to Charlwood Street, he described the place to Mabel and explained lesbianism to her, so that to one friend at least she appeared very knowing.[58] He was at the Moulin Rouge, where Yvette Guilbert had made her first appearance a year or two before. And he sat outside cafés, his long sensitive hands hovering over a small coffee cup and his head to one side as he watched throngs of strollers and every sort of horse-drawn carriage and omnibus. Beardsley strolled, too, simply because in sunshine the boulevards of Paris are irresistible. He spent hours in the Louvre, and if he was in Paris during the annual exhibition at the Champs des Mars, he lingered there as well.

That account of Beardsley's activities originates in numerous hints. There is some record, however, of his call on William Rothenstein. Another caller earlier that year, Grant Richards, the publisher, described Rothenstein as "small and put together with unusual neatness and . . . dressed with unusual neatness too. Spectacles. Black hair. An effect rather Japanese."[59] Only seven months Beardsley's senior, Rothenstein had come from Bradford, Derbyshire, to Paris in 1889 and after several moves, including an attempt to share working quarters with his compatriot Phil May, had set himself up in a bare, sunlit studio-flat. It was up a long flight of "sombre, even sinister" stairs at the top of a "tall, sombre house" in the rue Fontaine. There Rothenstein lived alone except for a boy who acted as *cuisinier* and an occasional young woman. There, too, Rothenstein worked diligently at painting with a concept of his art not far removed from Beardsley's, an acute awareness of the Pre-Raphaelites, especially Dante Gabriel Rossetti (tempered by recent French painters) and an interest in the Japanesque. Yet he was critical of Beardsley's drawings in their most characteristic derivation from the Japanese print, a "flattening of contours." Rothenstein said of Beardsley, "There was something hard and insensitive in his line, and something small and narrow in his design."[60] Nevertheless Rothenstein showed Beardsley something of his *quartier*, Montmartre, with the Chat Noir up the hill and the Moulin Rouge nearby. Their meeting ripened into a friendship which carried over to London, although Rothenstein had reservations. Later he described Beardsley as lovable, but in that summer of 1892, Rothenstein was uneasy with Beardsley. "At that time," Rothenstein said, "with his butterfly ties, his too smart clothes with their hard, padded shoulders, his face—as Oscar said—'like a silver hatchet' under his spreading chestnut hair . . . his staccato voice and jumpy, restless manners, he appeared a portent of change."[61]

The conservative, not the experimental, however, made the most gratifying encounter of Beardsley's stay in Paris, that is, his meeting with Pierre Puvis de Chavannes. Here was the president of the Salon des Beaux Arts, the dean of French painting. Even those painters who did not fall under his influence—Toulouse-Lautrec was one—regarded his murals in the Pantheon, the Sorbonne and elsewhere as masterworks and considered him the greatest living French artist. Armed with Burne-Jones' letter of introduction and his own portfolio, Beardsley appeared one day unannounced at Puvis de Chavannes' studio. No details of the call survive except the one incident which Beardsley recounted with great satisfaction. "I got great encouragement," he declared, "from Puvis de Chavannes, who introduced me to a brother painter as 'un jeune artiste anglais qui a fait des choses étonnantes.' I was not a little pleased," he added, "with my success."[62]

vii

Beardsley took back to London with him this success, Puvis de Chavannes' encouragement. It returned him to the drawing board at once, "working in the same method," the Japanesque, "only making developments." The immediate result was a drawing of Siegfried, which he then considered the "culmination" of his new style. He presented it to Burne-Jones, taking advantage of his visit to The Grange to talk of his success with the French artist.

Beardsley also made some "nice additions" to his portfolio. With these new drawings he began to go from one publisher to another seeking a commission. Most of them, as he told Scotson-Clark, "opened their great stupid eyes pretty wide. They were frightened . . . of anything so new and so daringly original."[63] This was the "airy assurance of a man conscious of genius."[64] It may well have evaporated when only one publishing house, Cassell's, showed enough interest to promise him work, and nothing came of that.

Although Beardsley had developed much more than his assurance from his stay in Paris, the externals of his life in London were unchanged. He was back at home with his mother, who was mildly

53

ill and complaining, his father, and Mabel, about to take up an uncongenial job. He went back sporadically to the art school, back to the Fire Office, and back to his noonday visits to Evans' bookshop, taking with him as a gift on one such visit a drawing he had had in his portfolio when he first visited Burne-Jones, *Hail Mary*.

And so again the conservative rather than the daring and new brought good fortune to Beardsley and with it, change. It brought him the opportunity he wanted. Evans and the ingenious publisher J. M. Dent were on very friendly terms. Together they had planned Dent's Temple Shakespeare series, and they often talked over numerous publishing projects. Evans had listened to Dent tell about his plans to produce a new, illustrated edition of Malory's *Morte d'Arthur* for popular readership and how so far he had been unable to find an illustrator who could draw with the spirit of the medieval text. He was accustomed to dealing with artists. Walter Crane and G. F. Watts were two among a host of others whose work he had published, but this time he needed something different. To clarify what he wanted, Dent referred to the books issued from William Morris' Kelmscott Press. Kelmscott used hand-carved wood blocks, however, and Dent meant to publish with line block illustrations, a commercial and far cheaper method. He wanted an artist who could match the Kelmscott decorations at a small fee.

Soon after this talk with Dent, Evans suggested to him that he come to the bookshop to inspect drawings left there by a young artist who might answer his requirements. Dent was examining Beardsley's *Hail Mary* when Beardsley walked into the shop. It was midday, and he had come as usual to browse among the books. Evans pointed to Beardsley, told Dent, "There's your man," and at once introduced the two: Beardsley, painfully thin and boyish, and Dent, a man of forty-three years with a large, dejected moustache and a long, graying beard. He was an energetic man whose well-made suits were always creased and wrinkled. He liked Beardsley's drawings and he trusted Evans' recommendation; but to be on the safe side, Dent wanted to see something from Beardsley designed especially for the *Morte d'Arthur*. Then if the design was appropriate, the two could talk terms. Beardsley was dazed and excited but adaptable. He asked to see one or two Kelmscott Press books on the shop's shelves and he examined them briefly, since he had to go back to the Fire Office. As he turned to go he shook hands with Evans and breathed to him, "It's too good a chance. I'm sure I shan't be equal to it. I am not worthy of it."[65] Without question, Beardsley was grateful to Evans; but such humility is vastly different from his remark to Scotson-Clark that

J. M. Dent *(From J. M. Dent*, The Memoirs of, *London, 1928)*

Dent, the "lucky dog," saw his "chance" and put Beardsley "onto a large edition de luxe."[66]

Of course that is exactly what Dent did. Beardsley's nightly efforts in the candlelight were intense and serious. As yet Beardsley had learned almost nothing about techniques for reproducing drawings, and he was ignorant of the fact that the line block might have been invented for him, so well did it suit his work. But he aimed at the highest he knew, an emphasis on his method derived from Burne-Jones modified by the Japanesque. What he produced was *The Achieving of the Sangreal*, work so fine that he may well have been amazed at his own powers. He signed it—the first piece so signed—with what he called his Japanese mark, his "trademark," a device which was a rough imitation of his candles and the light they gave.

When Dent saw this picture, this "marvellous design," he was almost speechless with amazement. It was rich in detail, a whole so composed as to belong on the printed page. The fact that it was done in wash and line and thus must be reproduced by photogravure instead of line block made no difference. There and then Dent and Beardsley concluded a gentleman's agreement whereby Dent was to commence publication within a year of the *Morte Darthur* in monthly parts, all ornamented with Beardsley's designs. Beardsley anticipated making "twenty full-page drawings (eight on copper and twelve on zinc), about a hundred small drawings in the text, nearly 350 initial letters and the cover"[67] over a period of twelve months. He told both King and Marshall, his former headmaster at Brighton, that for these he would receive £200. That was in late 1892; by mid-February 1893 a letter to Scotson-Clark reported the fee as £250, a figure which matched his exultation at his new circumstances.[68]

For the next few months, when Beardsley opened his peripatetic portfolio, he usually disclosed one or more of his designs for *Morte Darthur*. Although he was to develop his capability well beyond that of 1892 and early 1893 and thus came to resent this commission which ended as eighteen months of work involving "twenty full and double pages and nearly 550 borders, ornaments, chapter headings, initials and tailpieces,"[69] he began the work with great confidence and enthusiasm, eager as always to show what he could do. One of the first to see the new designs was Aymer Vallance, who was still active in his crusade for Beardsley's recognition. At once, he wanted Beardsley to go again to William Morris with the drawings, so increased in power and so appropriate to the Kelmscott Press. Beardsley refused; so Vallance took *The Lady of the Lake Telling Arthur of the Sword Excalibur* to Morris. Beardsley had prepared it with great care, making more than one kind of reproduction before he settled on a zinc process picture, and Vallance went to Morris with the expectation that he must now recognize the young artist's ability. But, forgetful of his own adaptation of medievalism, Morris flew into a tantrum, spoke loudly of Beardsley's "act of usurpation" and declared more loudly that "a man ought to do his own work." He threatened to protest such poaching to Dent, and only Edward Burne-Jones managed to quiet Morris. When Beardsley heard about the episode, his response to it was arrogant but honest. He said of Morris, "While *his* work is mere imitation of the old stuff, mine is fresh and original."[70]

Vallance, aware now that Morris and Beardsley could never work together, turned his efforts another way. On a Sunday afternoon, probably in November, he conducted Beardsley and his portfolio to Palace Court, where the Wilfred Meynells were at home to artists, writers, musicians. Wilfred Meynell was editor of *The Weekly Review*, a position which he filled most capably but which he had got through the intervention of friendly priests with Cardinal Manning. Alice Meynell, when she was not attending to one of their seven children was an essayist and a poet of quality, handling verse forms and statement with controlled lyricism. *Preludes*, her first volume of verse, had appeared in 1875. Usually dressed in black with a white ruffle at her neck, fastidious in thought and act, severe, sometimes self-righteous, unyielding, she was the dominant member of the Meynell household. The two are remembered partly for salvaging the poet Francis Thompson and for failing to make any effort in the direction of poor Frederick Rolfe, who called himself Baron Corvo. When Vallance and Beardsley entered the lofty, well-lighted and well-aired drawing room of the Meynell home, Vernon Blackburn, another guest, was singing his own musical setting of Mrs. Meynell's sonnet "Love of Narcissus." The listeners stirred as he reached the last line, "His weary tears that touch him with the rain," and after a pause began to move about; and Vallance with Beardsley in tow approached C. Lewis Hind, also a guest.

Hind, a sub-editor then of *Art Journal*, was preparing to launch a new periodical, *The Studio*. He had backing from John Lane, the publisher, and Charles Holme, a man in the "Japanese Trade." Holme thought the magazine ought to start with a "sensational send-off," a leading article which would make the new *Studio* "go." But Lewis Hind had found nothing which would serve. On this Sunday afternoon at the Meynells', Vallance introduced Beardsley. "I've brought a young artist here, Aubrey Beardsley. I wish you would look at his drawings: they're remarkable." Hind tells how he looked up to see, standing behind Vallance, Beardsley, "slim, self-possessed, a portfolio under his arm." He handed it to Hind, who looked through the drawings, some for *Morte Darthur* and others which were exercises in the artist's developing ability. Hind's thought was, "Either I'm crazy, or this is genius."[71]

Thanks to this meeting with Beardsley, *The Studio* was on its way. The next day, Hind took Beardsley and his portfolio to Holme. He bought the drawings Beardsley would let him have, and Holme and Hind signed an agreement. Holme wanted Hind to write an article to accompany Beardsley's drawings, but Hind, in full command as editor, insisted on Joseph Pennell as a man whose critical opinion carried weight.[72] The first issue of *The Studio* was planned with a cover design by Beardsley for February 1893.

Beardsley first showed his drawings to Joseph Pennell in December 1892 when they met at Robbie Ross' rooms. Ross introduced Beardsley to all kinds of people. Count Eric Stenbock is one example. An English-born Esthonian of Swedish background, he was bizarre in habits and appearance. W. B. Yeats described him as a "scholar, connoisseur, drunkard, poet, pervert," and charmer; Yeats might have added that Stenbock was also painfully self-destructive. By taking into his heart and purse Norman O'Neill, a young English musician whom he first encountered atop a London omnibus, Stenbock provided Beardsley with a pleasant acquaintance and the subject of various caricatures plus some cash.[73] But the meeting with Pennell was a special occasion. Thinking it advisable for Beardsley to dine with art critics, Ross invited both artists and critics to 54 Church Street in early December 1892. There were George Moore, an artist turned writer, Walter Sickert, the artist, D. S. MacColl, critic. All three were later fixed (with others) in William Orpen's painting, *Homage à Manet*. In addition to those three there were Justin McCarthy, who was historian, novelist, journalist; Gleeson White, author and editor recently come from Christchurch to London; Lewis Hind, and of course Joseph Pennell.

Every one of Ross' guests was older than Beardsley—McCarthy was forty years older—so that Pennell's immediate impression is not surprising. Pennell speaks of "a boy, almost a child" so simply dressed that he looked less like an artist than a "swell." He carried a portfolio "prettily decorated on the sides," such as a young woman might carry, and from it he selected drawings to show to his ready-made audience. MacColl characterized them as "a whole world of fanciful vision expressed in fine-spun lines and cunningly arranged blots." MacColl, who had encountered Beardsley at least once before this dinner party, later, after his death, spoke of Beardsley's "sweetness," but in fact found him trying as only a very young

58

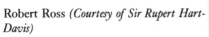

Robert Ross *(Courtesy of Sir Rupert Hart-Davis)*

person can be. What Ross called his vehemence of speech, MacColl described as a nervous, almost overbearing, impatient speech, wholly concerned with his "own ideas, and indifferent to everything outside them." Beardsley's sharp "admirations and indifferences" were disconcerting and his enthusiasm for the "naughty, witty extreme" was both too confident and too flippant. If Beardsley's green youth was abrasive to MacColl, and what he objected to was typical of a very assured and very young man, he nevertheless (with reservations) found Beardsley's work striking.

So did Pennell. Pennell especially admired drawings for *Morte Darthur* which combined in a "remarkable manner" Pre-Raphaelite influences with modernity. When he commented on it, Beardsley answered calmly that Burne-Jones and William Morris had also liked them. Fortunately Aymer Vallance was not present as Beardsley, carried away by his own fabrication, went on to disparage Morris' wood-cutting as a means of reproduction, saying that he much preferred the more recent method of line block. All this, according to Pennell, "waked . . . up" the group, and Pennell, "staggered" by the talk of Burne-Jones, decided that this young Beardsley was indeed worthy of attention.[74]

Aubrey Beardsley's gifts were great and his application to them, prodigious. Neither comes to much without the other, and in Beardsley they were admirably balanced. Unquestionably his illness aroused pity. MacColl spoke of Beardsley's "eager fire and hurry" as the "stamp of the consumptive"; to Gertrude Atherton, the American novelist, he looked as if he might die at any moment.[75] But so many of Beardsley's contemporaries were consumptive. Henry Harland and Ernest Dowson, the poet, are only two. Indeed, such illness even in Beardsley's case was so taken for granted that his friends Cochran and Scotson-Clark failed to realize its seriousness as Beardsley lay dying.[76] The attention given him before his success reached the point where briefly he needed no help is attributable, however, mostly to the "sweetness" which MacColl remarked. A mother's prejudice may be apparent in Ellen Beardsley's calling him "the dearest boy, gentle, affectionate, whimsical & Puck like." But few who knew Beardsley remained unaware of his amiability, his gentle and lovable nature. Jacques Emile Blanche, the French artist, included Mabel in his praise when he told her that both young Beardsleys were endowed with "the most divine gifts" and had "all possibilities," but yet both "smiled & chose just" to make themselves agreeable to their friends. Ross spoke of Aubrey's charming lack of sophistication, his "brisk and virile character" with all the "curiosity and gaiety of boyhood"; Edward Strangman, Irish-born and English-educated member of the

Bar, remarked on Beardsley's "dear charming ways and kind sweet sympathy." Even those who castigated Beardsley at the height of his later notoriety fell silent when they came to know him. Elizabeth Pennell summed up his gentle nature as simplicity; she said she found him as "simple and natural as are always the really great."[77]

Thus Beardsley's gentle, ingratiating boyishness as well as Joseph Pennell's approval and the recommendations of the Harlands made him a welcome guest at the Pennells' Thursday nights in their flat in Buckingham Street. This boyishness also gave Beardsley the opportunity to learn the necessary relationship between the techniques of drawing and reproduction. Pennell taught him. It also made him the object of the solicitude with which he was served in the years 1891 and 1892; that of Aymer Vallance, Robbie Ross, Evans, King, Burne-Jones, and Joseph Pennell, who agreed to write the article Hind wanted for *The Studio*.

CHAPTER III

i

THE first number of *The Studio*, scheduled for February 1893, did not appear until April. The delay was owing to the fact that Lewis Hind was seduced by William Waldorf Astor and Harry Cust, Astor's editor, to forsake *The Studio* for *The Pall Mall Budget*. Gleeson White moved into the editorship of *The Studio*, but not in time to produce its first number before April.

That first issue was a distinguished one, with articles by artists R. A. M. (Bob) Stevenson, Frank Brangwyn, and C. W. Furse and an article on Sir Frederick Leighton. It included, as well, a cover which Beardsley made expressly for *The Studio* and nine of his other drawings. Among them was the decorative and stylized piece, *Siegfried*, which he had given, soon after his return from Paris, to Burne-Jones. In addition there was a wonderfully detailed drawing made for the *Morte Darthur*, *Merlin Taketh The Child Arthur Into His Keeping*, and another made at the last minute after a reading of Oscar Wilde's play *Salomé*, published in French in both Paris and London on February 22, 1893. Beardsley's copy was a gift from Wilde inscribed "March '93. For Aubrey: for the only artist who, besides myself, knows what the dance of the seven veils is, and can see that invisible dance. Oscar."[1] Beardsley chose to illustrate lines from the play, making them an integral part of his design by lettering them in it, "J'ai baisé ta bouche Iokanaan/ J'ai baisé ta bouche." Although the drawing from *Salomé* is sensational in its depiction of lilies alive in a pool of blood dripping from John the Baptist's severed head, that and the design for the *Morte Darthur* are the most skillful of the nine pictures. Each of these two in its own way demonstrates Beardsley's capacity for line and manipulation of space and perspective. They are the work of a consummate artist.[2]

One of Beardsley's ornate initials introduces Pennell's article. It announces Beardsley as an artist, a new artist, of such quality that he is very likely to suffer from over-appreciation. But Pennell's admiration is as much for current methods of reproduction and Beardsley's good sense in taking advantage of them. After all, Pennell had demonstrated line block to Beardsley and Beardsley had indeed learned his lesson well. In any case, as Pennell said, he was writing for artists to whom Beardsley must appeal, and what was said about him, Pennell implied, must also appeal to them.[3]

Certainly the article pleased Beardsley. Often he was so amiable that his thanks might well be an act of good manners rather than gratitude. In this instance, he wrote to his friend Scotson-Clark about the article, so "grand" that he would "blush to quote" it; but Beardsley promised to overcome his modesty enough to send a copy of the magazine, which would also exhibit the "grand cover" he had designed. That he was genuinely appreciative was further demonstrated by a continuing association with Pennell and the fact that Beardsley dedicated his first book of collected drawings to Pennell.[4] To be noticed, to see his work in print, to have favorable comment from so authoritative a critic was most gratifying.

The article was too late to be of much practical use. That was always before Beardsley's eyes. In the latter part of 1892, he had told E. J. Marshall that the "money view" of his art work had "to be kept keenly in view."[5] But by April 1893, Beardsley had almost as many commissions as he could manage. Indeed, he had declared in December that he hardly knew how he was to "find time for them all."[6]

Beardsley's assertion was true although he devoted his time fully to his art work. Soon after receiving the commission from Dent to make the drawings for the *Morte Darthur*, Beardsley had given up his job at the Guardian Life and Fire Insurance Office. That decision, very likely carried out in October, was a momentous one. If his father had a job, it was uncertain and ill-paid. His mother suffered from chronic sciatica and even more from the insecurities of her life. The positions which Mabel and Aubrey held seemed essential, as usual. Family needs and the whole question of family survival outweighed the matter of Mabel's or Aubrey's suitability for their work or their satisfaction in it. But both Mabel and Aubrey were young enough or wise enough in 1892 to put personal satisfaction and necessity in perspective and to take risks to keep them there. When Aubrey consulted her, Mabel ardently supported his eagerness to end his clerkship. And so, much to the relief of both employer and employee, Beardsley left his job at the Fire Office. Only after he had done so did he tell his parents. They were aghast, especially Vincent Beardsley. What Aubrey called "ructions" erupted and apparently they went on for several weeks, diminishing at last in a flutter of interest in his work, a manifestation which he mistrusted. He knew that the fees from the considerable amount of work he had made a difference to his parents, especially his "revered father."

Having commissioned work from Beardsley, both Lewis Hind and Dent exercised a proprietary interest in him. They were both eager for many additional drawings. In the autumn of 1892, Beardsley was planning to work on "no less than four books" for Dent plus the *Morte Darthur*. For two of these four, Hawthorne's *Classic Tales* and Mackenzie's *Man of Feeling*, he ended by drawing nothing. For a reprint of Fanny Burney's *Evelina*, he made at least one drawing, *Evelina and her Guardian*, which was not used and a title page and designs for the front cover and spine which were. He had no time to do more for this book, partly because there was so much to do for others. Dent's fourth assignment was for a series of three volumes of *Bon-Mots*, which appeared one at a time, commencing in 1893, over a period of several months. In the latter part of 1892, Beardsley spoke of spending ten days for a fee of £15 in order to complete "a set of sixty grotesques" for the first volume of this series. He described his grotesques as "very tiny little things, some not more than an inch high, and the pen strokes to be counted on the fingers."[7]

Whatever their number, these and other designs made for the three volumes of *Bon-Mots*, and some were full page drawings, as well as the drawings Beardsley made for *Evelina*, are significant because they exhibit, so early in his professional career, motifs which were a part of his continuing concept of design both thematically and decoratively. Architectural ornamentation, derived either from the Regency grandeur of Brighton's Pavilion[8] or from monuments of Paris, such as the Arc de Triomphe or the Opéra, the Palais Garnier, and particularized by Beardsley's grotesque fancy, is present in the unused drawing, the cover design, and the title page for *Evelina*. Such architectural details occurred often thereafter and reappeared prominently in Beardsley's last and finest drawings. Another persistent compositional device in the drawing for *Evelina* is birds-in-flight, often visible through a window.[9] The grotesques for *Bon-Mots* make an early statement of a theme which Beardsley retained throughout his career. For his grotesques, Beardsley borrowed freely, even from himself. There is at least one figure got from his early Greenaway-like drawings made for Lady Pelham almost ten years earlier,[10] and another holding a severed head which drips blood as in the *Salomé*-drawing made for *The Studio*.[11] Outside his own work, Beardsley found various influences in Mantegna, always an object of his admiration, and in contemporary French artists who concentrated on visionary and exotic subjects. Odilon Redon may have provided

Beardsley with various spiders[12] and, without doubt, Félicien Rops offered the background for Beardsley's humanoid creatures with four cloven hoofs. Rops' illustration for Barbey d'Aurevilly's immensely popular *Les Diaboliques* show two such monsters, both women.[13] Beardsley derived other grotesques from Rops and from Mantegna, transforming them by the power of imagination and technique into his own, but the cloven hoof is one of the most obvious and the most persistent thematic concepts which occur first, as far as Beardsley is concerned, in *Bon Mots*.

That statement is based on the assumption that such concepts are thematic. When Beardsley told Scotson-Clark about the work "new in method of drawing and composition" which aroused Puvis de Chavannes' amazement, he also spoke of subjects which were "quite mad and a little indecent. Strange hermaphroditic creatures wandering about in Pierrot costumes or modern dress," a "new world" of his own creation.[14] Actually he had already illustrated letters written to Scotson-Clark in 1891 with strange creatures. In any case Beardsley's description of his work implies that he had happened on his subjects involuntarily and that to him they were no more than the products of his fancy. That point of view is supported by Beardsley's claim for himself that he was nothing if not grotesque, and by Rothenstein's claim that Beardsley's taste was for the "bizarre and exotic." Besides, he had recently learned from his drawing of Salomé with the head of John the Baptist that "Beauty is the most difficult of things" whereas the grotesque was arresting and, for him, comparatively effortless. Ross, who knew Beardsley as well as any of his associates and saw him frequently, declared that he had "no other than a decorative intention" and that each of his drawings explained itself.[15] Furthermore, that line and pattern were not his first and dominant consideration is difficult to accept. He was surely an artist, not a moralist.

On the other hand, Beardsley frequently exaggerated to his own advantage in reporting his activities to Scotson-Clark, and he may have amplified his inventiveness. Mrs. Beardsley and his sister Mabel testified to his acute awareness of that "side of human imagination and human instinct" which "Respectability" in his time had chosen to ignore. They testified further to his determination to exhibit it with a liberalizing intent. Mrs. Beardsley said her son told her that "people hate to see their darling vices depicted," that "vice is terrible and it should be depicted." She insisted that he was "clean-minded," and Mabel confirmed this years later when she told W. B. Yeats that her brother had a "passion for reality." She said, "He hated the people who denied the existence of evil, and so being young he filled his pictures with evil."[16] If they were correct then so was Mr. Yeats in associating Beardsley's "patterns and rhythms of line" with the coming of symbolic art.[17] Then Beardsley's cloven hoofs and other recurring motifs, the fetus, the satyr, Pierrot and various bizarre misshapen forms, are symbols of various aspects of man's thoughts and obsessions. They serve as gleeful satire of humanity's involuntary self-disclosure.

Whatever his intention (which in fact matters not at all except to his biographer), Beardsley's later work employing the motifs so profuse in the three volumes of Bon-Mots was regarded as wicked. Alice Meynell, capable of very polite letters to his mother while Beardsley lived, wrote after his death with no more asperity than many critics that he invariably expressed "an infernal evil . . . explicit evil standing alone, apart from human tumult."[18] Her attitude matched innumerable comments in his lifetime and, except in rare instances, he never bothered to correct or deny them. Instead he pretended to enjoy his lurid reputation.

These motifs are not always present in other assignments which filled his hands with "nice things" at this time and for which, Beardsley said, he did not "forget to be thankful."[19] On December 9, 1892, Beardsley accepted a commission from the publishers Lawrence and Bullen to illustrate Lucian's True History, an edition which appeared in 1894. He agreed to do "30 little drawings . . . 6 inches by 4" for a fee of £100. Beardsley began these designs at once so that by mid-February he could tell Scotson-Clark that he was working for Lawrence and Bullen in his "new manner, or, rather a development of it." He went on with a singular lack of modesty to describe the drawings as "the most extraordinary things that have ever appeared in a book both in respect to technique and conception. They are also the most indecent."[20] Beardsley's boasts of indecency were true, but they were also evidence of an adolescent pretense of worldliness. He was role-playing again, as much for himself as for Scotson-Clark. In any case, Beardsley made only five of these drawings, of which Lawrence and Bullen printed two.[21] A third was reproduced in platinotype by Evans and inserted in fifty-four copies of a special edition.

At the same time, Beardsley was producing drawings, mostly caricatures, for The Pall Mall Budget at the request of Lewis Hind. He had given up The Studio, but he retained Beardsley. Hind acknowledged, however, that he failed to make the most of Beardsley, who might better have made full-page, straightforward designs for The Budget, but neither William Waldorf Astor, who owned The Budget, nor Harry Cust, Astor's agent, had much enthusiasm for Beardsley.

So Hind kept him inconspicuous with the result that his work in *The Pall Mall Budget* was slight. Some of it was less Beardsley-like and less meritorious than any of his other drawings published after 1892. Nevertheless, Beardsley enjoyed making the drawings. To prepare for them, Hind and he made a number of excursions together. They went together to the mint to inspect casts for the new coinage of 1893, a "particularly hilarious" occasion which provided eight of Beardsley's caricatures of the new currency. Of these, *The Budget* published four; the others were too ludicrous for anything but suppression.[22] Other memorable visits were to the theater, where Beardsley found material for drawings of members of the cast of *Becket*, which included Ellen Terry and Henry Irving, and of the actors in *Diplomacy*, among them Arthur Cecil and Forbes Robertson.[23] But most of all, Beardsley enjoyed the effect of his drawings for *The Budget* after he had made them. He declared that he had "created some astonishment" when he "blossomed out" in both "caricature and wash-work." His portrait of Irving, Beardsley said, "made the old black-and-white duffers sit up." Indeed, with all this work and with offers from Clark of Edinburgh, from Elkin Mathews, from American publishers and from several periodicals, including *The Pall Mall Gazette*, Beardsley was justified in saying to Scotson-Clark, "My dear boy, I have fortune at my foot."[24]

For Beardsley, "fortune at my foot" was a happy expression. That was exactly where he wanted fortune to be, prostrate before him; and he used the phrase more than once to indicate the "oof and fame" he had achieved. In those months of 1893, life seemed endlessly gratifying. Pressure from his parents to hold on to the security of a steady job had evaporated. His mother's view of him as her baby, and sometimes a "naughty" one, was a nuisance but one he could usually ignore. Mabel, still at the Polytechnic but nowhere near the headmistress-ship Aubrey had predicted for her, was on hand for encouragement, admiration, or an evening at the opera. He rested often in the interest of his health, reading or writing letters from his bed. But, stimulated by his success and so many new experiences, his health improved. He ordered a top hat from Hatch and began to go to Doré for his suits.

Beardsley anticipated exhibiting at The New English Art Club in spring. Frederick Brown, who had gone from the Westminster School of Art to the prestigious Slade, had invited him, so that in early spring Beardsley was busily recalling the drawing *La Femme Incomprise* from the *Pall Mall Magazine* in time for "sending day."[25]

Beardsley had friends who sought his company and Mabel's, among them Ross, Vallance, Julian Sampson, first met at one of

Left, Drawing of Ellen Terry in *Becket* for *The Pall Mall Budget (Courtesy of The Bodley Head Ltd.)* Above, Cover design for *Le Morte Darthur (Courtesy of Brian Reade Esq.)*

Gurney's Sunday luncheon parties, the Pennells, and Henry and Aline Harland. Their homes were open to him, and in them he met more members of intellectual and artistic London. Some time in the spring, Beardsley began to visit the two artists Charles Ricketts and Charles Shannon. They were vastly different in appearance and temperament. Shannon was very fair and boyish; he was slow, quiet, reserved. Ricketts had golden-red hair and beard and such authoritative and eloquent speech that Beardsley was soon convinced that Ricketts was a man worth hearing. The two, Shannon and Ricketts, lived together and worked together in an old house once occupied by Whistler. The house, which took its name from its location, The Vale, a cul-de-sac off King's Road, Chelsea, was well within London but rural in atmosphere owing to a former deer park along one side and an open field before it as well as a tree in its yard. Inside this house, hosts and guests gathered in the kitchen for talk and argument in which, rightly in Beardsley's view, Ricketts usually had the last word.

When no one's kitchen or drawing room beckoned, Beardsley frequented the Crown, a pub in Charing Cross Road between the stage doors of the Alhambra and the Empire; or the Café Royal, where he enjoyed Château de Mille Sécousses, an inexpensive claret, with talk over marble tables; or Jimmy's—the St. James Restaurant in Piccadilly—or a good, cheap meal at Aux Gourmets. The writer Edgar Jepson says he saw Beardsley there, gay and noisy at his dinner; and once, also according to Jepson, Beardsley tried to "ravish" Henry Horne's "light o'love" Lucy in the supper room of the Thalia.[26] Beardsley loved noise and talk and laughter. He loved lavish gestures—literally—and movement. He had success and youth, and at his age, tomorrows are no more than dreams, especially if death lurks nearby.

In May, Beardsley went again to Paris. He told King that he was going with Oscar Wilde, but there was never such a plan and he went alone as he had done in 1892. He was forced to take unfinished work with him, completing it in his hotel and sending it off to England and *The Pall Mall Gazette* from there. With the drawing went a simple statement of his pleasure, "It is really *lovely* over here."[27] Paris in May is lovely, but it was also a place where, without challenge, Beardsley could express what Robbie Ross called an "artificial manner." He could be what he chose. Elizabeth Pennell saw him at the *vernissage* of that year's Salon coming towards her "with the tripping step that was characteristic of him, a little light can swinging in his hand." He was dressed in the costume he "thought Paris and art demanded of him." He had devised an entirely gray outfit, "a harmony carefully and

Sketch of Beardsley by D.S. MacColl *(Courtesy of The Gallatin Beardsley Collection, Princeton University Library)*

quite exquisitely carried out, grey coat, grey waistcoat, grey trousers, grey Suède gloves, grey soft felt hat, grey tie which, in compliment to the French, was large and loose." Without doubt, he was the "most striking figure at the galleries of the Salon, sharing the stares of the crowd with "the *clou*" of the year's exhibits, a portrait by Amman-Jean which changed the way women wore their hair that season.[28] No one admired Beardsley at that *vernissage* more than he did himself.

Thereafter he spent much time with the Pennells and with Bob Stevenson and the Henry Harlands, also in Paris for "sheer love" of it "in the May-time." One afternoon, Henry Harland led them on an expedition to St. Cloud where they played "living statues on the broken columns," enacting Mercury on one column and on another Apollo "in frock coat with silk hat for lyre." Afterward they went for dinner to a small restaurant, less notable for food and drink than for a parrot which welcomed guests, "Après vous, Madame." There Beardsley began to lament the prevalence of worn-out artistic principles and Bob Stevenson proceeded to defend *"les vieux"* pompously and ponderously, to the amusement of everyone except the two principals. Another time they were hilarious at feeding cake soaked with absinthe to a peacock and then watching the poor bird's uncertain gait.

Beardsley's pleasures were more relaxed when his only companion was Joseph Pennell. Together they visited the Luxembourg Gardens or strolled toward the Louvre through the Tuileries gardens and their recently restored pavilions of Marsan and Flore, and one Saturday evening they went together to the Opéra to hear *Tristan and Isolde*. According to Pennell, an early version of one of Beardsley's most remarkable drawings, *The Wagnerites*, resulted from this very performance.

When they left the Opéra, the two men crossed to the Café de la Paix, where they promptly noticed Whistler at a nearby table. Not to see him was difficult, with his foppish dress and careful white curl against the masses of his dark hair. A meticulous craftsman and a highly gifted artist, Whistler was demanding, often noisy and quarrelsome, and this time he was supercilious when Pennell and Beardsley joined him. Beardsley soon left, but Pennell stayed on while Whistler muttered complaints about "that young thing" and all the hair which he insisted grew on Beardsley from head to toe, even sprouting from his shoes. Pennell insisted on Beardsley's distinction and at last get a grudging permission to take Beardsley the next day to Whistler's flat in the rue du Bac. When they arrived, Beardsley very stylish in a straw boater such as Whistler wore, and joined the other guests in the garden, Whistler showed himself a poor host. Although

Beardsley had long admired Whistler, even to the extent of once spending an entire week's salary, 15s, on one of his etchings, his behavior now seemed a personal affront, and Beardsley was offended. He remembered it for a long time. From it came several caricatures of Whistler and one of his wife.[29] Beardsley gained much from his stay in Paris.

ii

When he returned to London in June, Beardsley managed with Mabel's cooperation to acquire a home for the Beardsley family, the first of their own. Together, Mabel and her brother bought an unremarkable house at 114 Cambridge Street, Pimlico. Aymer Vallance took over the decorating so that the interior was remarkable if not distinguished. Beardsley's studio, according to some accounts, had black doors, green rugs, black furniture upholstered in blue and white, and walls hung with blazing orange. William Rothenstein, who disliked Beardsley's or anyone's flamboyance, reported only walls "distempered a violent orange, the doors and skirtings . . . painted black."[30] Eventually Beardsley added to the decor of his bedroom a series of pornographic Japanese prints removed from *The Book of Love*, a book which Rothenstein found an embarrassment to own and so gave to a grateful Beardsley.

With the new home, the Beardsleys adopted Thursday afternoon as their own; on that day at tea-time they were "at home" with Mabel and Aubrey passing the plates of biscuits while Mrs. Beardsley "poured out." If Mr. Beardsley was ever present, he went unnoticed. Netta Syrett, Mabel's colleague at the Polytechnic and often at Cambridge Street on Thursdays, was surprised to learn that there was a Mr. Beardsley. But all the friends who had entertained Mabel and Aubrey were in turn entertained to tea and there were others— Julian Sampson, Count Stenbock (who wrote a set of verses about "Mabel and her Thursday teas"),[31] and later Max Beerbohm and William Rothenstein.

Some time that summer Rothenstein and Beardsley renewed the acquaintance first made in Paris the year before. Rothenstein had taken up a commission too exciting to refuse, an offer from John Lane to publish a series of twenty-four drawings of prominent Oxonians under the title *Oxford Characters*. After closing his studio in Paris and disposing of paintings, obligations, and the habits of a young artist in Paris, Rothenstein had returned to England to stay. Exactly when he reached London is uncertain. He says that he came in autumn; yet he was at Oxford during the Summer Term and he spoke of seeing Oscar Wilde's *A Woman of No Importance*, which closed on August 16, 1893. In any case, en route to Oxford, Rothenstein stopped in London to practice drawing on stone and to learn the fine points of lithography from Thomas Way and Son, a firm of lithographic printers recommended by Whistler. During this stay in London, Wilde took Rothenstein to The Vale, where he heard Shannon and Ricketts talk of Beardsley. And so Rothenstein remembered and went to call at 114 Cambridge Street. Beardsley welcomed him, and since Rothenstein had no studio in London, Beardsley offered one side of his work-table. Rothenstein made use of it repeatedly both during his short stay in London and later when he was resident in Oxford but in London for a few days.[32]

In turn, Rothenstein—Beardsley called him Billy—introduced Max Beerbohm to Beardsley. Beerbohm and Will Rothenstein met at Oxford, where Max was an undergraduate and Will an artist-visitor who had lived in Paris and reputedly knew everyone there, even Whistler and Edmond de Goncourt. Rothenstein designated Max as one of several undergraduates for inclusion in *Oxford Characters*, an opportunity for Max to exhibit himself in a bell-shaped hat, which Rothenstein had him remove, and green trousers. Max then decided to spend the next Oxford term in London, a practice sanctioned by the University for fourth-year men. It was during those months that Rothenstein introduced Beerbohm to life: to the "exuberant vista of gilding and crimson velvet," among the mirrors and "upholding caryatids," the tobacco smoke and the noise of the Domino Room of the Café Royal; to the less elaborate but lively Crown Pub; and to Beardsley, by taking Max to Cambridge Street.[33] Beerbohm was impressed by Beardsley's achievement without admiring his drawings unreservedly. But he liked Beardsley at once, seeing beyond his mannerisms to his "stony common sense," his responsible and affectionate attitude toward his family, his essential sincerity.[34] And Beardsley liked Max. He liked Billy Rothenstein, too.

Apparently Rothenstein was the odd man of the three, all born in 1872, all gifted, all young men of character. He still had reservations about Beardsley, as he recorded eventually in *Men and Memories*. Beerbohm confirmed that fact when, in mid-1939, he altered a radio script for the BBC by putting in Walter Sickert and taking out Beardsley for Rothenstein's sake. Max explained that the change was made "because W. R. never liked A. B. so much as most of us did (though the two were quite passably good friends)."[35] Neither of the other two put their feelings on paper. David Cecil, Max's biographer, remarked on Max's distaste for self-exposition, and the consequent

William Rothenstein and Max Beerbohm *(Courtesy of Mrs. Ensor Holiday)*

biographical puzzle he created.[36] Certainly, when Beardsley stopped writing to Scotson-Clark, as he apparently did early in 1893, he wrote no more letters as intimate as those, even to his sister Mabel. Yet the three young men were undoubtedly held together by the affection of Max and Beardsley for each other and for Rothenstein and his for Max, a relationship which survived for years. And in 1893, commencing in the autumn, they began to go about London together.

Rothenstein summarized their activities when he spoke of Beardsley as a tireless worker: "His work done, Aubrey loved to get into evening clothes and drive into the town. So did Max and I."[37] They went to music hall performances, especially at The Gaiety, where Max could dream of Cissy Loftus, London's answer to Yvette Guilbert. Together they enjoyed the theater, made especially accessible by Herbert Beerbohm Tree, Max's half-brother. Billy and Aubrey laughed uproarously at the opening night of Shaw's *Arms and the Man*. Beerbohm and Beardsley watched Rothenstein fence with Robert Cunninghame Graham at Angelo's. Each man made suggestions to the other two about techniques and reproduction of drawings. Both Rothenstein and Beardsley visited the Beerbohm home in Upper Berkeley Street. The family liked them, and Julius, Max's brother, was particularly pleased with Beardsley's patent approval of Max's writing and drawing.[38]

Beardsley's only hardship, seemingly, apart from the uncertain state of his health, was the very thing which had set off the pleasurable excitement and success, the drawings for the *Morte Darthur*. The quota of drawings due each month, according to his contract with Dent, became more and more difficult to supply. Invariably he put off this chore as long as possible and as the deadline approached he had to "strain every nerve working early and late" to get the work done.[39] Then he began to fall behind. In August he had to cancel plans for going to Hampton Court to see the Mantegna collection because he had to be "hard at work working off arrears for Dent."[40] Over and over, Beardsley threatened to repudiate the contract. He disturbed his mother so seriously with such threats in late September that she wrote to Robert Ross asking him to "shame" her son "into proper behaviour." She told Ross that she was "uneasy at the way Aubrey" was "treating Dent" over the *Morte Darthur* and "horrified at hearing him propose throwing it over altogether." She went on,

To me it seems monstrous that he should even contemplate behaving in such an unprincipled manner. His "Morte" work may be a little unequal—that is his own fault and because he is wilful enough not to exert himself over what he pretends he doesn't like . . . But that isn't the point, he undertook to do it, and Mr. Dent has spent money over it and subscribers too, and if Aubrey gives it up it will be disgraceful.

She ended by assuring Ross that she troubled him only because her son was not "small enough to whip."[41]

Beardsley was deliberately difficult with his mother, threatening what he had no intention of doing; her outrage at his behavior often drove him to greater extremes. Still he strongly resented working to schedule. It limited his development and restricted his choice of subject. He failed to fulfill a similar commitment for *Lucian's True History*, although in the case of the *Morte Darthur* he worked his way through the contract, however unwillingly and unevenly. Indeed, he was so disenchanted with this assignment that he never once referred to the exhibition of black-and-white drawings which Dent mounted in September and October 1894 and which included a number of Beardsley's drawings.[42] Vallance explained that Beardsley was reluctant to continue with the *Morte* because he was disappointed with its printing, with "finding how much beauty of drawing on which he had bestowed infinite pains was lost in excessive reduction." Furthermore, he was too impressionable and too restless "to acquiesce in a single convention."[43] In February 1893 he could honestly say that he still clung to the "best principles" of the Pre-Raphaelite Brotherhood, but *Japonisme* was already prominent in his work[44] and other influences began to touch it as the year progressed. In other words, Aubrey Beardsley found working in the convention demanded by the *Morte Darthur* tiresome.

That was increasingly so in view of a number of new opportunities. Soon after his return from Paris, Beardsley was approached by two periodicals eager to secure work from him. *St. Paul's*, a new magazine which commenced publication in March 1894 and ran until 1900, got Beardsley off to false starts with plans for a drawing to be called *The Procession of the Magi* (in which he expected to put somewhere a caricature of Charles Whibley, journalist and critic and one of Henley's "young men") and another, an illustration in "mystico-Oriental style" of the "Song of Songs."[45] Neither materialized, but in the remaining months of 1893 Beardsley produced instead one tailpiece and two headpieces for the first number of *St. Paul's*. One of the headpieces had to be altered so as to delete a drawing of a fetus under glass. A large drawing called *Girl at Her Toilet* appeared in the second number of Aprl 2, 1894. *St. Paul's* held a charming headpiece called *Pierrot and Cat* until July 20, 1895. *Pick-me-up*, the second journal, settled with Beardsley to publish a series of his drawings with occasional verse under the heading "Masques" and to bring them out later in book form.

Masks—or masques—were an intermittent theme of the years in which Beardsley lived. Robert Louis Stevenson's *The Strange Case of Dr. Jekyll and Mr. Hyde* and Wilde's *The Picture of Dorian Gray* are, after their fashion, investigations of masks in a society without the terminology of psychoanalysis. This motif, like so many subjects and modes which aroused Beardsley's interest, was in a sense a cliché of his intellectual environment. Such an observation in no way denigrates Beardsley's originality. That resides, rightly enough, in the execution of his drawings. But his subjects were an illustrator's. He began by exemplifying the text of some book, but he soon came to the view set down by George Moore, probably in 1887, "that in illustrating a book it would be much more artistic to do something that was not in the text than to try to reproduce in line what the writer had done in words."[46] In either case, Beardsley's concern was, of necessity, to "grace a page" and at the same time to impose a pattern on convention by means of predictable associations. The contrast between man's preoccupations and what he avowed, the mask he wore, was, of course, Beardsley's comprehensive subject. Immediate means of disclosing it were the clichés.

In August when he told Bobbie Ross about the undertaking for *Pick-me-up* and asked him to write verses to accompany the drawings, Beardsley explained, "Especially I want a prologue to be spoken by Pierrot (myself)."[47] Pierrot was one of the principal clues to Beardsley's attitudes as exhibited in his drawings. No single figure appeared more often in more forms and guises than Pierrot and there was none with which Beardsley identified himself as frequently. Pierrot, enacted by Gaspard Deburau in fanciful and often tragic playlets, appeared on the French pantomimic stage early in the nineteenth century. The character was marked by his dress, usually a loose white or white striped tunic with large flowing sleeves and ruffles at neck and wrists and loose white pantaloons. His face was heavily powdered and beneath the chalk-white mask he suffered from his own innocence, which defeated every yearning. By the late 1800s when he was reintroduced in pantomime, both French and English, he had changed. He had become Verlaine's *Pierrot gamin,*

> le subtil génie
> De sa malice infinie
> De poète-grimacier.

Although Pierrot remained a character who could say with Verlaine, *"Il pleure dans mon cœur,"* Pierrot's suffering now was from excess and from boredom with the limited ways of the world.[48]

Beardsley knew Paul Verlaine. The two met some time shortly after November 21, 1893. Although his mind was on Philomène Boudin and the twin questions of marriage and money, Verlaine came to London on that date to deliver a lecture under the auspices of Arthur Symons and William Rothenstein. That week or the next, Verlaine was taken to Henry Harland's flat in Cromwell Road and there Beardsley met the "dear old thing."[49] But the French poet had no direct influence on Beardsley, whose interest in pantomime had flourished since his school days when he went three times to see *L'Enfant Prodigue,* staged at Brighton.[50] And his presentation of Pierrot was sometimes merely for the requirements of composition, frequently traditional in concept, and increasingly a mask of self which suggested Beardsley's growing awareness that ". . . surfeiting, the appetite may sicken, and so die."

What concept of Pierrot Beardsley meant to emphasize in "Masques" is unknown. He turned from Ross to Max Beerbohm for the occasional verses, a suggestion which Max found flattering, and then Beardsley thought of writing them himself.[51] He worried the idea of the projected "Masques" for several months and as late as November reported that it would be "A-1"; but before 1893 was done, the book disappeared from his concern.

In any case, Beardsley was so busy with a number of other things that he could say honestly to King that he "hardly knew which way to turn for work."[52] Nevertheless, Beardsley had prepared a drawing, *Girl and a Bookshop,* for the New English Art Club's show, which opened on November 18. By late November, he had completed a frontispiece for *Virgilius the Sorcerer,* published by David Nutt that year; and on December 22, 1893, Stone and Kimball of Chicago commissioned four drawings for *The Works of Edgar Allan Poe.*[53]

iii

Beardsley's most important assignment in 1893, except for drawings still to do for the *Morte Darthur,* was to "picture" a translation into English of Oscar Wilde's *Salomé.* Although Ricketts thought Beardsley's "considerable talent" began with *Salome* and his drawings for it "never surpassed," and Ross thought them "collectively" Beardsley's masterpiece, they proved to be a disastrous assignment.

79

Thereafter Beardsley was coupled with Oscar Wilde in the public's mind and charged with Wilde's offenses.

John Lane of the firm of Elkin Mathews & John Lane, Vigo Street, commissioned the drawings. Lane was the self-educated son of a Devonshire yeoman who made himself a legendary publisher of his time, whether in partnership with Elkin Mathews or working alone under the imprint The Bodley Head. Lane was always a man with an eye to the main chance and a minimal consideration for his partner and their authors. While he was still employed as a clerk in the Railway Clearing House, Seymour Street, Euston Square, where he had worked since he was a small boy, Lane had used books instead of cash for capital and manipulated Mathews into a reluctant partnership. In 1892, Lane left his clerkship and became an active partner in the firm; but Mathews never trusted him. "Lane misrepresents and falsifies matters . . .," Mathews declared, "whenever it suits him to do so."[54] As for their authors, Lionel Johnson, the poet, was least critical when he called Lane "excellent but limited." Gertrude Atherton, the American novelist, said that Lane reminded her of a "fat white frog." She was never sure that he paid her all that was owing and what he did pay was "yielded . . . up grudgingly."[55] Frederick Rolfe, the English writer, was pleased to be in touch with Lane, a man who had enough sense to recognize genius (Rolfe's) when he saw it; but Rolfe described Lane as a "tubby little potbellied bantam, scrupulously attired and looking as though he had been suckled on bad beer,"[56] and they quarreled over money and publication dates.

Oscar Wilde, too, had his problems with Lane in the matter of the original, French-language publication of *Salomé.* In 1892, when Lane learned about the proposed edition of 250 copies to be issued by the Librairie de l'Art Indépendant in Paris, he suggested increasing the number of copies to 650 and adding to the title page the imprint of Elkin Mathews & John Lane for simultaneous publication in Paris and London. Wilde made the necessary arrangements, but despite repeated attempts, he could not bring Lane to put in writing his intent to publish. At last on February 21, 1893, the day before publication, Wilde had a telegram from Lane confirming their agreement. That was bad enough, but Wilde thought it far worse that Lane publicized this work of "tragic beauty" written "by an artist" as the "play which the Lord Chamberlain refused to license . . ."[57]

Beardsley knew little or nothing of such things, and he was eager for this commission which paid him £50 and associated him with the conspicuous Oscar Wilde and John Lane, a rising publisher. Lane

Illustration for Edgar Allan Poe's "The Mask of the Red Death" *(From* The Chapbook Semi-Monthly, *August 15, 1894)*

and Beardsley had met in late 1892 through Aymer Vallance. Beardsley had talked enthusiastically to him about making drawings for George Meredith's *The Shaving of Shagpat*. Vallance knew that Lane, too, admired Meredith; so Vallance invited the two to his rooms. For a time there was talk of Mathews & Lane publishing a new edition of *Shagpat* with Beardsley's illustrations, but the scheme fell through.[58] Here, however, was a firm and irresistible offer from Lane. Beardsley had already demonstrated his interest in *Salomé* with the drawing *J'ai baisé ta bouche Iokanaan*, published with Pennell's article about him in *The Studio*.[59] That drawing had secured the commission. Both Lane and Wilde were impressed enough by it and by Beardsley's growing reputation to prefer him to Ricketts or Shannon, who had provided decorations for a number of Wilde's books, among them *The Picture of Dorian Gray* and *The House of Pomegranates*. At the moment, Wilde's *The Sphinx* with Ricketts' drawings was in production.

That Wilde and Beardsley met first in Burne-Jones' garden at the time of Beardsley's great adventure is generally accepted. His letter to King describing the momentous visit is unclear; it says, "The Oscar Wildes and several others were there."[60] Mabel Beardsley, however, declared that Constance Wilde and the two boys, Cyril and Vyvyan, were present that afternoon without Oscar and then Mabel stated that Herbert Beerbohm Tree introduced Wilde and Beardsley in 1894. That second statement is mistaken. Wilde's gift of a copy of the French-language *Salomé* with an inscription dated March 1893 disproves Mabel's date. Where and when the two men first met may never be established, but they certainly encountered each other at The Vale, where Shannon and Ricketts lived; both Wilde and Beardsley visited there frequently. Furthermore they were often guests of Robert Ross in his rooms. William Rothenstein testified from his own experience that Wilde, Beerbohm, and Beardsley were never wittier than when at Ross' parties.[61] Certainly at least once, either late in 1893 or early in the next year, Wilde invited Beardsley to dine with Ross at Kettner's in Soho, and on August 16, 1893, at the last performance of *A Woman of No Importance*, Lord Alfred Douglas, Ross, and Beardsley were Wilde's guests in a box at the Haymarket. Max Beerbohm reported seeing them, all except Beardsley, who was entirely sober, wearing "rich clusters" of "vine leaves in their hair."[62] Obviously Mabel's statement that the "acquaintanceship" between Wilde and Beardsley lasted only six weeks was mistaken, too.

But their connection was hardly more than an "acquaintanceship." Neither Beardsley nor his friends was bedazzled by Wilde. He was too old for the company he kept and his habits were common knowledge. Of the three young men, Beerbohm, Rothenstein, and Beardsley, Beardsley seemed the most tolerant and the most indifferent at this time. Billy Rothenstein thought Wilde "gross" and "soiled by the world." As for Max, he disliked Wilde's "coy, carnal smile & fatuous giggle" and thought Wilde's play *Salome* beautiful but "terribly corrupt."[63]

Beardsley's drawings for *Salome* emphasized its corruption, especially in the person of the heroine, beautiful and cruel and obsessed. Among French literati, this was a popular conception of Salome which Beardsley understood very well but which in Wilde's text he found overblown and therefore worthy of ridicule. Beardsley began work on *Salome*, at the latest, immediately after his return from Paris, sketching in his usual way first in pencil and then with unfaltering hand, however dense the detail, in ink. Sometimes Rothenstein, up from Oxford and in need of a studio, sat across from Beardsley at his drawing table. They talked and worked together with ease. When Beardsley looked up he saw displayed prominently over the fireplace a photograph of Oscar Wilde. The picture is often thought to have been placed there as an aid to Beardsley's serious "attempt to transfer the atmosphere of *Salome* to his own peculiar art."[64] More than likely the photograph was there as an aid to caricatures of Wilde which Beardsley incorporated into four of the total of fifteen designs which he made. The first drawing for the play, possibly the title page, was finished some time in June, when Beardsley suggested to Ross that he stop at the Mathews-Lane bookshop to see it.[65] By late August or early September, even though he also worked at other commissions, Beardsley had completed ten more drawings for *Salome*. Of these ten, one was a redrawn and simplified version of *J'ai baisé ta bouche . . .*, the picture which had appeared in *The Studio*. Called *The Climax*, it marks an important stage of Beardsley's development in its sparse detail and its arrangement of black and white mass.[66]

The decorations for *Salome*, taken as a whole, also mark the first clear-cut exposition of certain of Beardsley's personal preoccupations. The caricatures of Wilde are, of course, the playfulness of an impudent boy, one who found life a "great game," as he once told Lewis Hind when he surprised Beardsley in a long yellow dressing gown and red slippers with turned-up toes "pirouetting" about his studio.[67] To play the game was magnificent. Was it not the game— another kind, to be sure—which helped drive Kipling's Kim along the Great Road? But the drawings also convey an intensity and a sense of beauty and horror, interfused, not hitherto present in

Beardsley's work. He had written to Scotson-Clark about the indecency of drawings for *Bon-Mots*, and *Lucian's True History*;[68] but any indecency in them is explicit and concentrated in set pieces. A difference in kind and degree of indecency is in the new drawings. Both the play *Salome* and its pictures are pervaded with an acute awareness of the power of lust and the pain and glut which are its rewards.[69]

None of this was objectionable to Lane. Indeed Lane understood that in Beardsley's drawings he had masterful decorations eminently suited to the play. But Lane and Mathews thought some of them too graphic, too specific, for general publication. The title page had to be redrawn, a task which Beardsley undertook willingly when Lane pointed out that the original title was hardly appropriate ("impossible," Lane said) for use as a poster in bookstore windows. The second title page, which Beardsley described as one with "rose patterns" and a "little grotesque Eros," was in his mind a great improvement on the first. But Lane decided to use the original drawing, first making it respectable by expurgating the prominently displayed genitalia; the second he published as a border for the list of pictures. There was a brief respite during the first ten days of September while Lane was in Paris under the guidance of Rothenstein, to the eventual distaste of both Rothenstein and Lane. When he returned, apparently Lane showed the drawings to various visitors to his shop in Vigo Street, and the result was what Beardsley called "a veritable fronde, with George Moore at the head of the frondeurs."[70] Consequently several drawings were altered or replaced. A fig leaf appeared tied with a cord over the genitals of a male figure in one drawing, *Enter Herodias*. The first *Toilet of Salome*, in which the heroine basked in her near-nakedness, was replaced with a spectacular decoration showing Salome in modern dress. In addition Beardsley prepared three new illustrations, "simply beautiful and quite irrelevant."[71]

None of the drawings pleased Wilde. Mabel Beardsley maintained that the caricatures of Oscar were "too delicate for him to resent, and in any case he was compelled to admire the beauty of the drawings." He may have, but he thought them too Japanesque for his Byzantine play and when "Dear Aubrey" was not at hand, Wilde likened the drawings to the "naughty scribbles of a precocious schoolboy . . . on the margins of his copy books." Furthermore, Wilde disliked the cloth Lane had chosen to bind the ordinary edition of *Salome* and reported to Lane that Beardsley loathed it too.[72]

Meanwhile a quarrel of major proportions having to do with the translation of *Salomé* from French to English was raging between Lord Alfred Douglas, lovingly called Bosie, and Oscar Wilde; and

The Woman in the Moon, illustration for *Salome*. The woman is a caricature of Wilde
(Courtesy of Fogg Art Museum, Harvard University, Grenville L. Winthrop Bequest)

Enter Herodias, the first state of an illustration for *Salome* (*Courtesy of The Gallatin Beardsley Collection, Princeton University Library*)

eventually Beardsley allowed himself to be involved in it. In early September, when Wilde returned from Dinard and Jersey to London, he reviewed the translation which Douglas had made and promptly pointed out its "schoolboy faults." Wilde's conclusion that the translation was as unworthy of Douglas "as it was of the work it sought to render" and that it could not be published was an incitement to Bosie's volatile temper.[73] Hearing of this from Ross, Beardsley, proud of his French and always eager to try his hand at writing, offered to make a translation. Wilde seemed to welcome the offer. Then Ross intervened with Wilde on Douglas' behalf, pointing out how very "hurt, perhaps almost humiliated" Bosie must be at having his translation sent back "like a schoolboy's exercise." As he always did with Douglas, Wilde relented and not wishing, he said, to discourage Bosie's "beginnings in literature," turned to revising Douglas' translation,[74] so that Beardsley's efforts were disregarded. The situation was so awkward that the publication of the book was doubtful. Beardsley even gave some thought to reclaiming his drawings from Lane but decided against doing so as impractical financially. All in all, as he told Ross, Beardsley had a "warm time of it between Lane and Oscar and Co. For one week, the number of telegraph and messenger boys who came to the door was simply scandalous."[75]

The melee was too much for Beardsley. He stated a firm conviction when he declared in November that he thought Douglas and Wilde "very dreadful people."[76] The parade of their personal agitation in a professional matter was outside Beardsley's tolerance. The commotion was exhausting. And so in September Beardsley was ill once more. He suffered "severe attacks of blood spitting and an abominable bilious attack." At the end of the month, he was still so ill and so feeble that he found letter writing a "terrible strain."[77]

By the time Beardsley was once more unremittingly at work and able as well to participate in the Thursday teas at 114 Cambridge Street, the matter of *Salome* was settled. Wilde's version of Douglas' translation served as text. Douglas' name did not appear on the title page, but Wilde dedicated the book to him as "translator" of the play. Twelve of Beardsley's drawings plus a design for the cover appeared in both the ordinary and the large-paper copies. The three additional drawings Beardsley had made for *Salome*, Lane rightfully kept as his property and issued in a later edition. The first edition appeared on February 9, 1894.

Few reviewers admired Beardsley's drawings. The *Times* was bewildered and described the pictures as "unintelligible for the most part and, so far as they are unintelligible, repulsive." The reviewer went on to say that they appeared to "represent the manners of Judaea as conceived by Mr. Oscar Wilde portrayed in the style of the Japanese grotesque as conceived by a French *décadent*" and concluded that the whole thing must be "a joke . . . a very poor joke." *The Saturday Review* called the pictures a "fantastic way of illustrating a Biblical tragedy" and Beardsley a "very clever young man" but concluded that his cleverness was not "quite agreeable to Mr. Wilde." Without question, the reviewer said, Wilde was "on the rack," and then asked whether Beardsley would "play the same pranks with *Samson Agonistes* as with *Salome.*"[78] Only *The Studio* valued the drawings as "so audacious and extravagant" and so powerful in "achieving the unexpected" that they act "as a piquant maddening potion, not so much a tonic as a stimulant to fancy." Remarking on the "irresponsible personality of the artist dominating everything"—a statement hardly pleasing to Wilde—*The Studio* raised the question as to "whether the compositions do or do not illustrate the text" and then disregarded conventional criticism as outweighed by the quality of Beardsley's designs. But in this matter most critics, as King said, "grew grave and began to resent the manner in which this daring young draughtsman flouted the accepted canons of art and stereotyped methods of interpretation."[79] In other words, Beardsley was roundly abused.

CHAPTER IV

i

B Y the time *Salome* appeared, Aubrey Beardsley was absorbed in preparations for a new periodical, a venture which he shared with Henry Harland and John Lane. The name of Elkin Mathews, Lane's partner, appeared with Lane's on the first two numbers, but in fact Lane carefully disregarded his partner and acted as publisher; Harland was literary editor and Beardsley, art editor. The project was novel and exciting and although Beardsley could not anticipate the consequences, it would become his token, his symbol, and they would be identified with each other. Because of this enterprise, Beardsley would be both famous and notorious; he would be gazed at with admiration, but he would also be credited with unfathomable perversity[1] and castigated for his part in the periodical. It was *The Yellow Book*.

Even before *The Yellow Book*, Lane had almost managed to monopolize Beardsley.[2] He still had contractual obligations with Dent, the periodical *St. Paul's*, and others. Furthermore, commissioned by Florence Farr, actress and writer, Beardsley designed the program for her production of John Todhunter's *A Comedy of Sighs*, which opened at the Avenue Theatre on 29 March 1894 with Yeats' *The Land of Heart's Desire* as curtain-raiser. Miss Farr used the design not only for the program but for a poster as well. T. Fisher Unwin similarly converted Beardsley's *Girl and a Bookshop*, a drawing exhibited in November at the New English Art Club, to a poster to advertise series of books called The Pseudonym and Antonym Libraries. These, with the placard for *Salome* derived from its title page, opened a new area for Beardsley's designs, the poster. This was a thriving graphic form, especially in France, where the work of Chéret, Anquetin, Bonnard, Caran d'Ache, and many more was on constant display. Beardsley's designs were especially suited to the poster. In the case of *Girl and a Bookshop*, slight changes in composition, possibly made on the lithographic stone, and the addition of color converted it into a poster design for which Fisher Unwin found numerous uses.[3] A commission from Singer Sewing

Machines in March testified to Beardsley's immediate success with the poster. But in late 1893, when Lane asked Beardsley to prepare the front cover and title page for *Keynotes*, a book by Mrs. Chevalita Dunne Clairmonte, who used her husband's Christian names and called herself George Egerton, Lane and Beardsley set in motion a whole series which took its name from this first book, *Keynotes*. Each volume in the series was a well designed but inexpensively produced book with a key-related monogram of its author drawn by Beardsley and blocked on the spine; his drawings also ornamented covers and title pages of the books in this series. The authors, in addition to Egerton, included most of the young and less young, aspiring authors of Lane's Bodley Head from Ella D'Arcy, Netta Syrett and Henry Harland to Richard Le Gallienne, George Moore (who wrote an introduction to Dostoievsky's *Poor Folk*, translated by Lena Milman), and Arthur Machen. Beardsley ornamented twenty-two of the thirty-four volumes in the series, which ended in April 1896, more than two years after the appearance of Egerton's *Keynotes* in December 1893. Before that date, Beardsley was making illustrations for John Davidson's *Plays*. In late November he told Ross about a "really wonderful picture" for "Scaramouch in Naxos," a picture which served as frontispiece for the plays when Lane issued them in 1894.[4]

On New Year's Day that same year, in Henry Harland's drawing room, *The Yellow Book* took shape. Harland's account of what happened runs,

> The *Yellow Book* was first thought of one fearful afternoon in one of the densest and soupiest and yellowest of all London's infernalest yellow fogs. Aubrey Beardsley and I sat together the whole afternoon before a beautiful glowing open coal fire and I assure you we could scarcely see our hands before our faces, with all the candles lighted, for the fog, you know. . . .
>
> So we sat together the whole day and evening and were a gay and cheerful couple I assure you. We declared each to each that we thought it quite a pity and a shame that London publishers should feel themselves longer under obligation to refuse any more of our good manuscripts. Fancy having our brains stowed away for so long in their editorial sideboards that we lost our chance of even having our ideas served up cold.
>
> "Tis monstrous, Aubrey," said I.
>
> "Tis a public scandal," said he. And then and there we decided to have a magazine of our own. As the sole editorial staff we would feel free and welcome to publish any and all of ourselves that nobody else could be hired to print.[5]

The gaiety, the insouciance of that account are typical of Harland, but it does not tell everything. First of all, Aline Harland, Netta Syrett, and Mabel Beardsley were also in the drawing room, and Max Beerbohm came in late in the day. Harland and Beardsley discussed the possibilities for this projected quarterly in which "Letters" and "Black and White Art might enter into their own." They talked about format, quality of production, and costs. They compared their idea of the quarterly with others already on the book stalls. Then there was the question of a name. Mabel states that "each one in turn suggested a title, Aubrey triumphing with 'The Yellow Book.'"[6]

The concept of *The Yellow Book* was not as spontaneous, either, as Henry Harland made it sound. At some time in the previous summer, Beardsley with his mother and sister joined the Harlands at Ste. Marguerite-sur-Mer, a Norman village close to Offranville and an hour's train ride from Dieppe. In June 1893, the Harlands had gone from Paris to Ste. Marguerite, where they spent most of the summer with a group of English friends at a pension which they called The Grob MacThornlander, a name concocted by lumping together the names of various lodgers. Other summer residents at The Grob included artist Charles Conder, Litellus Burrell Goold and A. H. R. Thornton (art students now lost in obscurity), and D. S. MacColl, as well as various guests who came for short stays, among them Frederick Brown, once Beardsley's instructor. Exactly when the Beardsleys were at Ste. Marguerite is uncertain, although July is most probable. In fact, that they were there at all is demonstrated by only one letter, undated, which urged Bobbie Ross to join the group. Everyone involved signed the letter—Goold, Thornton, Conder, MacColl, the Harlands, and the three Beardsleys.[7] Most of them spent their days at work on their writing or drawing or painting, but when tea-time came, everyone gathered in The Grob's sun-splashed garden. It was on one such occasion, said MacColl, that he first suggested the possibility of a periodical made up of fiction, poetry, essays and drawings unrelated to each other but all exemplary of the best and the newest. Everyone discussed it and agreed on the desirability of such a publication, but no one acted on it. That idea was the one which Harland and Beardsley revived on January 1, 1894.[8]

Despite Harland's gaiety, and according to Henry James, Harland "charged every thing he touched whether in life or literature" with "mirth" and "amusement,"[9] both he and Beardsley took this projected periodical very seriously. Harland was a "fanatic for Art with an immense A. It was his god." He had decided that the art of fiction

91

was dependent on the short story. In a letter of November 18, 1892, to Edward Stedman, his godfather, Harland had written, "I am coming to lose my faith in the novel as a form of fiction and to think of the short story more and more as the thing desirable." By the following spring he had decided (mistakenly) that he would very likely write no more novels. "I don't think the form," he said, "an especially good, an especially artistic one." In *The Yellow Book*, Harland meant to "graft" the short story, so masterfully written by the French, "on to the literature" of the English-speaking world.[10]

As for Beardsley, his first consideration as always was financial. He wanted an assured, regular income, and as art editor of *The Yellow Book* he would have it. Besides, he was increasingly eager for an opportunity to expand his subject matter, to have no limitations set by a text. In his preliminary talks about the new publication, Beardsley had maintained the condition first suggested at Ste. Marguerite the summer before, that the literary matter and pictures must have no reference to each other.

The scheme might have dissipated in talk had Beardsley not proved practical. At his urging, he and Harland got in touch with John Lane, who invited them to the Hogarth Club on Bond Street for lunch the next day. Harland declared that they sat down at "one o'clock precisely" and that by "five minutes after one" Lane had "consented" to back *The Yellow Book* with Harland as editor and Beardsley as art director. According to Harland, "exactly at half past one" he had talked on the telephone with Henry James, his literary idol, to arrange a meeting, at which he and Beardsley meant to solicit a piece of fiction for the first number.[11]

Word of the new periodical and arrangements for it actually moved almost as fast as Harland said. When the three men, Lane, Harland, and Beardsley, left the Hogarth Club they had settled that the "get-up" was to look like "the ordinary French novel," that each issue would contain about ten short stories and "discursive" essays by such writers as Harland, James, Hubert Crackanthorpe, George Egerton, and Beerbohm, and that the drawings, all "independent," would come from Beardsley, Walter Sickert, Wilson Steer, Rothenstein, "and other past-masters." John Lane would publish at 5s. a copy, with the first number planned for April 16. Before that, on January 1, the very day on which it was first discussed seriously, Max Beerbohm wrote to his friend Reggie Turner about the "new periodical to be called *The Yellow Book*," for which, Max said, he was "both to caricature and to write." He declared, "It is to make all our fortunes."[12] By January 3, the title had been registered at Stationers' Hall and both Bobbie Ross and Oscar Wilde invited to contribute.

Beardsley's sketch of Henry Harland
(Courtesy of The Bodley Head Ltd.)

John Lane *(Courtesy of The Bodley Head Ltd.)*

93

On the same day, at lunch again but this time at the National Club in Whitehall Gardens, Lane and Harland consulted with Edmund Gosse, whom Harland had admired since settling into London. At that same lunch, Arthur Waugh, invited to join the threesome, learned of the budding quarterly and the next day wrote about the "bold scheme" in his literary letter destined for *The Critic*, an American publication. The next day, too, Beardsley sent a note by Harland's maid to Ada Leverson, asking to bring Harland to lunch with her; they wanted to tell her their plans and to solicit a contribution.[13] And on Sunday afternoon, January 7, Harland and Beardsley kept their appointment with Henry James by going to his flat in the De Vere Mansions.

Years later James remembered the occasion, how his "young friend" Harland called "to introduce a young friend of his own and to bespeak" James' interest for "a periodical about to take birth, in his hands on the most original 'lines' and with the happiest omens." James continued,

> What omen could be happier for instance than that this *enfant recueil*, joyously christened even before reaching the cradle, should take the name of *The Yellow Book?*—which so certainly would command for it the liveliest attention. What, further, should one rejoice more to hear than that this venture was, for all its constitutional gaiety, to brave the quarterly form, a thing hitherto of austere, of awful tradition, as was indeed in still other ways to sound the note of bright, young defiance?[14]

James was inclined to condescend to Harland as a delightful, amusing, and trivial young man; but what to make of Beardsley was a puzzle. James recalled his "rather embarrassed inability to measure the contributory value of Mr. Aubrey Beardsley," presented as Harland's "prime illustrator, his perhaps even quite independent picture-maker." This slender, pale young man, "delicate, unmistakeably intelligent," seemed detached and pleasantly remote about the entire "proposition." James had seen an example or two of Beardsley's "so curious and so disconcerting talent," but, as he looked back, his appreciation of it seemed "to have stopped quite short."[15] Nevertheless, when Harland and Beardsley left De Vere Mansions, they had their first firm promise of something on the "literary side" for the new *Yellow Book*. Although Beardsley had urged Ross to participate in the new venture, had told him how long to make his contribution—five to six thousand words—and anticipated something for the first issue, Ross produced nothing then or later for *The Yellow*

Book. Neither did Wilde, despite encouragement from Beardsley. "I long to see your contributions to the Yellow Book," he wrote to Wilde early in the year.[16] Mrs. Leverson offered nothing for many months. But from Henry James, Harland's literary idol, they had secured "The Death of the Lion." It must give elegance and literary stature to the first number.

Preparations for that first number went on steadily. Before the end of January, Beardsley had drawn what he called a "most wondrous cover," a design related to poster art in the gaiety and the arresting disposition of black-white (or black-yellow in its appearance on *The Yellow Book)* in the central figure, but still typically Beardsley's in those same characteristics as well as in certain details such as a taper, a second ambiguous figure, and the balancing of lines and masses.[17] That was for the upper cover and was intended for the first number only. For the spine and lower cover, he drew a design exhibiting small flowers of his own making and a frieze of women's heads. This served five issues before it was replaced. He showed these cover designs to friends and associates and from them, to his real satisfaction, received "universal admiration."

Beardsley took his editorship seriously; it was an opportunity he meant to warrant. He postponed a visit to Paris, planned for January, and began to prepare his further contributions with great care. His title page is a masterly departure from the usual, symmetrical title. The information on it is ornamented by a slender panel on the left showing a standing female figure before a piano, all placed within a field. In addition Beardsley supplied at least five other drawings for the first issue plus a poster with the words "Sold Here" for bookshop-display and a cover for a *Yellow Book* prospectus. Except for a depiction of Elkin Mathews in a Pierrot's costume on the prospectus' cover, there are no caricatures in any picture. That is owing to John Lane. Beardsley made one drawing for the new quarterly which he called *The Fat Woman*, easily recognizable as a picture of Beatrix Godwin Whistler, the artist's wife. Lane refused to publish it despite Beardsley's protests. "I shall most assuredly commit suicide," he told Lane, "if the *Fat Woman* does not appear . . ." Beardsley said that he had shown the drawing to "all sorts and conditions of men—and women," and all agreed as to its merits and its wit. He was certain it could hurt no one's "sensibilities."[18] But Lane was adamant, and the drawing went unpublished until Jerome K. Jerome accepted it for the May issue of *To-Day*. Nor are there the usual ambiguities or naughty innuendoes in Beardsley's pictures, except possibly in *A Sentimental Education*, amusing in any case. In mid-March Beerbohm described this "*marvellous* picture" to Turner:

A fat elderly whore in a dressing gown and huge hat of many feathers is reading from a book to the sweetest imaginable little young girl, who looks before her, with hands clasped behind her back, roguishly winking.

Max went on to say that her face haunted him.[19] That nothing more suggestive occurred in the Beardsley drawings was owing to Lane, too. He realized, he said, that Beardsley's youth prevented his taking himself seriously, that as a draftman he was "almost a practical joker" and that his drawings had to be examined with infinite care, "so to speak" placed "under a microscope and looked at upside down before they could be passed for publication."[20] Perhaps Beardsley's most notable drawing within the covers of the first issue is the portrait of Mrs. Patrick Campbell, the actress then playing the lead role in Pinero's *The Second Mrs. Tanqueray* at the St. James Theatre. Wilde had introduced Beardsley to her as "a very brilliant and wonderful young artist"[21] during a performance of the play in February, and soon afterwards Beardsley arranged for a sitting at the theater.

But Beardsley, as Harland did, gave considerable attention to securing others' work for *The Yellow Book*, so that the first number had a representative selection of art being produced in England. Sir Frederick Leighton, P.R.A., conventional and highly regarded, drew the frontispiece. Work from Pennell, Sickert, Charles Furse, Nettleship, Rothenstein, Laurence Housman, and R. Anning Bell made up the impeccable list of artists. The list of contributors to the "Letterpress," similar to that of the artists, was a mixture of the established and the eager young. Great writers rarely appear in periods of transition and most of the few who approached greatness in the 1890s are not on the list. Only two or three who are—George Moore, Max Beerbohm (for several reasons), and Henry James— warrant more than passing notice. But still the "Letterpress" had quality. Its writers included Hubert Crackanthorpe, Ella D'Arcy (who also assisted in the production of *The Yellow Book*), Pearl Craigie writing as John Oliver Hobbes with George Moore, John Davidson, William Watson, Edmund Gosse, Mary Chevalita Dunne Clairmonte writing as George Egerton, Richard Le Gallienne, others. All in all, the editors had made every effort to fulfill the aims which they had set forth in an interview quoted in *The Sketch* of April 11. They had spoken of "distinction, moderness." They had stressed that literature and art were to be "on precisely the same level." The only limitation on contributors, they said, would be quality; everything was to be judged on "the absolute rule of workmanship."[22] All in all, the bright yellow volumes with which Frederic Chapman, Lane's assistant, filled the windows of the Bodley Head in Vigo Street on the morning of Monday, April 16, were eminently respectable and well worth the 5s. each cost.

The birth of *The Yellow Book* was celebrated that night with a dinner which the editors gave in an upper room of the Hotel d'Italia in Compton Street. There were notable absentees, such as Henry James, who chose that time to go to Italy, and Joseph Pennell, who was in Dalmatia. Crackanthorpe, with his wife, was en route to Avignon; Le Gallienne was in Liverpool, Edmund Gosse and George Egerton were ill, but her husband, Mr. Clairmonte, attended in her place. Netta Syrett stayed away owing to family demands and Elkin Mathews, whom Lane had represented as uninterested in "the working of the *Yellow Book*," was not invited. But the room was crowded with other Bodley Head authors and *Yellow Book* contributors with their friends and relations: Kenneth Grahame, Beerbohm, Ella D'Arcy, the Beardsleys, the Harlands, George Moore with Olivia Shakespear on one side and Pearl Craigie on the other, Richard Garnett, Ernest Dowson, Theo Marzials, the Ernest Rhyses, Yeats, Sickert and Steer, and of course Lane. He was at the head table with Ménie Muriel Downs on his left. At the head of the head table sat Henry Harland and Beardsley with Elizabeth Pennell between them. The two men, such voluble and charming conversationalists, neither talked nor ate. Elizabeth Pennell said that both, "shrinking from the shadow cast before by their coming speeches" had not so "much as a word to throw" to her. She ate, for something to do, while "plate after plate was taken away untouched" from Harland and Beardsley. But at last when they had made their speeches—Beardsley commenced by announcing as his "most interesting subject" himself—the "strain was relaxed" and talk flowed unstanched. Only one incident marred the evening's euphoria. When Lane got up to speak for the publishers, he began by regretting Mathews' "unavoidable absence" and some one shouted, "That's a lie."[23]

After dinner, a few chosen people went to the Bodley Head with Lane. And after that, Elizabeth Pennell, the Harlands, Max Beerbohm, Beardsley, and one or two others ended the night around a "little table with red-and-white checked cover" in the beer-saloon of the Monico, a restaurant in Shaftesbury Avenue. All in all, it was a triumphant evening aglow with enthusiasm. Those involved were "thrilled" by the new experiments "in art and life. It was indeed a kind of expansion, a Renaissance on a small scale."[24]

Although the first printing of *The Yellow Book*, some five thousand copies, sold out in five days and it was twice reprinted, the "hue of jaundice" did not provoke unqualified admiration. Oscar Wilde declared that he thought *The Yellow Book* "dull and loathsome, a great failure," and then added, "I am so glad."[25] And some of the contributors to the new quarterly were seriously affronted by it. Henry James wrote from Venice late in May to explain his failure to send a copy of the first number to his brother. "I haven't sent you *The Yellow Book*—on purpose . . ." he wrote; "I say on purpose because, although my little tale which ushers it in ('The Death of the Lion') appears to have had, for a thing of mine, an unusual success, I hate too much the horrid aspect and the company of the whole publication. And yet I am to be intimately, conspicuously associated with the 2nd number. It is for gold and to oblige the worshipful Harland (the editor)."[26] Charles W. Furse, whose portrait of Miss Butcher, his fiancée, was in that first number, objected to Beardsley's drawings, quarreled with Harland about them, and disappeared from *The Yellow Book*'s scene. It was difficult for Furse and James to recognize that Beardsley was first of all an illustrator and decorator. Often in his drawings he was merely gay and lighthearted, however concerned with pattern and technique. At other times he was intent on exposing the discrepancy between propriety and the truth beneath it. The very young rarely go beyond exposure. They rarely have solutions to problems, they rarely offer anything new on which to build. Satires of *The Yellow Book* flourished with such titles as "The Yellow Boot," described as a product of the "Blodey Head," and "The Bilious Book."

Few reviews were as laudatory as that in the *Weekly Irish Times*, which remarked on an "exquisite" new quarterly, very likely to "charm the eye and mind," a publication "goldenly interesting and joy-dispensing to the cultured mind."[27] Most reviews took the same attitude as the *World* in its issue of April 25, when it spoke of "Mr Henry James in his most mincing moods" and of "a Mr. Beerbohm" whose "Defence of Cosmetics" was called "pure nonsense" owing to "such humorous phrases as 'the resupinate sex,' 'the veriest sillypap,' 'Rome in the keenest time of her degringolade.'" The *World* was no happier with Beardsley's art work. It asked, "Who wants these fantastic pictures, like Japanese sketches gone mad, of a woman with a black tuft for a head, and snake-like fingers starting off the keyboard of a piano; of Mrs. Patrick Campbell with a black sticking-plaister

Beardsley's portrait of Mrs. Patrick Campbell for *The Yellow Book*, Volume I, April 1894 *(The National Gallery of Berlin)*

hat, hunchy shoulders, a happily impossible waist, and a yard and a half of indefinite skirt. . . ."[28] The drawing of Mrs. Campbell prompted *The Daily Chronicle* to complain that, although a portrait of her was listed in the table of contents, none was present. *The Pall Mall Budget* objected to the title-page and the *Times* began with the cover, which they found repulsive and insolent, "a combination of English rowdyism and French lubricity."[29]

Beardsley took a perverse pleasure in his critics and even more in replying to them. If critics must be answered, then perhaps Beerbohm followed a better procedure when he wrote a polite essay which commenced with amazement that the critics had failed to understand his "A Defence of Cosmetics" and continued with a discussion of the obligations of the critic. The essay, in the form of a letter to the editor of *The Yellow Book*, appeared in the second number.[30] Beardsley, on the other hand, sent impudent and sometimes silly letters to the periodicals which carried disparaging comments. His first such letter had been a response to *The Daily Chronicle*'s lament at his poor taste in caricaturing Wilde and the theater manager Sir Augustus Harris as well as others in the frontispiece to Davidson's *Plays*. Beardsley's letter read in part, "I cannot help feeling that your reviewer is unduly severe. One of the gentlemen who form part of my decoration is surely beautiful enough to stand the test even of portraiture, the other"—meaning Harris—"owes me half a crown."[31] Now, with *The Yellow Book* he wrote again to *The Daily Chronicle* in the matter of Mrs. Campbell's portrait and to the editor of *The Pall Mall Budget*, who had published Beardsley's drawings a year earlier. On April 27, he defended his title page, representing "a lady playing the piano in the middle of a field," against the *Budget*'s charges of "unpardonable affectation" and decadence by citing a fictitious authority for similar practice on the part of Gluck when he was composing his operas.[32] Perhaps Beardsley was pretending again. Certainly at best such replies are a futile business. The artist or writer is put on the defensive and almost inevitably the critic has the last word, so that the supposed faults are only emphasized. Yet Beardsley apparently found genuine enjoyment in prodding his critics and in the give and take of such bickering. Perhaps it helped assuage the charges of "lubricity" and poor taste.

After all they were only the consequence of Beardsley's sudden prominence. With the appearance of *The Yellow Book*, Aubrey Beardsley had leaped to the pinnacle of success. Unwarned, he found himself in the midst of the Beardsley Period, and the next twelve months were the few in his all too few years in which Beardsley seemed indeed to have fortune at his foot. Both fame and notoriety

Design for the title page of *The Yellow Book*, Volume I, April 1894 *(From* The Yellow
Book, *April 1894)*

were his. Tall, thin, gracefully melancholy, with his too-smart clothes and his face "'like a silver hatchet' under his spreading chestnut hair, parted in the middle and arranged low over his forehead,"[33] he was highly visible. Indeed, he was almost impossible to ignore, and he liked that. "I . . . wish to be stared at," he told William Butler Yeats,[34] and wherever Beardsley went, people stared at him.

In London, Beardsley went everywhere. He enjoyed opera, especially Wagnerian opera, at Covent Garden. He attended meetings of the Rhymers' Club at the Cheshire Cheese to hear Yeats, long-haired, bespectacled and gaunt, read his poems in a harsh and high chant. Beardsley was often at the music halls—the Empire, the Tivoli, the Oxford, or even the Mogul in Drury Lane or Gatti's at nearby Charing Cross Station—with Max Beerbohm or Herbert Horne or William Rothenstein. There they enjoyed Dan Leno and Marie Lloyd or someone singing "You Cannot Tell Cigars by the Picture on the Box," and afterward they often indulged in a dish of jellied eels. Max caricatured Beardsley; Rothenstein made two drawings of him in the house in Cambridge Street. Strangers talked about his perversity and "acquaintances all recognized his simple boyishness."[35]

And so, either for his notoriety or for his charm, what Henry James designated as the "perfect case" of the artistic spirit, Beardsley was invited everywhere, often with Mabel. They were both tall. He was very emaciated, his eyes were brilliant; and his beautiful hands, "very long, very thin, very sensitive," he used "dramatically, with the hint of affectation from which his entire personality was by no means free."[36] Mabel, still unfulfilled as to her theatrical ambitions, had developed a "grotesquely affected" manner. She had real prettiness, however, with the "colouring of a sweet pea,"[37] and she was extremely sweet-natured. So was Aubrey. Thus they were welcomed by the Meynells on Sunday afternoons and by the Edmund Gosses on Sunday evenings. The Dearmers were at home on Mondays. Thursay evenings belonged to the Pennells. John Lane had authors' parties at the Bodley Head and "smokers" in his chambers in the Albany. Ada Leverson, Wilde's "Sphinx," invited the Beardsleys to dinner and took them to the theater. Frank Harris of the *Saturday Review* entertained Beardsley with Wilde, Beerbohm, Bobbie Ross, and Rothenstein at the Café Royal. Gertrude Atherton remembered seeing Beardsley at a party in the Chelsea garden of the T. P. O'Connors, who entertained lavishly, especially people who had a name in the world of art and letters. Pearl Craigie, Marie

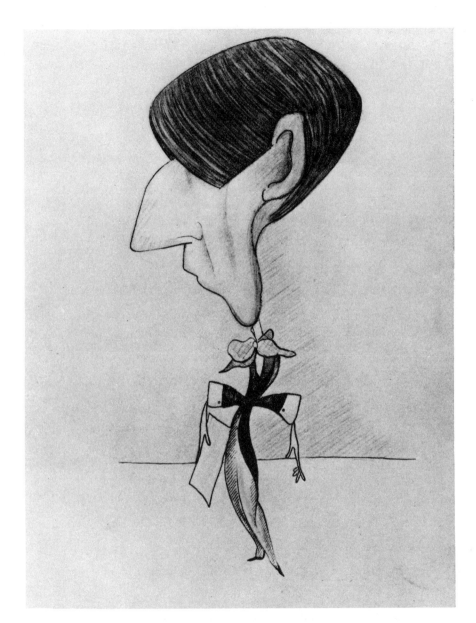

Caricature of Beardsley by Max Beerbohm *(Courtesy of Ashmolean Museum, Oxford)*

Corelli, Arthur Conan Doyle, Shaw, and Anthony Hope were regulars.[38]

The best parties were at the Harlands' where on Saturday nights the fever of aesthetic achievement infected each guest. Beardsley often dined with the Harlands, and afterward, he and other dinner guests, such as Mabel and Percy Dearmer and Aubrey's sister Mabel, joined the frequenters of the Harlands' drawing room at 144 Cromwell Road. Those associated with *The Yellow Book* and a number who were not drifted in about nine for coffee and cigarettes and talk. James, Edmund Gosse, Charlotte Mew came now and then. George Moore sometimes surged into the room, going on with the monologue about Wagner or Manet or Balzac already commenced silently in the street. For a time, Theo Marzials, the poet, was a regular, but his habit of adapting the Harlands' teaspoons for his morphine proved unpleasant. Usually Richard Le Gallienne, looking "like Narcissus," and Arthur Symons, like a girl, with his "yellow hair and pink and white cheeks" could be counted on. Among the other regulars were Kenneth Grahame, Max Beerbohm (he and Beardsley were younger than anyone else), Bertie Crackanthorpe, Netta Syrett, and Ella D'Arcy. In other words, in Harland's pink drawing room with its Persian carpets, its pictures and old furniture gathered the "salt of the earth." Had not Henry Harland so classified artists, by which he meant *The Yellow Book* set, and decreed that *"il faut souffrir pour être sel"*?

That most of the people who came to Harland's Saturday Nights had yet suffered comparably with most of humanity is open to question. Evelyn Sharp, one of their number, wrote years later that it was part of their middle-class, Victorian pose to have experienced everything, though most of them "were so young in actual fact" that they had difficulty "in maintaining even the necessary appearance of vicious depravity popularly attributed" to them. She justified their "gay absurdities" by their real objectives, to attack the "sentimentalities and hypocrisies of a dying age" and to establish "a new standard of beauty and sincerity in art." In the interest of these aspirations, they defiantly accepted the tags "precious" and "decadent." Here was an ambiance which reflected exactly what Beardsley was projecting in his drawings. And as they talked and talked, Beardsley contributed his "peculiar kind of brilliance." It was vehement, witty, "a salt, whimsical dogmatism, equally full of convinced egoism and of imperturbable keen-sightedness."[39] Even more articulate than Beardsley was Henry Harland as he stood on the hearthrug or sat on the floor, "waving his eye glasses on the end of their cord, or refixing them on his short-sighted eyes," making every lady think herself brilliant and beautiful and every gentleman, whatever he wanted to be. Sometimes in the large drawing room lighted by lamps and candles, Aline Harland sat down at the piano to accompany herself as she sang; and she often ended the evening at the kitchen stove, preparing an omelette while the guests discussed the best way to cook one.[40]

iii

According to Mabel Beardsley, Aubrey soon grew tired of all the noise and chatter. "In the season of '94," she said, "he went out a good deal—he was a brilliant talker and much sought after, but he soon got weary and gave up people altogether." She explained that Beardsley "cared very little for people. His only companion was his sister."[41] In one respect Mabel was correct. Aubrey's only companion was his sister. He kept everyone at arm's length, but if he had a confidante, it was she. Certainly after Beardsley ended his letter of mid-February 1893 to Scotson-Clark, who seemed settled in America, with an appeal to "come out from among" the Philistines and to return to England, and after Beardsley attempted unsuccessfully in May 1893 to arrange for his friend to work with Gleeson White on *The Studio*, Beardsley wrote no more letters to Scotson-Clark.[42] And thus he wrote none even suggesting honest self-exposition. His letters to Mabel and his mother are cursory and to almost everyone else, businesslike or role-playing or role-serving. Beardsley's only intimacy after the correspondence with Scotson-Clark ended was apparently with his sister.

That Mabel and Aubrey were loving friends, each interested in the other's welfare, is unquestionable. How far beyond such interest this intimacy extended is problematical. At one extreme is the charge that Mabel and Aubrey engaged in an incestuous relationship. Numerous situations and surmises have been presented in evidence. One is their forced reliance for companionship on each other when, at an impressionable and inquisitive age, they lived in Brighton with their aunt, Sarah Pitt. Another is a conversation with both Beardsleys reported in *My Life and Loves* by Frank Harris. There he says that Beardsley declared he had learned about sex from his sister and that Mabel blushed but made no denial. Frank Harris, of course, was a notorious liar. Still another is Beardsley's repeated depictions of fetuses in his drawings, commencing with those in *Bon-Mots;* presumably Beardsley was made familiar with the fetus when Mabel aborted his or someone's child. Also advanced as proof are portraits

105

of Mabel in the nude drawn by Beardsley and one of her in a man's suit painted by W. Graham Robertson, a picture which has raised the question of transvestism compounded by a fixation for Aubrey's clothing. Robertson's disclosure that the suit was his has generally been ignored. Aubrey's drawings of Mabel, naked, include most notably the frontispiece to Davidson's *Plays*, where the portraits of Wilde and Augustus Harris also occur, and the magnificent *The Mysterious Rose Garden*, published in the fourth number of *The Yellow Book*. The latter piece is an adaptation of a design originally intended to represent the annunciation; but the messenger in the final version is hardly a holy one and apparently its implication is plain to those who see Mabel in it.[43] Scotson-Clark, who knew Mabel as well as Aubrey, testified to such "wonderful sympathy between brother and sister" that when Aubrey died, "Mabel, the real Mabel, died also." And Beardsley's benefactor in the last year or so of his life, André Raffalovich, hints at incest when he speaks of Mabel as having "recalled or inspired the beautiful Venus" in Beardsley's story of Tannhäuser.[44] But Mabel has been charged with so much: an illegitimate son, an abortion which her brother observed, lesbianism with Pauline Tarn, better known as Renée Vivien.[45] And she may have practiced incest. Who knows what goes on behind closed doors? Thousands and thousands of words have been written about this supposititious relationship and yet there is not one word of proof.

No other woman's name has ever been associated with Beardsley's except in the story, admittedly questionable, that Ada Leverson attempted to seduce him. Despite his friendships with homosexuals—Robbie Ross is the most obvious—and his association with Oscar Wilde, Beardsley's sexual preference reputedly was what the 1890s considered normal. W. B. Yeats tells of Beardsley's having had a beautiful mistress and recalled his coming once to the flat which Arthur Symons and Yeats shared "of a morning, with some painted woman," with whom Yeats assumed Beardsley had spent the night. But Yeats supplied no identifications. In another instance, he associated Beardsley with a harlot called "Penny Plain." On a cold winter night she came with Beardsley and several other young men to Yeats' flat. In order to enjoy fully the warmth of the fire burning at his hearth, she removed her clothes and sat naked before the flames, now and then interrupting the talk and her pleasure in the fire to go with one or another young man into the bedroom. Later Yeats changed his tale and put the poet Ernest Dowson in Beardsley's place.[46]

Still, Beardsley supplied ample evidence of his thoroughgoing knowledge of sex and near-obsession with it. The fetuses in his

Mabel Beardsley *(From* The Idler Magazine, *March 1897)*

drawings, so often cited, may have been no more than a symptom of his addiction to the grotesque, and the recurring cloven hoof, a derivative symbol of sexuality. The enormous phalluses which appear in illustrations made for the *Lysistrata* at a time of continuous illness possibly indicate the fantasy of unsatisfied desire. In those drawings, however, symbolic necessity for an artist who was not a realist can hardly be ignored. But in *The Story of Venus and Tannhäuser*, Beardsley's "romantic novel," is undeniable evidence. It is also, incidentally, the most obviously decadent of all Beardsley's productions, whether that word is defined in terms of style, as Havelock Ellis did, or in terms of Maurice Barrès' *"le Culte du Moi,"* an immoderate cultivation of exotic experience for its own sake.

Beardsley first mentioned *The Story of Venus and Tannhäuser* in a letter to Evans, the bookseller, written between the performances of *Tannhäuser* on June 26 and *Tristan and Isolde* four days later. These were two presentations in a season of German opera at Drury Lane, where Mabel and Aubrey "used to sit on the gallery stairs surrounded by enthusiasts from 4:30 to 7:30," awaiting the performance. As Mabel said, "Never was German opera enjoyed more." Beardsley told Evans that Max Alvary, who took the title role, was "scarcely a singer" but Katharine Klavsky in the part of Elizabeth, "beyond all praise." After writing about his drawings prepared for the second number of *The Yellow Book*, Beardsley explained that he had put aside other things until he could finish a "big long thing of the revels in Act I of *Tannhäuser*." He was sure it would "simply astonish" everyone.[47]

Beardsley never finished *The Story of Venus and Tannhäuser*, although he worked sporadically on it the rest of his life. He soon began to carry around with him, as he had once done with his drawings, a portfolio containing the large notebook in which he was writing. He used only the recto of each leaf in the notebook until he began to make revisions and insertions. Most of these went on the versos. Unfortunately several changes have been made in the manuscript in a hand other than Beardsley's. Some are unimportant, but a major one is an alteration of names of characters, so that Beardsley's meaning is sometimes blunted and his story confused. That is especially true when another character, Sporion, is substituted for the hero. Further confusion comes from his own failure to be consistent in the use of the name of his hero.[48]

The opera *Tannhäuser* is the tale of a man who, having spent a year in the Venusberg, has grown weary of endless revels with Venus and returns to the world to find salvation. Beardsley's *Venus and Tannhäuser*, in a series of brilliantly baroque scenes composed as though they were drawings, tells of the revels which took place when

Tannhäuser first arrived at the Venusberg. As infinite variety of sexual activity goes on without pause. Although Beardsley's middle-class notion of Venus in drawers must be disregarded, he presents the anticipation of intercourse between Venus and her guest with voluptuous tenderness. Venus, already much used that evening, is described moments before Tannhäuser, "pale and speechless with excitement, pressed his gemgirt fingers brutally over the divine limbs":

> Her frail chemise and dear little drawers were torn & moist & clung transparently about her, & all the body was nervous & responsive. Her closed thighs seemed like a vast replica of the little bijou she held between them; the beautiful tetons du derrière were as firm as a plump virgin's cheek & promised a joy as profound as the mystery of the Rue Vendôme, & the minor chevelure, just profuse enough, curled as prettily as the hair upon a cherub's head.

Compelling aberrations in sexual activity are at times suggested and at times described. At the first banquet which Beardsley's Tann-häuser attends sit Venus' minor satellites whose talk is of "the infidelities of Cérise, Sarmian's caprices, that morning in the lily garden, Thorilliere's declining strength, Vulva's affection for Rose-ola, Falix's impossible member, Cathelin's passion for Sulpitia's poodle, Sola's passion for herself, the nasty bite that Marisca gave Chloe, the epilation of Pulex, Cyril's diseases and a thousand amatory follies of the day . . ." Such a passage is twice removed from action, but the drunken scene as the banquet progressed is alive in its account of Sophie, who "became very intimate with an empty champagne bottle"; of Bellmour, who "pretended to be a dog and pranced from couch to couch on all fours biting and barking and licking"; of Aubrey, "just a little grisé," who "lay down on the cushions & let Julia do whatever she liked."

Was Beardsley a voyeur of the underside of London and Paris? A weak suggestion that he was survives in his facetious letter to John Lane, in Paris as a guest of Rothenstein in September 1893. Beardsley wrote,

> I hope that William Rothenstein has done no more than take you to the Chat Noir in the daytime and shown you the outside of the Moulin Rouge.
> I am going to Jimmie's on Thursday night dressed up as a tart and mean to have a regular spree.[49]

Certainly Beardsley had observed the lesbians at play in the Rat Mort and he had penetrated the mystery of the rue Vendôme. Furthermore that congenital fraud Sir Trelawney Backhouse reported Beardsley's awareness, got from Wilde, of the enormous trafficking in telegraph boys and the savor of their dirt among English connoisseurs. But whatever Beardsley listened to and whatever he saw in London and Paris, he cannot have observed the communion between Venus and Adolphe, her pet unicorn, which makes up the eighth chapter of his "romantic novel." It tells how Tannhäuser joined Venus on the morning of his second day on the Venusberg and stood outside Adolphe's enclosure while Venus went in to feed him with "spicy buns." After Adolphe had eaten, Venus pretended to leave him and then, as was her custom, went back "passionately to where he stood" and made "adorable amends for her unkindness." Beardsley's tale continues:

> How happy he was, touching the Queen's breasts with his quick tongue-tip. I have no doubt that the keener scent of animals must make women much more attractive to them than to men: for the gorgeous odour that but faintly fills our nostrils must be revealed to the brute creation in divine fulness. Anyhow, Adolphe sniffed as never a man did around the skirts of Venus. After the first charming interchange of affectionate delicacies was over, the unicorn lay down upon his side, and, closing his eyes, beat his stomach wildly with the mark of manhood!
>
> Venus caught that stunning member in her hands and lay her cheek along it; but few touches were wanted to consummate the creature's pleasure. The Queen bared her left arm to the elbow, and with the soft underneath of it made amazing movements horizontally upon the tight-strung instrument. When the melody began to flow, the unicorn offered up an astonishing vocal accompaniment. Tannhäuser was amused to learn that the etiquette of the Venusberg compelled everybody to await the outburst of these venereal sounds before they could sit down to déjeuner.
>
> Adolphe had been quite profuse that morning.
>
> Venus knelt where it had fallen, and lapped her little aperitif!

Beardsley depicted an equally lascivious but more violent encounter between satyrs and the residents of the Venusberg, but he preferred the incident with the unicorn. He talked of several unicorns and even spoke of a picture in preparation showing them with Venus.[50] Certainly Beardsley's baroque manner is nowhere more suited to his matter than in this episode of the unicorn. It is a verbal reflection of the detail and grotesquerie of his drawings.

After Beardsley's death, his friend Aymer Vallance likened Beardsley to his favorite opera-character Tannhäuser,[51] and indeed their lives and deaths can be reconciled in kind if not in detail. In *Venus and Tannhäuser*, Beardsley identified himself with the hero. He began his tale, "The Abbé Aubrey having lighted off his horse, stood doubtfully for a moment beneath the ombre gateway of the Hill of Venus." Later Beardsley changed the name Aubrey to Fanfreluche and on the next page of the manuscript, to Tannhäuser. Two or even three of these characters may take part in the action all at once; but one or all, Beardsley is intended. In an obvious self-portrait, he described Fanfreluche as a "tall slim diseased young man with a slight stoop, a troubled walk, an oval impassable face with its olive skin drawn tightly over the bone . . ." And the activities of Fanfreluche or Tannhäuser, once named Aubrey, may well reflect Beardsley's sexual desires and their enforced frustration. If those activities are only role-playing, a fantasized view of himself as he wanted to be or wanted to be thought to be, or if they are conceived from an enforced sexual deprivation, Beardsley chose a lurid part for himself. That is apparent in the scene in which Aubrey, in the person of Fanfreluche, enacted a version of his attention to little girls, to which Mrs. Beardsley testified.[52] When a group of children thrust themselves into the midst of woodland revels, "clapping their hands and laughing immoderately at the passion and the disorder and commotion," Fanfreluche,

> sprang to his feet gesticulating as if he would say "Ah the little dears" "Ah the little ducks" "Ah the rorty little things!" for he was so fond of children. Scarcely had he caught one by the thigh than a quick rush was made by everybody for the succulent limbs; & how they tousled them & mousled them. The children cried out, I can tell you.

Beardsley added, "Of course there were not enough for everybody so some had to share, & some had simply to go on with what they were doing before." That incident is less bizarre than almost any other in Beardsley's "novel," but it may be more truthful.

From his *Venus and Tannhäuser*, Beardsley's sexuality and his sexual practices can be assumed. Venus, of course, is physical love in all its enchantment. That Beardsley knew its magic is clear in the "novel." The fact is emphasized in his drawings of Tannhäuser's return to the Venusberg, first designed in 1891 and redesigned in 1896. They comprehend the essence of desire. In the practice of such love, Beardsley showed himself the passive partner. He took the initiative in the "novel" only with children, with little girls. Doubtless he was aware of their charm. But is the scene with them fact or role-playing?

iv

How far Beardsley had progressed with *Venus and Tannhäuser* when he left London in August with his mother for a rest at Haslemere, Surrey, is impossible to say. By August, in addition to beginning the novel, Beardsley had worked at several things. In April he had accepted a commission to design a cover for the *Cambridge A.B.C.*, a new magazine produced by three undergraduates, Austen Leigh, Maurice Baring, and Warre Cornish. The first number, with Beardsley's cover, appeared in June. In July his contribution to an article "The Art of the Hoarding," to which Jules Chéret and Dudley Harding contributed, appeared in *New Review*.[53] More important, Beardsley shared in the great flurry of activity at the Bodley Head in preparation for the second *Yellow Book*.

The first *Yellow Book* was still in the book stalls when the second got under way. Almost at once, Harland struck out in all directions. He proposed a suit against *The Speaker* for its abuse of the first number. From numerous unsolicited manuscripts as well as urgent letters from friends of would-be contributors, Harland singled out a "remarkable" manuscript from an unknown, Charlotte Mew. Use of such material helped keep costs down to the eventual £200 spent for this number. Moreover, Harland decreed that Beardsley must "modify himself" for the second volume.[54] Meanwhile, John Lane rushed off to Paris to solicit from P. J. Hammerton, retired editor of *The Art Journal*, a criticism of the first number to appear in the second. After getting an indignant refusal from Andrew Lang, Lane turned to Hammerton, another "staid critic," to write an adverse comment.[55] By the end of April, only two weeks after the first *Yellow Book* appeared, Beardsley was soliciting Sargent's portrait of Henry James, choosing other drawings by other artists, and preparing his own. At the end of June, Beardsley could write to Evans that the second *Yellow Book* was "going to be a glorious number . . ." After seeing Réjane in *Madam Sans-Gêne*—"She is ravissante," he said— Beardsley had made her portrait. In addition he had a suite of three drawings called *The Comedy-Ballet of Marionettes as performed by the troupe of the Théâtre Impossible*. He told Evans that it looked "superb." Beardsley's letter to Evans went on,

Cover design for *The Cambridge A. B. C.*, 1894 *(Courtesy of W. G. Good Esq.)*

113

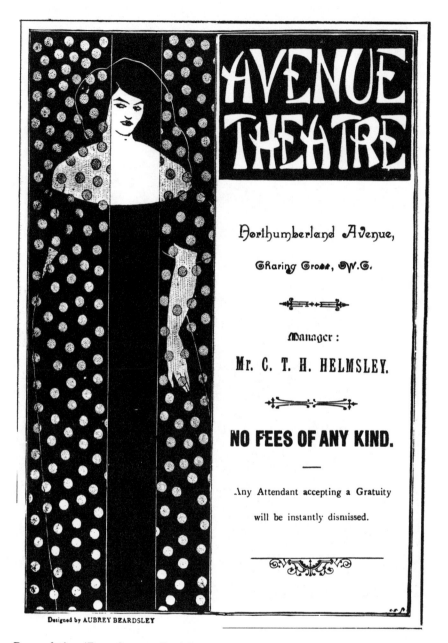

Poster design *(From the cover of a program for George Bernard Shaw's* Arms and the Man *and Louis N. Parker's* The Man in the Street, *April 1894)*

Then I have an astounding piece of decorative realism which I call *Les Garcons du Café Royal* and a thing called *The Slippers of Cinderella*. Then there are three amazing Sickerts, quite his best stuff, three admirable Steers, a divine Walter Crane (his only great thing) and about a dozen more pictures—some very amusing.[56]

In June, too, and at least a week before he wrote that letter to Evans, Beardsley's doctor had examined him with a "grave face" and Beardsley had acknowledged that he must have a rest. He did not agree to it, however, until early August, when he had located a place to go near at hand, Valewood Farm, Haslemere, Surrey, suggested by a Mrs. Williams. Even then he went reluctantly, sure that he would need to return to London once or twice and expecting, as he said, to have a "vile August." But on August 8 or 9, he and his mother went to Valewood Farm, taking along his book. About August 20, he wrote again to Evans to say that it went well but slowly. The fact that the farm and its surroundings were the "pick of scenery" and thus provided "backgrounds" for his *Tannhäuser* pleased Beardsley, but it was the only aspect of Haslemere which did. It was "too peaceful" for his "restless brain,"and he determined to leave. "I simply long for London again," he told Evans, "the only place where you can live and work (which comes to the same thing)."[57] Contrary to Mabel's statement that he soon got "weary and gave up people altogether,"[58] he wanted to go to London at once. But his mother managed to keep him at Valewood Farm a day or two longer even though for almost two weeks he had been greatly depressed and had made her life a misery.

At last she gave up, and Aubrey returned to London. Mrs. Beardsley went for a week to Woking and then, on August 30, she too returned to London. She was in time to see Mabel in rehearsal. Mrs. Beardsley approved of neither Mabel's ambitions nor the company with which they threw her, but she went to see Mabel leave for Malvern, where she made her official debut. Then on September 6, Mrs. Beardsley went off with Mr. Beardsley to Brighton;[59] and Aubrey, happily alone in the house in Cambridge Street, concentrated on London and his work, especially the work he still had to do for the third volume of *The Yellow Book*. He was already busy asking for others' drawings, such as Sargent's portrait of Edmund Gosse, and preparing his own contributions. By early October, he had apprised Evans of the forthcoming *Yellow Book*, and without undue immodesty Beardsley declared that by "general consent" it had in it his best work to date. For this number, Beardsley had designed four drawings in addition to the covers and title page, but he referred especially to *The Wagnerites*, first conceived in Paris more than a year before and still in progress when the second *Yellow Book* went to press in June.[60] Possibly Beardsley's best known drawing, it is indeed remarkable in its manipulation of black and white and in its implicit tension between the romance and idealism of Wagner's *Tristan and Isolde* and its disillusioned audience made up almost wholly of women. Another of the four drawings is called *Portrait of Himself*. It shows the tiny head of a boy in a vast, curtained bed. As usual with Beardsley's drawings, it is noteworthy for its workmanship first and then for the lack of resemblance of the figure to Beardsley but a correspondence between its legend, *"Par les dieux jumeaux tous les monstres ne sont pas en Afrique,"* and its sexual symbols.

No sooner was one issue of *The Yellow Book* published than Beardsley must start on the next, making his own designs and selecting work from other artists. As long as Beardsley was art director, Walter Sickert appeared in each number. Wilson Steer's work was in the second and following numbers. Max Beerbohm as artist rather than author was in number three for the first time and Charles Conder in four. Sargent, Leighton, Walter Crane were sporadic contributors. Rothenstein had work in the second and fourth issues. After the fifth, he severed all connections with Lane, whom he had never regarded very highly anyway. As for his own work, Beardsley made a new upper cover (the lower cover was repeated on five numbers) and title page for each number of *The Yellow Book*. For each of the first five issues, he made no less than three other drawings and for the second, he made six. Furthermore, the designs for Lane's Keynotes series was a continuing assignment, and in that autumn of 1894, Beardsley was also preparing a bookplate for Frederick Evans and a poster to advertise Fisher Unwin's Children's Books Library.[61] And constantly nagging at him was his wish to get on with his "beloved Venusberg."

All this was forced to a halt in mid-November. Before November 12, Beardsley had suffered "terribly from hemorrhage of the lung" which left him "horribly weak" and, sadly, he had lost the capacity to contend with his illness. Dr. Thompson had recommended Dr. Grinrod's clinic at Wyche Side, Malvern, and there Beardsley went to stay on November 14. From Malvern, he wrote to Evans later in the month that he was "buried in the country getting back a little" of his "usual nerve," that all his work had been stopped, and that he sat about all day "moping and worrying" about his novel. He confided that he was "just doing" a picture to accompany it, one of Venus feeding pet unicorns garlanded with roses.[62]

The Wagnerites, in *The Yellow Book*, Volume III, October 1894 *(Crown Copyright. Victoria and Albert Museum)*

Beardsley improved rapidly. He spent some part of the Christmas season with Max Beerbohm and William Watson, all guests at St. Mary's Abbey, a house which John Lane had hired at Windermere. While there, Lane and Beardsley discussed the possibility of his accompanying Lane when he went at the end of March to New York. The prospect was intoxicating, and Beardsley tentatively agreed to go. Meanwhile he started a series of five designs intended for a large quarto edition of Edmund Gosse's "little romance" *The Secret of Narcisse*. Beardsley had approached William Heinemann, Gosse's publisher, with the idea, but they had not yet reached a final agreement. Nevertheless, Beardsley had told Gosse, "I mean to do something very beautiful for you," and commenced the work at Windermere.[63] He also began work on *Frontispiece to Juvenal*, a drawing for the January *Yellow Book*.

Before the end of the year Beardsley was back in London and back in the pleasant patterns of life which he had so enjoyed in the past months. On January 1, a Tuesday, the Beardsleys welcomed the New Year with a few friends in their Cambridge Street drawing room. Two days later, Beardsley was the guest of Ada Leverson in her box at the Haymarket Theatre when Oscar Wilde's *An Ideal Husband* opened. Aubrey and Mabel were both with Mrs. Leverson at the St. James' Theatre on February 14, 1895, for the opening of Wilde's *The Importance of Being Earnest*. Mabel came late, shortly after nine, but Aubrey accompanied the Leversons in their carriage through a raging blizzard to the theater, where a fashionable audience, fashionably dressed, awaited Wilde's second success in little more than a month. Because the Marquess of Queensberry, Alfred Douglas' father, had threatened to force his way onto the stage and to address the audience on the subject of Wilde, Wilde stayed in the wings at the back of the stage. The police had been alerted; but if the marquess had come in some disguise, such as a policeman's uniform, Wilde could have recognized him instantly. By the end of the second act, however, the possibility of a disturbance had evaporated; so Wilde, a devoted friend of the Leversons, visited their box. He was elaborately dressed with a velvet collar on his coat, a green carnation in his buttonhole, a large scarab ring, numerous seals on a black ribbon watch-chain hanging from his white waistcoat, and white gloves in one hand. Wilde began his visit by teasing Aubrey: "Don't sit on the same chair as Aubrey," Wilde said; "it's not compromising." Then he contrasted Mabel with her brother, one a "daisy, and Aubrey the most monstrous of orchids." Only the year before, Beardsley had sometimes imitated and even tried to outdo Wilde in his formalized wit, but that attitude had not survived the

Ada Leverson, The Sphinx *(Courtesy of Francis Wyndham Esq.)*

difficulties with *Salome*. Now, only his good manners made Beardsley pretend amusement. This night, with its splendid success, belonged to Wilde, and the Leverson party as a whole regretted that he failed to end it with them at supper after the theater. They went to Willis', a small nearby restaurant as famous for its decor as for its food.

Mrs. Leverson later saw the entire evening, with its contrast between the glittering theater and the mud and blowing snow outside, as a forecast of what was to come for Wilde.[64] She certainly could not know that, regardless of his distaste for the playwright, Beardsley's future was tied to Wilde's. The Beardsley Period, the Beardsley Woman, signifying not only Beardsley's security and comfort but the very pattern of his daily affairs as well, in this glorious twenty-third year of his life, was coming to an end.

Beardsley's acquaintance had widened and briefly he was in a position to help others. From the Leversons—Ernest Leverson, in particular, this time—Beardsley solicited an introduction to Sir Arthur Sullivan for Raymond Roze, a young musician-composer. With Brandon Thomas, author of *Charley's Aunt*, Beardsley commenced a play which went unfinished. After Aubrey's death, Thomas spoke to Mabel about completing it, but the suggestion was only a sentimental one. To the Reverend C. D. R. Williamson, another new acquaintance, Beardsley sent a ticket for the New English Art Club show opening in April with his *Black Coffee* on exhibition.[65]

v

Black Coffee was one of the drawings which Beardsley planned for the fifth number of *The Yellow Book*. John Lane had gone to New York without Beardsley while he and Harland worked at putting this number together. Harland had selected, from a large number of manuscripts in both verse and prose, pieces by the regulars such as himself, Ella D'Arcy, Kenneth Grahame, Crackanthorpe, Le Gallienne and a few not-so-regular contributors. In this volume Ada Leverson appeared for the first time and there were two pieces in French, a discussion of Anatole France by Maurice Baring and a story by the master himself. Similarly, Beardsley mixed the well-known Steer and Sickert with less prominent artists. His own contributions included as usual a cover and title page. In addition to those and *Black Coffee*, he had produced a portrait of Letty Lind in *An Artist's Model*, *Frontispiece to the Nocturnes of Chopin*, and the beautiful *Atalanta in Calydon*.[66]

Atalanta in Calydon (Courtesy of the Trustees of the British Museum)

121

The fifth number of *The Yellow Book* was in print and ready for distribution when Oscar Wilde's counsel in his libel suit against the Marquess of Queensberry advised withdrawal from the prosecution, and the suit was terminated before noon on April 5, 1895, with a verdict of "not guilty" for Queensberry. At about half past six on the evening of the same date, Wilde was arrested on a charge of committing indecent acts. As he prepared to leave the room in the Cadogan Hotel, where he was served the warrant of arrest, Wilde picked up *Aphrodite* by Pierre Louÿs, a novel in yellow paper covers. The next morning the newspapers heralded "Arrest of Oscar Wilde Yellow Book Under His Arm." The reaction to that statement was dramatic. Elkin Mathews and John Lane had terminated their partnership at the end of summer 1894, with Mathews retaining the premises and Lane, The Bodley Head sign. He moved across Vigo Street to number 8, taking the sign with him. Outside these offices an angry crowd gathered, shouting and smashing the office windows.

Then the champions of Victorian decency began to gather. Wilfred Meynell and Sir William Watson, whose verses called "Hymn to the Sea" occupied a prominent place in the forthcoming *Yellow Book*, visited The Bodley Head and demanded to see the drawings Beardsley had made for the fifth issue. The cover upset them. It showed a faun reading to a girl; in the background, sparse as always, was a tree whose trunk with some of the branches could be construed, after very careful examination, as a female torso. Watson and Meynell were horrified. They insisted that *The Yellow Book* must not be issued with Beardsley's drawings. Frederic Chapman, left in charge of The Bodley Head when Lane went to New York and badly frightened by the street-demonstration and by these two gentlemen, acquiesced in principle.

When Lane reached New York he was greeted with headlines announcing Wilde's arrest. At his hotel he found a cable demanding that he withdraw Oscar Wilde's books from The Bodley Head's list; it was signed by the Meynells, their protégé Francis Thompson, John Davidson, and Richard Garnett. On the afternoon of April 8, Lane had a cable from Watson. It read, "Withdraw all Beardsley's designs or I withdraw all my books."[67] Lane replied by sending his own cable to *The Daily Chronicle*. In it he declared that Beardsley "had no more sympathy with Oscar Wilde and the vices of the Nineties than Hogarth had with the vices of his period."

But Lane deferred to his authors. He sent another cable which reached Chapman on the afternoon of April 11. In it Lane directed suppression of the offending drawings, and Beardsley's association with *The Yellow Book* came to an end. On April 16, Easter Tuesday, Ella D'Arcy, who saw in Beardsley's drawings "nothing . . . but repellancy" anyway, tried to reassemble the fifth number of the periodical, but she soon summoned Harland from Paris. By 9:30 on the morning of April 18, he was at The Bodley Head, and in two days every trace of Beardsley's art work was removed except the lower cover, retained by an oversight. It still had on it Beardsley's design, a sad remnant of an important association.[68] Mabel said that her brother was "bitterly humiliated" at the suppression of his pictures. If that is all he felt, perhaps Beardsley already understood that only first success is sweet and that his glorious year was done.

CHAPTER V

i

A UBREY Beardsley was in Paris when the fifth number of *The Yellow Book* appeared at the booksellers' stands on April 30. From the time of Wilde's arrest, a number of uneasy Londoners found reasons to travel to Paris and elsewhere on the Continent, and they stayed at least until his trials were finished. Unlike those gentlemen, however, Beardsley's compulsion to go to Paris was not from guilty fear occasioned by Wilde's misfortune. In fact, in letters to Mrs. Leverson, Beardsley had expressed sympathy for the "poor dear old thing" and real interest in his trial, which Aubrey called "Oscar's new tragedy. . . ."[1] Rather, Beardsley left London to escape the bewilderment he felt at the injustice done him and the necessity for dealing with the collapse of his pleasant, secure world. And so on April 20, probably with Harland, Aubrey Beardsley journeyed to Paris.[2]

Because the Harlands had been in France since the latter part of March, Henry had had no part in the decision about *The Yellow Book*–Beardsley crisis. Until Ella D'Arcy summoned him to London, he had not been consulted and he very likely knew nothing about Beardsley's dismissal. Even now he seemed to think Beardsley's severance from the periodical temporary. In a letter to Edmund Gosse written early in May, Harland deplored Beardsley's absence from the recently published fifth number and then added, "He'll be in the July number, I hope, larger than ever."[3]

Surely Harland's remark is equivocal. That Harland was still uninformed as to Beardsley's status with *The Yellow Book* is hard to credit. In any case he was faithful to John Lane and his publishing house. Ella D'Arcy maintained that if Harland had been at hand when the ultimatum about Beardsley reached Chapman at The Bodley Head and Lane in New York, "everything would have been different"; but she was very likely mistaken. His position with *The Yellow Book* was too important to Harland to risk it for Beardsley. In the first place, Harland firmly believed that he was editing a journal representative of the most cultured work which was then being done in England. With John Lane, too, Harland had connections which were almost sacred to him, because his godfather and literary patron, Edmund Stedman, and John Lane were friends and associates. Eight years earlier, Harland had withdrawn his second novel, *Mrs. Peixada*, from the publisher Samuel S. McClure, until McClure pleaded for reconciliation and publicly apologized for misquoting Stedman. Harland was capable of unfaltering loyalty, but in this instance it was to himself and John Lane, not Aubrey Beardsley. "What is one to do," Harland asked Edmund Gosse, "with a capricious boy whose ruling passion is a desire to astonish the public with the unexpected?"[4]

Fortunately, Beardsley did not test Harland's loyalty, and Lane's behavior had only strengthened an earlier suspicion of treachery.[5] Beardsley went on with his work for Lane's Keynotes series, sending at least one drawing back to The Bodley Head on May 2. Except for his position with *The Yellow Book*, nothing seemed changed. But Beardsley's financial security, such as it was, had disappeared. Equally important was the public estimate of Beardsley. The gleeful bawdiness of his drawings now confirmed an association in the public mind between Wilde and Beardsley which had arisen with the publication of his drawings for *Salome*, pictures which Beardsley maintained he "in no way" regretted.[6] The whole series of events and their implications may have been humiliating, as Mabel said, but they were also shocking. Beardsley did not luxuriate in his problems; "he's capital company," Harland reported.[7] But Beardsley was troubled. Something, very likely a lack of funds, so beset him that late in April he hurried to London to consult André Raffalovich and probably to ask his help.

André Raffalovich, born in September 1864, was the third and youngest child of Herman and Marie Raffalovich, Russians who had emigrated to Paris in 1863 to evade the Russian decree that all Jews must accept Christianity. In Paris, Herman Raffalovich had become a successful banker with an international reputation. His wife, a woman of beauty, charm, and intelligence, held a regular *salon* at their home at 19 Avenue Hoche, where the guests included Henri Bergson, Colette, Sarah Bernhardt, the Ernest Renans, and Claude Bernard. Mme. Raffalovich's children were supervised by Florence Truscott Gribbell, who also acted as governess to André. Indeed, he was more Miss Gribbell's child than his mother's; according to some reports Mme. Raffalovich thought him so ugly that she disliked looking at him. In 1882, when he determined to come to England with a view to taking a degree at Oxford, his parents provided him with a generous allowance and Miss Gribbell to take care of him and make a home for him. Once in England, Raffalovich soon gave up the idea of Oxford and settled in London, first at Albert Hall Mansions and then at 72 South Audley Street. He was too studiedly elegant in dress and manner, too eager for social prestige. He began to entertain lavishly, however; and people as unlike as Lily Langtry and Walter Pater, George Meredith and Ella Hepworth Dixon were happy to sit at Raffalovich's dinner table. But his attempts to emulate his mother's salon had meager success. Before he was eighteen, when he left Paris, he had contributed to French literary periodicals, and two years after his arrival in London his first collection of poems appeared,[8] *Cyril and Lionel*, a book of love songs ambiguous in their direction, to say the least.

At some point, perhaps through Whistler, Raffalovich met Oscar Wilde. After a fashion he was attentive to the younger man, taking him to various places and once, after telling him in detail the story of Rachilde's new novel, *Monsieur Venus*, assured Raffalovich that he had the "right measure of romance and cynicism" to provide Oscar with a "new thrill." But Oscar was sometimes deliberately offensive in remarks both to and about Raffalovich, as when Wilde suggested to André that he be careful of his associates since he was not *"le premier venu."* At last Wilde went too far. He told his wife that he and André had "such improper talks together." She repeated it to Raffalovich in the way of a compliment, and thereafter Raffalovich saw Oscar Wilde as a threat. The rift eventually reached the stage where no friend of Wilde could be a friend of André Raffalovich.[9]

In their dislike for each other, there may well have been some rivalry for the affection of John Gray, the poet. Gray, two years younger than Raffalovich, was born in Woolwich of humble parents. After several lesser positions, he began as a librarian at the Foreign Office in November 1888 and very likely he and Raffalovich first met in that year through Arthur Symons. Gray was gifted, handsome, charming, much sought after. He is thought to have been the prototype for Wilde's *Dorian Gray*, although he denied it to the extent of bringing suit for libel against *The Star*, the newspaper which made the identification. In any case, Oscar Wilde paid for the publication in March 1893 of Gray's book of verses, *Silverpoints*. Gray no longer needed Wilde's patronage after he entered fully into the affection of André Raffalovich. The relationship between him and Gray developed slowly, but it never lessened and it never faltered until Raffalovich died in 1934.

That the paths of these two had not intersected with Beardsley's is owing to Raffalovich. He had taken a dislike to Beardsley without knowing him. Raffalovich had met Mabel somewhere—at "the home of the Bruntons and then in Waterloo Place," he said—and she had urged him to hear her brother talk on art at an "at home" of the Annan Bryces. By other accounts, Beardsley was lively and amusing on that occasion, but Raffalovich found neither "the slender youth" nor his lecture attractive, and he left the Bryces, he said, "without any wish to encounter the Beardsleys again."[10]

Yet on that morning in late April 1895 when Raffalovich returned to South Audley Street from an early call, he found Beardsley "in the drawing room near Gustave Moreau's Sappho. . . . He had travelled through the night from Paris. He was in a fix."[11] Mabel had suggested that he consult Raffalovich. The two men "conversed amicably" and then Beardsley returned to Paris.

By May 5, Beardsley was ready to go again to London, this time to get back to work, or so he told Harland. After Beardsley reached London, Raffalovich began to court him. That meant courting Mabel, too, and Raffalovich now enjoyed taking her to lunch at the Ritz, when she wore the "first turban of that season or the earliest modish colour. . . ." But with Beardsley, the attraction was irresistible. "He arrested me," Raffalovich confessed, "like wrought iron and like honeysuckle; hardness, elegance, charm, variety." Raffalovich, a small, homely man with sharp black eyes, "delighted" in Beardsley's "fame, his notoriety," delighted in appearing publicly with Beardsley, wanted him at the elaborate dinner parties at South Audley Street.[12] Once, briefly, they quarreled when Beardsley failed to rebuke a fellow guest, Hugh Dearborn, for discourtesy to an American woman. And once Beardsley forgot an appointment with Raffalovich. But each time, after a brief unpleasantness, the episode was dismissed and invitations and gifts from Raffalovich flowed again. There were chocolates which served Beardsley as "a great support" in work he was doing; there were walking sticks, a sonnet, seven letters which George Meredith had written to Raffalovich, flowers from Bond Street's most elegant florist. There were invitations to lunch, to dinner, to tea, to the theater and the opera, and invitations to join Raffalovich in Berlin. When he produced *L'Uranisme, Inversion Sexuelle Congénitale*, Beardsley saw it before publication, and he read at least part of Raffalovich's savage *L'Affaire Oscar Wilde* in manuscript.[13] Raffalovich wanted his portrait made, and Beardsley planned "a pastel on brown paper—full length"; but it was never drawn.

Beardsley did, however, make a frontispiece for Raffalovich's volume of poems *The Thread and the Path*, which David Nutt scheduled for publication that year. Beardsley chose to illustrate the first line of the first poem, "Set in the heart as in a frame Love

Mark André Raffalovich *(Courtesy of the National Library of Scotland)*

liveth. . . ." and for it he drew a magnificent, winged Amor set in a heart which in turn is part of an elaborate candelabrum. It was completed by May 25, and when Beardsley showed it to the author, he liked it. But Nutt refused to publish the picture, maintaining that the figure was hermaphroditic. Beardsley explained the rejection to Raffalovich by saying that Nutt disliked the frontispiece because it contained a "nude Amor. . . ." Although Raffalovich threatened to withdraw the book from Nutt, he published it that year, 1895, without a frontispiece.[14]

Beardsley's letters about the drawing, and indeed the general flurry of letters which marked his association with André Raffalovich in 1895 and early 1896, Beardsley addressed to "Dear Mentor" and in 1895 signed, "Télémaque. . . ." Raffalovich accounted for the use of these names in terms of their ages (he was thirty and Beardsley nearly twenty-three when it began) and "affectionate playfulness" rather than a tolerance on Beardsley's part of "interference or guidance".[15] Raffalovich may have been "arrested" and charmed, but he was obviously perplexed by Beardsley as well. That he was is no wonder. Beardsley's motive in the use of those names is puzzling. Beardsley's satiric turn of mind, especially when faced with Raffalovich's assumption of suavity and superiority, may explain their use. That possibility cannot be ignored, although it is not consistent with Beardsley's usual response to kindness. Another explanation is a strong temptation. Télémaque, or Telemachus, Odysseus' son by Penelope, traveled far in search of his father. Telemachus had help from Athena, who appeared to him in the guise of Mentor, a friend of Odysseus in the *Odyssey* and a man whose name is synonymous with faithful adviser. Did Beardsley, shocked by the hostility of the public as well as that of the Meynells, William Watson, and other Bodley Head authors and alarmed by the threat to his financial security travel from Paris overnight at the urging of his sister to find in Raffalovich both the wisdom and generosity a young man might normally expect from his father—but not from Vincent Beardsley?

In many respects such a notion fits in well with the fantasy which the psychologists Otto Rank and Sigmund Freud named the "Family Romance. . . ." An intense daydream, it recurs especially among the gifted and creative. It involves the imaginary substitution of a more satisfactory parent or parents for actual ones. The father suffers such substitution more frequently than the mother, perhaps for reasons suggested by these words which Telemachus spoke in the *Odyssey:*

> My mother saith that he is my father;
> For myself I know it not,
> For no man knoweth who hath begotten him.

130

Ludwig van Beethoven, a classic example of a man who fantasized in terms of the "Family Romance. . . ." copied these lines into his diary before he was eighteen and treasured them throughout his life. On the strength of their implications and their relation to his own situation, Beethoven created for himself a whole new and unreal genealogy.

Of course Beardsley did not go to such lengths as Beethoven, if indeed such a fantasy lay behind his bestowal of the name "Mentor" on Raffalovich and the assumption of the name Télémaque. But as the possible causes for father substitution are limitless, so are the possibilities of the shape it may take. In need of a father's help, Beardsley found a wise friend.[16] Such an explanation coincides with Vincent Beardsley's position in the family and his relations with his son, Aubrey. It even takes into account Beardsley's frequent role-playing. Ellen Beardsley's description of her son as eager to "shine & please" the person for whom he was enacting a part gives weight to the idea of a deliberate use of the names Télémaque and Mentor as an affirmation of the older man's view of himself and Aubrey's current view of their association.

By the end of January 1896, Beardsley had stopped addressing Raffalovich as Mentor, and some months before, he had abandoned the use of Télémaque for himself. Either he had grown weary of his role or he no longer needed to be bolstered by a real or imaginary father. The assumption is not unreasonable that by January 1896 his faith in himself, in his gifts and their possibilities was strong once more. Without question, by that time, the obviously practical details of his life were in as much order as they were ever to be again.

ii

In the first place there was the question of the Beardsley home at 114 Cambridge Street, Pimlico. With Beardsley's income reduced and his prospects uncertain and with Mabel's doubtful career as an actress, the two young Beardsleys concluded that they could not afford the house. When Aubrey returned from Paris in May 1895, the house went up for sale with the agreement that the new owner could have possession at once; and by early June, Beardsley could report the house as "on the eve of sale. . . ." Later that month, he took a lease on a house at 57 Chester Terrace, and by early July, Mabel and he had removed almost all the Beardsleys' effects from Cambridge Street to Chester Terrace.[17]

Beardsley left behind a canvas with unfinished oil paintings on both sides, the only two oils he is known to have made. They were no more than experiments, one a contrast in red and green, in keeping with his success with the black-white contrasts of his drawings. Walter Sickert had offered to teach Beardsley oil painting, but there is no trace of Sickert's influence in these two, *A Caprice* and *A Masked Woman*, a painting of a masked woman dressed in black behind a table which held a white mouse.[18]

Beardsley left even less evidence of his stay in the house in Chester Terrace. The Beardsleys lived there very briefly, and Aubrey was away much of that time. Many mornings during his brief stay, he went "hastily dressed and without a collar" to Billy Rothenstein's studio off the King's Road at 50 Glebe Place. On one such visit, Beardsley began "scribbling some verses about musicians. . . ."[19] He completed a version of these soon thereafter in his studio in Chester Terrace, and in 1896, after considerable revision, they appeared as "The Three Musicians" accompanied by two of his drawings in a new periodical, *The Savoy*.[20]

The Savoy was conceived by Arthur Symons to supplant *The Yellow Book*. Symons, some seven years Beardsley's senior, had come in his twentieth year to London, where he gratified his evergreen taste for women and his interest in literature. It was Symons, with Rothenstein, who had brought Verlaine to London in 1893. Symons had a particular enthusiasm for French writers, especially the Symbolists. As a critic, however, he was the disciple of the arch-aesthete Walter Pater, whom he liked and admired. After dinner at Pater's London home in Earl's Terrace, Pater and Symons exchanged photographs, and Symons watched Pater fondle his great black Persian cat. Through Symons, Pater was asked to contribute to the first *Yellow Book* but, wishing it all success, he honestly pleaded overwork. At about this time, possibly after reading Symons' "Stella Maris" in that first issue, Pater's friendship began to cool. Symons, however, had numerous other friends; he listened so well, "as a woman listens" according to W. B. Yeats. And so Symons could turn for companionship to George Moore, Dowson, Yeats, Havelock Ellis, Wilde (before and after his imprisonment), as well as the Coras and Bellas and Elises who were dancers at the Empire Music Hall and at others which he frequented. These were the women about whom he talked as he sat at the Crown after theater hours and whom he described years later in an essay written for Nancy Cunard's Hours Press.[21]

Symons was astute enough to recognize that *The Yellow Book* without Beardsley was inconsequential. Symons was convinced, however, that there was a place for a periodical such as *The Yellow Book* had claimed to be, a showcase for what was new and

132

experimental in art and ideas. He saw himself as editor and Beardsley as art editor for the projected quarterly, at first amorphous and nameless. Mabel Beardsley took credit for naming it "The Savoy," but Symons said it was Aubrey's suggestion, made when he first consulted with Beardsley, and "finally adopted after endless changes and uncertainties."[22]

That consultation took place before Beardsley moved from Cambridge Street, almost certainly before June 14, 1895. Possibly for literary effect, Symons said afterwards that was his first meeting with Beardsley. In fact the two first met in the late summer of 1893, to the distaste of Symons. An undated letter of Symons docketed "P. M. 24 Aug. 1893" by its recipient, Herbert Horne, states, "I saw Lane tonight, who brought Beardsley to the Crown; the thinnest young man I ever saw, rather unpleasant and affected."[23] Furthermore, they had acquaintances in common; from the meetings of the Rhymers' Club to the music hall and the Crown, they went to the same places; they were both associated with *The Yellow Book*. In any case, Symons called on Beardsley by appointment and was shown into his studio. There Symons found Beardsley "lying out on a couch horribly white" and Symons wondered whether he had "come too late. . . ."[24] Troubled by financial problems and the difficulties of house-selling and house-moving, Beardsley was exhausted. He had suffered a hemorrhage which forced him to rest. As he told Raffalovich, it was a "rather trying time."[25] But Beardsley reacted promptly to Symons. At once, Beardsley was brimming with ideas and enthusiasm.[26] The project appeased his resentment of Lane's expediency and at the same time put him back to work. He still had drawings to do for Lane's Keynotes series, but new commissions were scarce. *The Savoy* also put him again into the midst of the intellectual fervor which accompanies and fosters innovation.

But it had an adverse effect, too. According to many reports, especially his mother's, it commenced an unfortunate association which damaged Beardsley's health and took advantage of his financial need. That was the association with the publisher of *The Savoy*, Leonard Smithers.[27] Smithers was a native of Sheffield, where, after attendance at the Wesley College for the Law, he practiced as a solicitor. In 1891, when he was thirty, he moved to London and took an office in Wardour Street. From there, in addition to his work at the law, he began publishing in a quiet way with H. S. Nichols, a rare book dealer with the same address. From Wardour Street, Smithers apparently moved with Nichols to Soho Square and then to Effingham House, Arundel Street, the Strand, and there he abandoned his law career to trade in a few *objets d'art*, rare and secondhand

133

books of choice quality, often in fine or unusual bindings, and "absurd and ill-written pornography. . . ." At the same time he was commencing as "publisher of the most beautiful books ever issued in any country. . . ." books which caused him to be named "the cleverest publisher in London. . . ."[28]

As a man, Smithers was as various as his stock in trade, a remarkable mixture of vast learning (he was an authority on Napoleon and the French Revolution), unusual and discriminating taste in literature, enterprise with kindliness and generosity, great daring in his publishing ("I'll publish anything the others are afraid of . . .," he said). At the same time he was a man of infinite vulgarity and excesses. He drank more brandy in a day than most men consumed in a month; he also liked absinthe, and he developed an addiction to chlorodyne. He enjoyed every available woman from his wife to the coarsest tart, and he was sometimes unscrupulous in money matters.

He was "a most disreputable man" to Yeats, who agreed to contribute to *The Savoy* because Symons, with whom he shared a flat, urged it, but only on condition that he never again be asked to meet Smithers after the birth of the quarterly was celebrated. Charles Cochran, Beardsley's old schoolfellow, described Smithers as a "fat Yorkshire man. . . .", not at all the sort to publish "those beautiful editions" which emanated from his offices. "The most delightful and irresponsible publisher" he had ever met was Robbie Ross' description. Beerbohm long afterward remembered him as "a strange and rather depressing person. . . ." To Rothenstein, Smithers was a "bizarre and improbable figure—a rough Yorkshireman with a strong local accent and uncertain *h*'s, the last man to be a Latin scholar and a disciple of M. le Marquis de Sade. . . ." Rothenstein and Smithers quarreled and went to court but neither had a clear-cut decision.[29] Perhaps Oscar Wilde, who thought Smithers "a very good fellow" when they were not squabbling, provided as just a compendium of Smithers as can be found. It reads,

> He is usually in a large straw hat, has a blue tie delicately fastened with a diamond brooch of the impurest water, or perhaps wine, as he never touches water—it goes to his head at once. His face, clean shaven . . . is wasted and pale . . . He loves first editions, especially of women: little girls are his passion. He is the most learned erotomaniac in Europe. He is also a delightful companion and a dear fellow . . .[30]

That was the man who was thereafter Beardsley's publisher and very often his companion. As Wilde did, Beardsley enjoyed Smithers

Leonard Smithers *(From Malcolm Pinhorn, "The Career and Ancestry of Leonard Smithers"*
Blackmansbury, *August 1964)*

far more than he had enjoyed Lane. Smithers was indeed a delightful fellow. His characteristics, which some of Beardsley's friends found unpleasant, Beardsley enjoyed. *The Yellow Book* set affected weariness with the world; Smithers was infatuated with it. His disregard of conventional expectations, his restless energy and self-indulgence, his downright vulgarity made life joyous. He appealed to what Arthur Symons called Beardsley's "boyish defiance of things. . . ." Unfortunately Beardsley was determined to "shine" with Smithers, even to investigating the older man's vices. Possibly Smithers' taste for little girls, to which Wilde referred, provided the impetus for the scene with the children in *Venus and Tannhäuser*, a sexual indulgence which Beardsley attributed to himself, his novel's hero. The same implication is in these lines written later by an acquaintance, Aleister Crowley, the occultist who matriculated as an undergraduate at Cambridge in 1895:

> Aubrey attained in sleep when he dreamt this
>> Wonderful dream of women, tender child
>> And harlot, naked all, in thousands piled
> On one hot writhing heap, his shameful kiss
>> To shudder through them, with lithe limbs defiled
>>> To wade, to dip
> Down through the mass, caressed by every purple lip.[31]

Possibly, in talking to Wilde, Smithers pretended to emulate his good friend Beardsley.

At the end of July, Smithers and Beardsley were still on formal terms. Owing to another hemorrhage, Beardsley required bed-rest and thus he had to change an appointment with Smithers, whom he addressed as "Mr. Smithers. . . ."[32] The formality of that letter, dated July 30, 1895, vanished in August when they were both in Dieppe. As soon as he could after his enforced rest, Beardsley went with Arthur Symons to Dieppe. At least one account says that Beardsley crossed to Dieppe several times in July and August; probably nearer the truth, though not exact, is Symons' statement that they met daily in Dieppe for a month,[33] and certainly both were there in August. In Dieppe, Beardsley recovered to the fullest his "feverish brilliance," his "frail and intense vitality."[34]

It was a glorious time, "the first time," Beardsley said, that he had "ever enjoyed a holiday," and he remarked on the "Petits Chevaux and everything most pretty and amusing."[35] Beardsley had considerable devotion to the "petits chevaux" and even more to their setting. Symons says that Beardsley was at the casino almost every night.

Although he was often at the tables, he spent less time playing than watching others with a sort of "hypnotised attention." He liked to go to the casino as well for the afternoon concerts, but most of all he enjoyed the rooms when they were empty, "the sense of frivolous things caught at the moment of suspended life." Often he went into the writing room, where he set down a few words of his *Venus and Tannhäuser*. Beardsley worked at it, too, when Symons and he went to stay briefly at Arques-la-Bataille, where they spent "two whole days on the grassy ramparts of the old castle."[36] There, with the ancient ruins, its walls flecked with yellow *giroflée*, behind them and with an almost tangible silence around them, they worked, Symons on a poem, possibly one comparing the sea at Dieppe with absinthe, and Beardsley on his version of *Tannhäuser*. Once they went together to Puys to visit Alexandre Dumas *fils* at his seaside house so that Beardsley could tell its author how much he admired *La dame aux camélias*. Most of the holiday, however, was spent in Dieppe, where they were joined by Smithers en route to Paris. About August 14, 1895, Charles Conder the artist, wrote to Rothenstein about Smithers, designated as X, as well as Symons and Beardsley:

At present Symons and Beardsley and X are here but I hope they do not intend to remain. In fact I am almost sure they will be leaving tomorrow; X is too awful for words but very good hearted. He has decked himself out in a whole suit of French summer clothing from the Belle Jardiniere, and although it suits his particular style very well one is not exactly proud of his companionship.[37]

Whatever Conder hoped, Beardsley did not go. He planned to, but he missed the boat and "lingered on." To stay in Dieppe with its quiet streets and old churches, its sea air (Beardsley never went into the sea), "like some drug that makes one satisfied with . . . desire" was all he asked. His drawing seemed to be in suspension; he maintained, anyway, that he could draw only in London. Once, in the studio of the French painter Jacques-Emile Blanche, Beardsley prepared a canvas for painting, but he abandoned it. Blanche liked Beardsley; he was so witty, so learned, so removed from the glib eloquence of many "polished strangers" in France. He met Blanche's friends and those of his family, most notably the Duchesse Caracciolo. She lived on the sea front of the Bas Fort Blanc in a villa given her by the Prince of Wales. He was godfather of her young daughter, Olga Alberta, "that enchanting Olga," Henry James called her and maintained that at Dieppe she learned far more than his Maisie knew.

Both men enjoyed the sittings for a portrait of Beardsley which Blanche painted in his family's villa, also built on the front of the Bas Fort Blanc.[38]

But Beardsley was in Dieppe with Symons to plan *The Savoy*, and Smithers joined them to have his say about it as well. Apparently— or so Conder said—there was a "great deal of excitement" about the new quarterly and much discussion. The talk offended Beardsley and he let it be known. "Beardsley is very pompous about it all," Conder said. But Beardsley contributed his share of talk when he sat down with Symons and sometimes with Smithers at a table in the Café des Tribunaux to design the new periodical. And in the Café des Tribunaux (its ambiance was captured in a number of Walter Sickert's paintings), *The Savoy* took shape.

By late August, when Beardsley returned to London, Symons and Beardsley, with the occasional help of Smithers, had planned the first issue.[39] Working in the Café des Tribunaux, Symons had already written the "slightly pettish and defiant editorial note" which introduced *The Savoy*. He had also translated "Mandoline" from Paul Verlaine's *Fêtes Galantes*, and in late August he was writing his prose impression of Dieppe. In addition, Symons had planned for literary contributions from Shaw, Ernest Dowson, Edgar Jepson, Yeats, Pennell, and others. The first number was to include, too, Beardsley's "The Three Musicians" and an expurgated version of three chapters of his *The Story of Venus and Tannhäuser*. Lane had already advertised it, but Beardsley meant it to appear in *The Savoy*. So that Lane would not suspect that it was his book when Smithers announced *The Savoy*, Beardsley suggested changing the title to *The Queen in Exile*,[40] he settled on *Under the Hill*. For it, he made three drawings and two for "The Three Musicians." He had also to provide designs for *The Savoy*'s cover, and for its title and contents pages. He produced, too, a large Christmas card, *The Virgin and Child*, for insertion in the first issue. And he solicited contributions from Rothenstein, Beerbohm, Pennell, even Whistler. Beardsley secured from Jacques-Emile Blanche a painting made that summer of his fellow artist Fritz Thaulow with his family. Both Ricketts and Shannon, fearful of causing complications for their own publication, *The Dial*, had refused to contribute to *The Yellow Book*, but Shannon agreed to produce a lithograph for *The Savoy*.

Although Beardsley at least once referred to Symons as "Simple Symons" and later came to resent his behavior in the matter of a Beardsley contribution,[41] they began by working well together, accepting each other's suggestions and one providing material for the other to illustrate. At Dieppe, Beardsley had found the subject for

La Dame aux Camélias, a watercolor and pencil sketch on the flyleaf of a copy of the book given to Beardsley by its author, Alexandre Dumas *fils (From* A Second Book of Fifty Drawings by Aubrey Beardsley, *London, 1897)*

MOSKA

The Moska, an illustration for Arthur Symons' "Dieppe" in *The Savoy*, Number 1, January 1896 *(From* The Savoy, *January 1896)*

two drawings, *The Bathers* and *The Moska.* The second shows a young girl poised in the moska, a dance performed at the *Bal des Enfants* held periodically at the casino. Both drawings, made after Beardsley left Dieppe, accompanied Symons' essay on Dieppe.

Beardsley's stay in London was short and busy. With little more family opposition than might be anticipated, Beardsley disposed of the lease on 57 Chester Terrace. Ellen and Mabel took Vincent and their household goods back to Charlwood Street, where they had lived in 1891. Aubrey's only possessions were his books. Although he offered Rothenstein whatever books he wanted, Beardsley disposed of most of them and of his erotic Japanese prints, a gift from Rothenstein, by putting them at Smithers' disposal. For himself, Beardsley had rented a small flat which Oscar Wilde had once used for work at 10 St. James's Place.[42] Beardsley chose it for its location in the center of London and its proximity to Smithers, in Arundel Street.

Then, in the last days of August or the first ones of September, Beardsley again left London. He set off for what he once described as "touring all over the world."[43] Being Aubrey Beardsley, he doubtless had definite ideas as to where he meant to go and what he thought was enough money to get him there. In mid-August he had sold a drawing intended as a cover for *La Plume,* and although it was never published, it was paid for.[44] Somehow, he secured the rest or at least the promise of it in case of necessity. Very likely it came from Raffalovich. But for all the information which survives, either as to his plans or as to where he went, he might almost have been "touring" in space. From the time he left London until he reached Dieppe three or four weeks later, only two places he visited can be designated with certainty. They are Cologne and Munich. In a letter written to Raffalovich in 1896, Beardsley mentioned a painting by Francia which he had seen in the Alte Pinakothek of Munich. He wrote a draft of "The Ballad of a Barber," verses which appeared in the fourth *Savoy,* on the letterhead of a hotel in Cologne, the Englische Hof. There, too, he made additions, partly abandoned later, to *Venus and Tannhäuser.*[45] No other tangible evidence of his travels remains except perhaps the Gothic character of the terms he used for balance from time to time in the composition of a drawing. Surely he gazed at the magnificence of Cologne's cathedral, and he must have indulged in its Cologne 4711. Despite his singular appearance, he escaped notice. If he sent letters from either place, they no longer exist. He went to Cologne and Munich and he came away. More than likely he visited other cities in Germany, too. Raffalovich had praised Berlin highly earlier that year and urged

Beardsley to join him there; perhaps he went to Berlin and then at last crossed from Germany into Belgium and from there moved on to France, to Dieppe.[46]

By that time, late September, Beardsley had all but emptied his purse, and he had freed himself of the notion that he could not draw away from London. Almost his first act after reaching Dieppe was to send Smithers a design for the cover of *The Savoy*, to thank him for sending clean clothes, and to ask for money "as charity and not by right." Beardsley wanted to stay on in Dieppe's "quite perfect" weather, but the need for money was pressing. "My travels and *petits chevaux*," he wrote to Lane, "have cleaned me out." That fact explained his asking for payment in advance for the covers of Grant Allen's *British Barbarians*, one of the books in Lane's Keynotes series. It doubtless explains Beardsley's acceptance of a new commission from Lane, drawings to be used in the new Pierrot Library. Since they were certain to involve "a great deal of work," Beardsley wanted £15 for them.[47] While he lingered in Dieppe and waited for Smithers to send money, Beardsley was occupied with *Tannhäuser* and another drawing for *The Savoy*, possibly the one reproduced on the lower cover of the prospectus. At last Smithers' check came, but it was so small that Beardsley had to demand another one in order to get himself back to London. Once there, he promptly asked Jerome Pollitt, who wanted a bookplate, to pay in advance.[48]

London had become to Beardsley "this desolate city." To dismiss this phrase as the pretense of a young man fresh from his travels abroad does Beardsley an injustice. He had come back reluctantly, and except for his family and his work, he had little reason for enthusiasm. Since his "sudden leap" into fame with *Salome*, Beardsley had been the butt of some artists and most journalists. His presumed association with Wilde had made Beardsley even more vulnerable. Although he was indifferent, as his mother said, to things said about him, they sometimes limited his associations. Soon after his return to London, he renewed his friendship with André Raffalovich and the Leversons and as always he enjoyed the music London had to offer. But the Sunday afternoons at the Meynells and the Thursdays in the Beardsley drawing room at 114 Cambridge Street were both ended for him. The days with the Harlands were over. He rarely visited the Bodley Head. In other words, Beardsley now saw few of the people with whom he shared memories, dreams, discoveries.

Beardsley had hardly returned to London when he had a resounding quarrel with Lane and Elkin Mathews. Mathews had asked Beardsley to draw a frontispiece for Walt Ruding's *An Evil Motherhood* for publication in 1896. A portrait of Ruding was stipulated, but

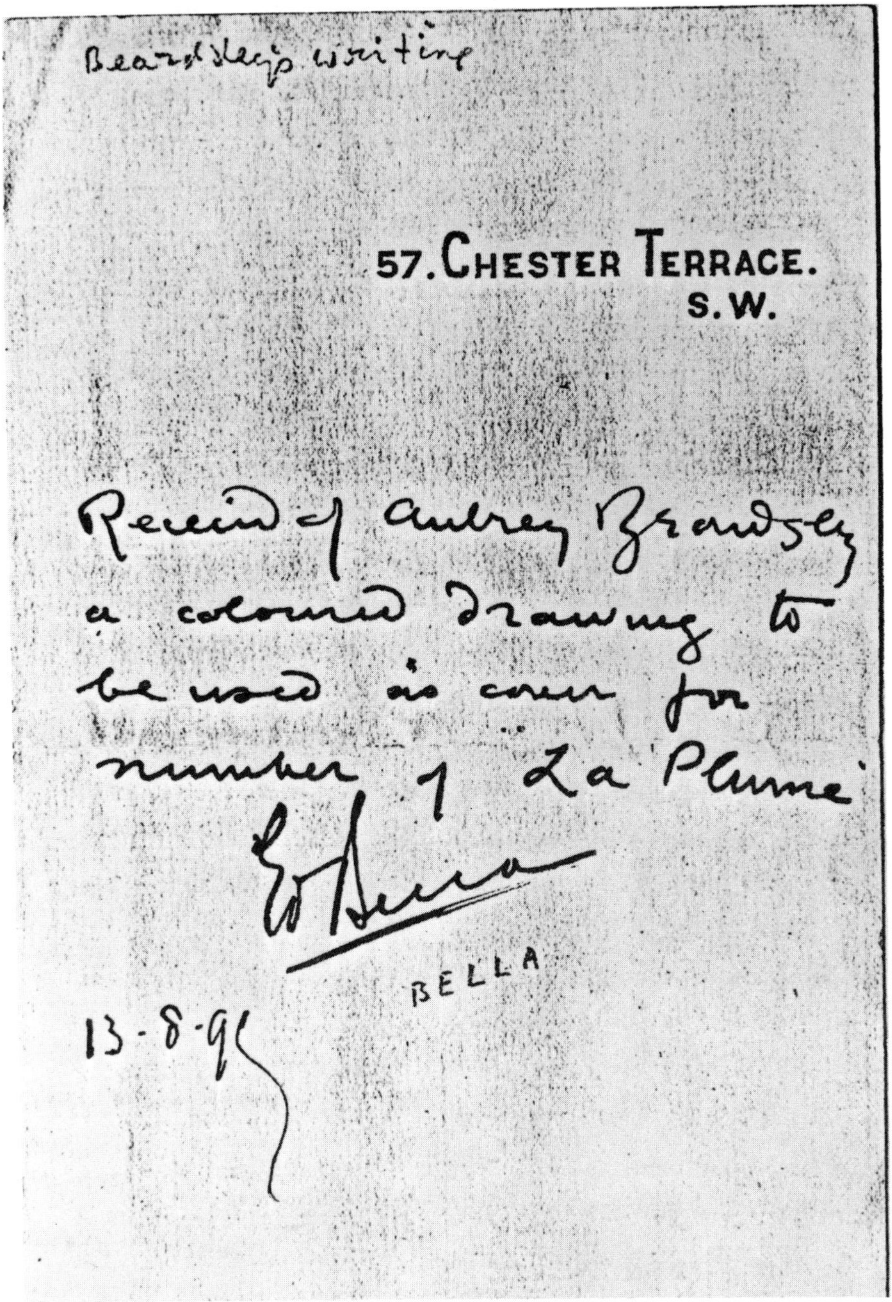

Beardsley's writing

57. CHESTER TERRACE.
S.W.

Received of Audrey Beardsley
a coloured drawing to
be used as cover for
number 1 La Plume.

Ed Bella
BELLA

13 - 8 - 95

A receipt in Beardsley's hand, signed by Ed Bella, for a cover design which Beardsley made for *La Plume (Courtesy of The Gallatin Beardsley Collection, Princeton University Library)*

Hôtel
Englischer Hof
KÖLN %Rh.

Unmittelbar
Central-Bahnhof, der festen Rheinbrücke
und gegenüber dem Dom.

Knotenpunkt
sämmtlicher Strassenbahnen.

Joseph Strunk.

Mit dem
neuesten Comfort eingerichtet
Central-Heizung
Personen Aufzug
Separat-
Neue Speise-Wirthschaft
Table d'hôte IX Uhr
Civile Preise.

Münchener Bier-Restaurant ersten Ranges.

Under the Hill ① Köln %Rh., den 189 ②

Chap. IX

"The ballad of a barber"

Here is the tale of Carrousel
The barber of Meridian Street.
He cut & coiffed & shaved so well
That all the world was at his feet.

The King, the Queen & all the court
To no one else would trust their hair
And reigning belles of every sort
Owed their successes to his care.

With carriage & with cabriolet
Daily Meridian Street was blocked
Like bees about a bright bouquet
The beauty about his doorway flocked.

Such was his art he would with ease
Curl wit into the dullest face
Or to a Goddess of old greece
Add a new wonder & a grace.

All powders, paints, & subtle dyes,
And costliest scents that men distil,
And rare pommades, forgot their price
And marvelled at his splendid skill

The curling irons in his hand
almost grew quick enough to
~~   ~~ (speak)
The razor was a magic wand
That understood the softest cheek.

Yet with no pride his heart was moved :
He was so modest in his ways!
It seemed his craft was all he loved
And now & then a little praise.

Equal respect alike he paid

To courtiers in or out of place,

Priest, poet, Dandy, or old maid,

in disgrace.

An equal care he would bestow

On problems simple or complex,

And nobody had seen him show

A preference for either sex.

How came it then one summer day,

Coiffing the daughter of the King,

He seemed to love the least delay,

And loitered in his hairdressing.

The Princess was a pretty child;

Thirteen years old, or thereabout.

She was as joyous as wild

As spring flowers when the sun is out.

Her gold hair fell down to her feet,

And hung about her pretty eyes,

She was as lyrical & sweet

As one of Schubert's melodies.

Three times the barber curled a lock,

And thrice he straightened it again;

And twice the irons scorched her frock,

And twice he stumbled in her train.

His fingers lost their cunning quite

His way combs obeyed no more.

Something or other dimmed his sight

And moved mysteriously the floor.

The flowers on the toilet Table

He felt as foolish as a fable

and feeble as a pointless jest.

He leant upon the toilet table

His fingers fumbled in his breast

He felt as foolish as a fable

& feeble as a pointless jest.

Beardsley's worksheets for "The Ballad of a Barber" (Courtesy of The Gallatin Beardsley Collection, Princeton University Library)

145

A design which Beardsley made for his own bookplate but instead provided for the use of Herbert J. Pollitt *(Courtesy of Fogg Art Museum, Harvard University and John L. Clark Esq., administrator of the Scofield Thayer Estate)*

Beardsley delivered instead *Black Coffee*, one of the drawings deleted from the fifth *Yellow Book* during the Wilde furor. *Black Coffee* had appeared in at most a dozen copies of *An Evil Motherhood* when Lane pointed out that he still held rights in the drawing. Mathews, prickly in any dealings with Lane, went indignantly to Beardsley's rooms in St. James's Place and refused to leave until Beardsley had started a new drawing, "a drawing," he said, "to be produced at sword's point."[49]

Then, Smithers disliked Beardsley's design for the cover of *The Savoy*'s prospectus. Beardsley had drawn a winged Pierrot stepping onto a stage to announce the new periodical, but Smithers thought it too flippant. He declared that "John Bull" would prefer "something more serious." Thereupon Beardsley drew a winged John Bull stepping onto the stage with the announcement. John Bull, however, was in a visible state of sexual excitement, and after some eighty thousand copies of the prospectus had been printed, somebody complained. Several people have been charged: Selwyn Image, George Bernard Shaw, Herbert Horne and George Moore, who is accused most frequently. Edgar Jepson said that he was so disgusted by the "silly and blatant" vulgarity of the announcement that he organized the protest, but he failed to name the protester. Smithers at first was angry and he insisted that the public needed Beardsley's excited John Bull, but having already distributed all eighty thousand copies of the announcement, he decided he might as well be agreeable.[50] He then distributed a second prospectus with the winged Pierrot on the cover and used John Bull, somewhat altered and sexually calm, for a page preceding the lists of contents in the first *Savoy*. He objected, however, to the cover for that issue. At its lower center, it showed a putto ready to void on a copy of *The Yellow Book*. Eventually the putto's genitalia and *The Yellow Book* were excised, and the cover duly appeared.

None of these occurrences means that Beardsley's world was out of joint. His financial position was as sound as it had ever been. He still had work to do for Lane, he had *The Savoy* for a steady income, and Smithers was ready to take as much work from Beardsley as he could do. The publisher's son, Jack, insisted, however, that in addition to his assignments, Beardsley brought Smithers drawings of so pornographic a character as to be "truly awful." Jack Smithers cited Leviticus XVIII, 23, to justify his opinion: "Neither shalt thou lie with any beast to defile thyself therewith: neither shall any woman stand before a beast to lie down thereto . . ." His charge is substantiated by Beardsley's statement in an interview reported in *The Sketch* for April 10, 1895, "I'm at work upon a set of illustrations to the Book of Leviticus, which suits me admirably." The drawings, young Smithers said, were "too devilish in subject" for his father to sell, but what became of them, Jack could not say.[51] Now, too, Beardsley had a wealthy collector of his work, H. C. J. Pollitt. About a year older than Beardsley, Pollitt was at Cambridge. He enjoyed acting, with "a special preference for transvestism under the stage name of Diane de Rougy, a soubriquet presumably taken from Liane de Pougy, a dancer of the Folies-Bergère."[52] Pollitt was always eager to know of Beardsley's work available through Smithers or directly from the artist, and Pollitt paid what was asked, sometimes in advance. Furthermore Beardsley liked having the center of London at his door, or more precisely, at the bottom of his staircase. His flat was comfortable. When he was not at work, he sat before his fireplace in a large chair covered with some sort of flowered material and, at its head, an oversized antimacassar. He took pleasure in the elaborate dressing gown and "Pierrot style" slippers (the sort he put on Walt Ruding in the second frontispiece for *An Evil Motherhood)* in which he often worked. Certainly, Beardsley enjoyed the stratagem of his drawings and he thought it most amusing when he was found out.

Besides, all of Beardsley's work did not involve difficulties. Indeed, much of it went smoothly and rapidly, so that by early December he had completed his illustrations for *The Savoy*, including those for "The Three Musicians" and *Under the Hill*, changed the name of its hero from Aubrey to Fanfreluche, and dealt with other contributors' drawings, which he carefully listed for Smithers. On December 9, 1895, Beardsley could tell King that *The Savoy* was "quite ready" but would not appear until January 4.[53]

The publication date for the first number of *The Savoy* was January 11, 1896. Among the people for whom it was intended, as Rothenstein said, it "created a stir." Comparison with *The Yellow Book* was inevitable, and Ernest Dowson, who saw an advance copy of *The Savoy* in December, declared that owing to its "type & excellence of reproduction," it licked "the 'Yellow Book' hollow." He thought Beardsley was "at his best" in his drawings for *The Savoy* and "really abominably clever" in his literary contributions, even though Dowson did not like them.[54] Dowson's comments doubtless reflect informed opinion. Symons was a better editor than Henry Harland, and Beardsley's drawings were among his finest. With Smithers, the two editors had attracted a number of gifted young men, from Beerbohm and Shaw to Yeats. Smithers kept after his authors, encouraging them to submit their work and then start a new piece. He was not always successful, as in the case of Jepson, who withdrew his contribution, but Smithers always had another writer to try.

148

The Toilet, later called *The Toilet of Helen*, an illustration for *Under the Hill (From* The Savoy, *January 1896)*

Symons had worked tirelessly, making changes even after the second prospectus was issued. He had altered titles and replaced a story by H. S. Byng with two others, one from Humphrey James and one from W. B. Yeats. George Moore's "After Parsifal" had been dropped.[55] Beardsley had secured from Max Beerbohm a caricature of his actor-brother, Herbert Beerbohm Tree. Pennell was represented by *Regent Street, London*, a pen-and-ink drawing, as well as an article on English art in the years 1860 to 1870; three drawings, one by Whistler, were reproduced from *Once a Week*. One or two others, in addition to Blanche, Shannon, and Beardsley, were listed in "Art Contents."

The press's reception of *The Savoy* was mixed. Well before its appearance, *The National Observer* and *The Globe* had prepared the journalists' way. Announcing *The Savoy* for December, *The Globe* wrote, "It was hardly to be supposed that the young decadents who once rioted . . . in the *Yellow Book* would be content to remain in obscurity after the metamorphosis of that periodical and the consequent exclusion of themselves." Early in November, *The National Observer*, after quoting that passage from *The Globe*, carried a parody of the last chorus in Shelley's *Hellas* about "The New Quarterly Blue Book." The latter half runs,

> O cease to brew your Bodley pap
> Whence all the spice is spent!
> The splendour of its primal tap
> Was gone when Aubrey went;
> Behold that subtle Sphinx prepare
> Fresh liquors fit to lift your hair.
> Absinthe in larger mugs! and let
> New *Esther Waters* spout;
> Degas is with us; we shall get
> G. Moore to join the rout;
> *Enfin*, the Villonous Verlaine
> Has got a little thing in train.
> Another Quarterly shall rise
> And knock the former down;
> Of happier hue, of simpler size,
> And sold at half a crown:
> Please note the pregnant brand—"Savoy,"
> And don't confuse with *saveloy*.

When the first number of *The Savoy* appeared, *The Sunday Times* described it as "a 'Yellow Book' redeemed of its puerilities" and spoke of the "splendid decorative effect" of Beardsley's "composition, his pattern, his 'idea.'" *Punch* carried Ada Leverson's "Dickens Up to Date," a friendly takeoff of *Under the Hill*. But on the whole enthusiasm was tempered. *The Star* was especially critical. They regarded the entire issue as "dull—at once eccentric and insipid"; and Beardsley's *Under the Hill* provoked strong distaste.[56]

The dinner which celebrated the birth of *The Savoy* was masculine and boisterous and totally lacking the euphoria of the dinner for *The Yellow Book*. Symons was deliberately provocative in reading aloud two letters which Yeats had had rebuking him for contributions to *The Savoy*. After hearing the first, Smithers was furious and he threatened to sue. The second letter, in which George Russell— AE—called *The Savoy* "the organ of the incubi and succubi," reduced Smithers to silence. Beardsley could do nothing to lessen the unpleasantness; he was too ill. Afterwards, Smithers and Beardsley went to Smithers' flat, where Yeats, a most unwilling guest, and Symons joined them. Yeats says that when they arrived, Beardsley was "lying on two chairs in the middle of the room and Smithers was sweating at his hurdy-gurdy piano. . . . Beardsley was praising the beautiful tone, the incomparable touch—and going into the lavatory at intervals to spit blood—and Smithers, flattered, sweated on."[57]

iii

Before *The Savoy* made its first appearance, Beardsley had two other projects in hand. One was for William Heinemann, who wanted the story of Cinderella in twelve pictorial installments for use in a monthly publication. Beardsley settled on the twelve drawings in accordance with Perrault, but the scheme came to nothing.[58] The second project was another matter. Edmund Gosse, the man of letters whom Beardsley had first known in connection with another Heinemann publication, Gosse's *The Secret of Narcisse*, had urged Beardsley to turn his talents to the illustration of more worthwhile literature than he had previously done. The titles Gosse suggested were Gautier's *Mademoiselle de Maupin*, Ben Jonson's *Volpone*, and Pope's *Rape of the Lock*. The whole idea, in Beardsley's view, rested on a logical perception of his talents; and so he chose the one which coincided with a recent influence in his art, the neoclassicism of the eighteenth century and especially French prints of the latter part of that period. He chose Alexander Pope's *The Rape of the Lock*. Smithers agreed at once to publish it. In a letter to Raffalovich written either late in December 1895 or early in January 1896, Beardsley spoke of starting the pictures for *The Rape*.[59]

Beardsley had very likely completed as many as five drawings for *The Rape of the Lock* when he went to Paris some time in the first week of February with Smithers and Yvonne, a girl whom Smithers brought from The Thalia, the London supper-club. Beardsley invariably tried at least to match Smithers' raffishness, so that they indulged in a lively time with Gabriel de Lautrec, a journalist, and Ernest Dowson, then living in Paris. Dowson told how the three Englishmen and the girl went on a Sunday to visit Lautrec in his flat near the Palais Royal and there Beardsley took hashish for the first time. He was unaffected for some hours, but then it began to act. Dowson's account went on,

> while we were dining with Smithers at Margery's the haschish began to work very powerfully. Luckily we were in a *cabinet* or I think we would have been turned out—for Beardsley's laughter was so tumultuous that it infected the rest of us—who had *not* taken haschish & we all behaved like imbeciles.[60]

On February 11, Beardsley went with Dowson to see the first performance—a "triumphant" one, he said—of Oscar Wilde's *Salomé* produced by A. M. Lugné-Poe at the Théâtre de l'Oeuvre. By that time Smithers had attended to his business affairs, among them arrangements for publication of Dowson's *Verses*, and returned to London. The next day Dowson left Paris for Pont-Aven.

But Beardsley stayed on. He had taken a room at the Hôtel St. Romain in the rue St. Roche and, having concluded that Paris suited him "quite well," he planned to stay "a deuce of a time." With that in mind, he determined to save money by having his meals at a nearby Duval and to concentrate on his work. The meals at Duval went on for little more than a week; they soon became "loathsome and impossible." But he worked almost incessantly. He avoided Jacques-Emile Blanche, one of the "boresome people" whom Beardsley had enjoyed in Dieppe as recently as September, and very reluctantly faced the prospect of an afternoon with Clara Savile Clarke. He was indeed, as he told Smithers, "the same old hardworking solitaire" he knew and loved "so well." And so, with "meticulous precision and almost indecent speed," Beardsley completed the drawings for *The Rape of the Lock*. About March 9, 1896, he listed them for Smithers and, no later than March 12, Beardsley sent all nine and a cover. On that day he told Mabel that they were finished and he believed "with great success." Beardsley was right. These were the drawings, or at

152

least those made before Beardsley came to Paris, which prompted Whistler to admit at last that Beardsley was indeed an artist and Beardsley, in thankfulness, to burst into tears. Gosse, to whom Beardsley dedicated this edition in gratitude for suggesting it, maintained that in Pope's poem, Beardsley had never had a subject "better suited" to his genius or one "in the embroidery of which" he had "expended more fanciful beauty." These drawings may be the height of Beardsley's achievement. The variety and disposition of ornament, the variety of tone and texture, the "centralized composition," the spatial balance, all contribute to the quality of the work, hardly surpassed afterwards, with which he "embroidered" *The Rape of the Lock*.[61]

Beardsley was ready now to get on with preparations for the second *Savoy*. He had already written about it to Smithers and had told Mabel that it would keep him "dreadfully" hard at work. But first he wanted to find rooms to which he could move from the Hôtel St. Romain. At the end of his month there, he had asked for his account. He had no intention of returning to London, which he described as a "filthy hole" where he got only "snubs and the cold shoulder." But he was convinced that he was being overcharged at the St. Romain, and he meant to take other rooms. He anticipated help from Smithers in finding them, since Smithers was due in Paris shortly, en route to Brussels.

But when Smithers came to Paris, his stay was brief and rowdy, with Beardsley constantly at his side. In a final show of good fellowship, Beardsley went with Smithers to see him board the train for Brussels. Not only Smithers but Beardsley as well was on the train when it puffed out of the Gare du Nord. At the station, Beardsley had decided he might as well go to Brussels, too; and with nothing besides the clothes in which he stood, he went. In Brussels, Beardsley embarked on a tender interlude with a young woman named Rayon, and with Smithers he fully expected to continue the gaiety started in Paris. But their laughter had hardly sounded when Beardsley fell ill. According to Dowson, Beardsley was ill from "congestion of the lungs." He had, in fact, suffered another tubercular hemorrhage. By order of some doctor, hastily summoned, Beardsley was confined to his room at the Hôtel de Saxe for an indefinite period of time.[62] Precisely when he fell ill is uncertain. In fact the date on which he went to Brussels cannot be fixed. Although Dowson spoke of a letter from Smithers written in Paris about March 21, 1896, Smithers and Beardsley may have left Paris on March 17. And before March 26, when the action which Rothenstein brought against Smithers was heard in court,

The Battle of the Beaux and the Belles, an illustration for Pope's *The Rape of the Lock* (*Courtesy of The Barber Institute of Fine Arts, University of Birmingham*)

Smithers had returned to London, leaving Beardsley in Brussels. Neither knew how serious Beardsley's condition was. Although he continued to work, he would be an invalid for most of the short time left to him. In effect, Beardsley had commenced his last illness.

CHAPTER VI

i

BEARDSLEY remained in Brussels until May 4. During most of that time, he was not allowed to "cross the hotel door," and even in the hotel he had difficulty in getting around. As late as April 28, stairs were almost beyond his strength. He had stopped using a walking stick, but his breathing was still laborious. Nevertheless, on that date, against his doctor's orders, Beardsley went for a walk, his first since his illness, and returned to the hotel in a hansom cab. He was not enthusiastic about his doctor anyway, especially his practice of continually applying blisters. But Beardsley kept quiet about it for fear he might provoke the doctor to increase his bill. Beardsley was worried enough about money as it was, although he had payments from Smithers at frequent intervals for drawings and for the sale of a few of the books left with Smithers in the summer of 1895. Once at least, Beardsley borrowed from a chance English visitor. All in all, it was a bad time. Vincent O'Sullivan, the gentle American poet and storyteller educated in England and a contributor to the second *Savoy*, was in Brussels in early April, but his presence did little to lighten Beardsley's gloom. When Mabel came to Brussels, also in early April, her brother's spirits improved considerably during her stay, especially when she managed to give him a good lunch with good wine (also forbidden to him), the "most insidious and satisfactory thing imaginable." When she went back to London, she left him to conclude that Brussels was an "impossible place on the whole."[1]

One constant source of distress throughout Beardsley's stay in Brussels was the fate of "The Ballad of a Barber," the verses he had written in Cologne for incorporation into the fourth chapter of *Under the Hill*, which was scheduled for the second number of *The Savoy*. Early in April, Smithers reported that Symons thought the verses poor. Beardsley then directed that they be printed separately from *Under the Hill* and signed with a pseudonym, only to learn that unless the last part of "The Barber" was revised they would not be printed at all. Symons was in an awkward position. To a man who had

157

discussed poetry with Verlaine and Swinburne, as Symons had, and who had intimate knowledge of Yeats' poetical aims, since he shared a flat with Yeats, Beardsley's verses at best surely seemed little better than doggerel. Even his precious prose *tour de force*, *Under the Hill*—or *Venus and Tannhäuser*—is far from peerless in its expurgated form, however ingenious both in concept and form it may be. When unexpurgated, it is at least as remarkable for what it exposes about Beardsley's knowledge of sexual possibilities and his interest in them as for its baroque presentation. His verses very likely could not have appeared without his illustrations in a periodical such as *The Savoy*. On the other hand, Beardsley declared rightly that Symons should have written to suggest revision. Beardsley was convinced that Symons' decision was arbitrary, and he lamented that he would now be "thinly represented" in *The Savoy*. Smithers made peace by reproducing one of the drawings from *The Rape of the Lock* in *The Savoy* and by promising future publication for "The Barber" with two drawings,[2] but Beardsley thereafter distrusted Symons. It was an ungenerous attitude, rare in Beardsley, but it was bred in part by his illness and the long, slow days.

Beardsley told Smithers, "If it wasn't for my work I shouldn't know how to kill my time."[3] Fortunately, when Beardsley reached Brussels he had much work to complete for the second number of *The Savoy*, so that throughout his stay he was busy making drawings and sending them off with instructions to Smithers. Beardsley's particular concern as far as his own productions went was for a fourth chapter of *Under the Hill*. He gave infinite attention to details which would insure its artificiality. Briefly he played with an idea for an addition, a section with "Hop-o-my-thumb" as hero, and even began it. And by April 20 or thereabouts, he was preparing to start a set of eight drawings which Smithers had commissioned for an edition of the *Lysistrata*.[4]

Beardsley planned to take any drawings he might complete for *Lysistrata* to London with him. He was still taking creosote pills and still forbidden fish and wine, but by April 28 his doctor had told him he could go to London early in May. He talked of going on Sunday, May 3; then André Raffalovich arrived in Brussels and "pressed" Beardsley "to a lunch" on that day. He wired Mabel to come to Brussels to "pilot him over" on Monday, but Mabel could not get leave from the play in which she was appearing. His mother then asked Robert Ross to fetch Aubrey, but Ross, too, was unable to go. So Mrs. Beardsley went despite the fact that she was not well. When she got to Brussels, she was "so knocked up," they were forced to delay their return a day.[5]

158

The next six weeks or two months were difficult. Beardsley's stay in London was brief. On his arrival he went directly to rooms which Ross had taken and arranged for him, even to sending in a sofa, at 17 Campden Grove. Beardsley went that same day to his doctor, Symes Thompson, who "pronounced very unfavourably" on his condition and advised "absolute quiet and if possible immediate change." In a letter to Raffalovich, Beardsley admitted that he was both depressed and frightened, but before doing much about his illness he had other matters to see to. He invited Ross to tea and sent copies of the new issue of *The Rape of the Lock* to Yvette Guilbert, appearing in London, and to Edmund Gosse, who pronounced himself "truly proud to be connected with such an ingenious object."[6] Beardsley had also to confront the prospect of considerable work. Smithers had decided to announce in the July number that *The Savoy* would thereafter appear monthly, a decision which Dowson hoped would cause John Lane's hair to "glow green with Envy" but which Beardsley faced with uncharacteristic dread of a "tremendous amount" of work. There was still the bookplate promised Pollitt and the possibility of making illustrations for John Gray's play *Northern Aspect*.[7]

But at the end of May, when he had hardly drawn a line, Beardsley was forced to leave London. He went to a guest house called Twyford at Crowborough, Suffolk, for rest, as ordered by Dr. Thompson. To Pollitt, who wanted the bookplate for which he had paid almost a year ago, Beardsley said that his drawing had stopped by doctor's orders and that he was taking "an entire rest" in the "depths of country stillness."[8] But he urged Robbie Ross to visit him in Crowborough, and to Smithers Beardsley wrote about a continuation of *Under the Hill* and declared his health would improve so rapidly in Crowborough that he would soon be strong enough to kick Symons' backside. Mabel came down for a Sunday, to find her brother restless and unhappy. By mid-June, still without strength to do much of anything, Beardsley was back at Campden Grove and concerned about final revisions for his "Ballad of a Barber." He was unaccustomed to outright rejection of his work, and it troubled him. He intended to return to Crowborough, but after two delays he went instead, about June 25, 1896, to The Spread Eagle Hotel at Epsom. Beardsley remained at Epsom considerably longer than at Crowborough. As usual in his illness, each move promised more than it fulfilled. Epsom had been beneficial to him as a boy, and he certainly started his stay there this time with real enthusiasm for his rooms, the hotel dining room, the air, the view, the cost of things, and his work.

Beardsley was able to work now as he had not done since leaving

Brussels, and he began to produce illustrations for the *Lysistrata* with considerable rapidity. By August 11, 1896, he had made eight drawings. In nothing are they more extraordinary than in the tension between the delicacy of execution and their bold indelicacy of subject. The apparent ribaldry of the drawings derives as much from Beardsley as from Aristophanes. The artist's symbols such as the obvious one of the greatly enlarged phalluses need not be admired, however laughable they are, but they must be accepted as the artist's privilege so long as they communicate, in this instance the urgency of swollen desire, a part of Beardsley's reality as well as a part of the play. Here the symbols exist in dotted lines, firmly closed lines, and ornamented blacks against unblemished white. The result is strength and sensitivity.[9] While he worked at the *Lysistrata*, Beardsley talked of a sequel to "The Ballad of a Barber";[10] it is now unknown and may have been fabricated in a thrust at Symons. Beardsley was certainly busy, however, with a collection of aphorisms which commented largely on the arts and which he planned to illustrate and publish as "Table Talk of Aubrey Beardsley." When Smithers came to Epsom on the last Sunday in June, he and Beardsley discussed the book's format; and within the week Beardsley had completed *Tristan and Isolde*, the first of the several pictures he meant to make for the projected book. The opera *Tristan and Isolde* was much in his thoughts at this time. By the end of June, it had already had two performances at Covent Garden that season and was scheduled for two more. Beardsley had read newspaper announcements of it "with jealous eyes," but he had to be content with his own drawing. In no time, he had finished a second drawing for "Table Talk," "a portrait or what you will" of Carl Maria von Weber, and four days later three more were ready for inking. He was still busy with the illustrations for the *Lysistrata*, he was preparing to make a drawing for Smithers' fifth catalogue of rare books, and he was deciding that the story of *Ali Baba* and the forty thieves would give him "plenty of chance," that it would make a "scrumptious" Christmas book. Although Beardsley abandoned or left half done more than one of these enterprises, his activity was feverish. He was wholly accurate when he told Smithers early in July, "There doesn't seem to be any time to lose over work."[11]

Beardsley could well have been prophetic in that statement. It was affirmed by the fact that both the April and July numbers of *The Savoy* had notes about work omitted owing to his illness. A "Publisher's Note" in the second number regretted the absence of *The Bacchanals of Sporion*, a full-page drawing to accompany the fourth chapter of *Under the Hill*. It was promised for the third number of *The*

Savoy, but it did not appear there and is now unknown. The third number, issued in July, announced that serialization of *Under the Hill* was discontinued but promised the piece in book form as soon as Beardsley was well enough to complete it. *Under the Hill* was never completed and it did not appear in book form until 1904, and then under John Lane's imprint. When the August issue of *The Savoy*, the fourth, appeared, it carried nothing by Beardsley except an indifferent design for the cover and title page. His drawing *The Death of Pierrot* was scheduled for August, but he withdrew it; he preferred to have no drawing if he could have only one.[12] Each of the next three issues, however, had one design by Beardsley, *The Woman in White* in September, *The Death of Pierrot* in October, and *Ave atque Vale* in November.

Beardsley had acknowledged time's "winged chariot" at his back by making his will. Dated July 17, 1896, it named Mabel Beardsley as sole beneficiary and executrix of his estate, which proved at last to consist of £1015 plus a few shillings and pence. Whether he had that amount in July 1896 is unknown. Whatever he had, he told no one. His mother, his sister, Smithers, Raffalovich—they knew nothing of Beardsley's pounds and pence; and to preserve them, he resorted to what he thought necessary. Beardsley borrowed, he accepted gifts and the obligations they entailed, he railed against his creditors and evaded them when he could, but he kept intact the sum meant for Mabel.[13]

Beardsley's awareness of the pressure of time was given further substance by the gravity of his doctor's prognosis. Both lungs were now affected. In mid-July when he wrote to Raffalovich about the "great fun" of illustrating *Ali Baba* and the delightfully hot weather of Epsom, Beardsley added that the only trouble was his entire inability to walk or otherwise exert himself. Some ten days later he suffered a mild hemorrhage, and his doctor began to talk about the advantages of sea air. Beardsley proposed Brighton, but the doctor objected. Smithers suggested Dieppe, but Beardsley had not paid the hotel bill at the St. Romain when he boarded the train for Brussels, and it was still unpaid. The capacity for such a carefree decision was behind him now, and he thought he had better not risk trouble. He confessed that he had "alarming notions of the perfection of the French police system." He told Smithers, "I don't believe there's a gendarme in France who hasn't either a photograph or a model of my prick about him."[14] But when a serious hemorrhage occurred early in August, Beardsley was strongly urged to leave Epsom. Fortunately Mabel was with him and she took charge, administering medicine and going to Boscombe, near Bournemouth, to find living quarters in a hotel called the Pier View. When he moved to Boscombe on August 12, 1896, Mabel went with him, and she stayed after their mother arrived less than a week later. That Aubrey was dangerously ill was unquestionable, and thereafter Mrs. Beardsley willingly left his side only twice until he no longer needed her or anyone.

If Beardsley had worked feverishly before coming to Boscombe, his efforts were frantic now. As he said of himself in September, his "genius for work" possessed him "in an extraordinary degree" throughout the rest of the year.[15] He had brought with him from Epsom two projects. One was to make a "permanent" picture for Smithers' catalogues. The publisher had arranged to move from Arundel Street to the Royal Arcade, Old Bond Street, and Beardsley had in mind a drawing of the Arcade "from some point . . . that would admit the introduction of figures." On September 11, Beardsley declared that he was about to start the drawing; but a week later he suggested that the bookplate he had made for himself but which later went to Pollitt could serve Smithers as "a fine and eternal catalogue cover."[16] In October, Beardsley wrote again about trying to draw the Arcade for a cover, but eventually Smithers decided on the drawing *Et in Arcadia Ego*, owing to the pun in its title. It appeared as the final illustration in the final number, the December number, of *The Savoy*. The second project brought from Epsom was a translation of Juvenal's Sixth Satire with illustrations. Beardsley talked of acquiring a Latin dictionary and he may have set to work with it; but if he made a translation, no remnant of it survives. He had at hand more than one translation made by others and from these his six drawings for Juvenal derived.

A few days after Beardsley's move to Boscombe, Smithers, bringing his wife with him, came for the day to talk about a new and exciting scheme, the publication of fifty of Beardsley's drawings in one volume, an album to be called *Fifty Drawings*. Beardsley was extremely pleased. "I am so anxious," he told Smithers, "for it to be an entirely pretty monument to my work and to contain my latest work especially."[17] Fearful that Smithers might listen to "Symons and such persons," who preferred his less recent work, Beardsley insisted that the "early stuff" be used very sparingly. To demonstrate his improvement, he called Smithers' attention to the workmanship in the bookplate which eventually went to Pollitt, pointing to the quality of the nude, the trees and the "general handling" of the line. Beardsley took great pains in selecting the pictures he wanted to include. He had once made several drawings of Réjane, but he insisted on one and only one; it had appeared in a book Joseph Pennell brought out in 1894, *Pen Drawing and Pen Draughtsmen*. To

Madame Réjane *(Courtesy of The Metropolitan Museum of Art, Rogers Fund, 1952)*

get exactly what he wanted, Mabel and Aubrey, almost before Smithers left Boscombe, had commenced asking permission to reproduce drawings to which he had sold the rights. In return for permission to use pictures from *Morte Darthur* and "in payment for a long-standing debt," Beardsley drew for Dent *The Return of Tannhäuser to the Venusberg*. Dent told Mrs. Beardsley that "all the spirit" in him was "moved to its depths by this most beautiful most pathetic drawing." But when Beardsley wanted, later, to include it in the album, Dent refused.[18] By the end of August, Beardsley wanted Smithers' help in making a selection from the illustrations for *Morte Darthur*, and he was concerned as to which picture of himself should appear in the album. By that time, too, he had arranged for Aymer Vallance to prepare a complete iconography of Beardsley's drawings. The iconography was a constant worry. Vallance was too casual or too slow or he might "give the public the idea" that Beardsley was forty-five and had "been working for fifteen years" whereas he preferred the impression that he was "only two" and had "been working for three weeks." After all, "youth and beauty" were his "only boasts."[19] In all seriousness, however, the selection of drawings already made and the making of new ones and a cover for *Fifty Drawings* were to occupy and interest Beardsley until he saw the book shortly before Christmas. Indeed, on September 26, when he had not left his room for a month owing to illness and only the day before had been "laid out like a corpse with haemorrhage," he regarded as "balm" any news of the album. "How furious I should be," he wrote to Smithers, "if I went away without ever having seen it."[20]

That month's confinement to his room resulted from at least a day in London on or about August 26. Beardsley took with him to London drawings for Juvenal and what material he had for the album. While he was there, he had H. H. Cameron photograph him for the frontispiece of *Fifty Drawings*. But the exertion and the imperative of returning to Boscombe, which he already thought dull, exhausted and angered him. Although he believed he had recovered from both fatigue and "tantrums" immediately after his return, a day later, that is on August 28, he "broke down again" and "stained many a fair handkerchief red with blood."[21] By September 22, he was better but still too weak to travel, so that he resigned himself to a winter at Boscombe. And the bleeding, the "continual leaking," as he called it, would not stop. When at last it did and he was allowed to take short walks, he had been ill so long that in November, in a letter to Robbie Ross, Beardsley described himself as "an agonized wreck of depression, a poor shadow of the gay rococo thing" he had been.[22] Mabel had gone to America with an acting company led by Arthur

Aubrey Beardsley *(Courtesy of The Bodley Head Ltd.)*

Bourchier, and Aubrey had been too ill to say goodbye. His poor spirits were driven still lower by toothache. Then, on December 10, in the midst of a morning walk with his mother, Beardsley had a violent hemorrhage. Mrs. Beardsley told Ross that it occurred as they approached the top of a hill leading to a cliff. She added, "You might have traced our path down, the bleeding was so severe." Beardsley said later that he had expected to "make an 'al fresco' croak of it," but he managed to find a drinking fountain, and the cold water helped. Leaving him in the care of a couple who happened to be near, Mrs. Beardsley found a donkey chair to "drag him" back to the hotel. Aubrey declared sadly, "There seems to be no end to the chapter of blood."[23]

Throughout his anguish, Beardsley kept at his work. "A fit of hard work," he said at one point, "dispelled" his depression.[24] In late August he talked of reading a "sentence or so" of Vincent O'Sullivan's *A Book of Bargains* in order to make a frontispiece. He spoiled two drawings, but the third, a picture which Beardsley called "radiant and compelling," went to Smithers on September 17. He had already made a cover design for *The Souvenirs of Léonard*, and a week later Beardsley was ready to start the cover for the October number of *The Savoy*, *The Fourth Tableau of Das Rheingold*. The tableaux of the Rheingold were a part of *Under the Hill*. Its hero's reading when he awoke on the first morning of his stay with Venus commenced with the score of Wagner's *Rheingold*. Beardsley had drawn a picture to illustrate the reading and to accompany the fourth chapter of *Under the Hill* in the April issue of *The Savoy*. Now, in September, Beardsley was writing his own version of *Das Rheingold*, which he called "The Comedy of the Rhinegold." He had elaborate plans for it, envisioning it as the first of a series of "Playbooks" giving "versions of famous or curious plays in story form." He mentioned Lamb's *Tales from Shakespeare* as an example of what he meant and suggested Symons, Yeats, and John Gray as possible authors.[25] For his own playbook, Beardsley planned four full page and eight or ten smaller pictures. The writing dwindled away, however, and he made only four of the pictures. Although all four appeared in the eighth *Savoy*, that number demanded an enormous effort for additional drawings.

After his move to Boscombe in August, Beardsley had designed covers and title pages for each issue of *The Savoy* commencing with the September number, but only one additional drawing appeared in that and the two following numbers. His arresting *Ave atque Vale*, which appeared in the November *Savoy*, illustrated his translation of Catullus' "Carmen CI." But the eighth *Savoy* was a particularly heavy assignment. Late in September Smithers decided to end publication of *The Savoy* with the December issue, the eighth. In it, he wanted work only from his two editors, Symons and Beardsley, and Beardsley promised to do "some scorching drawings" for it. In fact his contributions to the last *Savoy* numbered twelve, plus the usual cover and title-page. These were finished by October 29.

On that same date Beardsley decided against making a cover for Balzac's *La Fille aux Yeux d'Or*, which Charles Conder was illustrating. Beardsley had accepted the assignment only three days earlier, but in view of his "feelings against" Conder (neither man currently approved of the other), Beardsley decided that his "artistic conscience" would not let them cooperate. On the grounds that his agreement with Smithers prohibited work for another firm and that there was no way around it, Beardsley had already refused to design a poster for Fisher Unwin. Earlier in September, Beardsley had made an ornament for the title-page of H. Henry and Company's *The Parade*, but he was content not to work for Unwin.

Beardsley still had not completed a bookplate for F. H. Evans, started in 1894, and there were several new projects afoot. Smithers was planning to publish Yeats' *The Shadowy Waters* with Beardsley's illustrations as soon as it was complete. Beardsley was eager to make drawings for *Les Liaisons Dangereuses*, and by October 7 he had completed a picture of Count Valmont with a "beaded border to go round him."[26] Between them, Smithers and Beardsley settled on Dowson to translate it, and on November 24 Beardsley reported that he had almost finished the frontispiece. He expected to work on the pictures for *Les Liaisons* until some time in March—a frontispiece for each of two volumes, ten full-page illustrations, and 170 decorative initials, one for each of the "epistles" by which the book is told. He sketched some of the initials while he waited for Dowson's translation, but he finished neither the initials nor the other drawings, although they stayed alive in Beardsley's thought well into the next year. The only further series of drawings which Beardsley completed in that year, 1896, or in subsequent years was the series for Dowson's *Pierrot of the Minute*. Happy to have something to "set" his "hand going again at work" after his prolonged stay in bed, Beardsley began a frontispiece on November 6.[27] Ten days later, he posted the *cul de lampe*, the last of five drawings.

Two weeks later Beardsley was anticipating publication of *Fifty Drawings*. By December 22, he had examined the book and found many faults in its "'get up' owing to perfectly indecent haste in preparation"[28] as well as more serious and inexcusable faults. These had to do with the selections for the album. Beardsley thought them too limited. Although from the moment he planned it, Smithers had determined on fifty drawings, Beardsley's suggestions went well beyond that number. Once he pointed out that fifty was an arbitrary number, that there was no limit to what could be published in the album. Smithers, however, stuck to his first concept and produced *A Book of Fifty Drawings*. In doing so, he also produced an incontrovertible record of Beardsley's individuality and inventiveness and their constant renewal.

As an artist, Beardsley belongs to no category. Because his gallery of images derived from the facts of human existence conventionally inadmissible in his own time, no man is more relevant to the nineties. But as an artist, that is as a superb penman and a designer, Beardsley was his own man. By 1892, when Dent commissioned Beardsley to make the drawings for *Morte Darthur*, the impressionists were the establishment of French painting, and in literature Wagner had led Mallarmé to Symbolism and Verlaine to his faith in "music before all things." Beardsley was, of course, aware of the significance of French painting, and if he had not been, he had Sickert and Rothenstein to tell him. But Beardsley showed no interest in the play of light and shade. His pictures are dominated by figures drawn without nuance. As for Wagner, although Beardsley passionately admired the musician, derived subject matter from him and fashioned his beloved *Venus and Tannhäuser* after Wagner's, and at times resorted to symbols such as the cleft foot first used in *Bon-Mots* and the enlarged penis in the *Lysistrata*, nevertheless his images are his own. They reflect how and what Beardsley saw. Such a statement does not deny that he knew the influence of Burne-Jones, Mantegna, the Japanesque, the Greek vase, and certain artists, especially French ones, of the eighteenth century; but Beardsley was faithful to no one of them.

Even to classify him as a decadent, as Havelock Ellis defines it, is only to point to his love for the "mysteries of style," his infatuation with "paradox and *'marivaudage.'*" Decadence refers more specifically to the baroque details of Beardsley's design, his manner of imposing white on black, his interest in imbalance in composition, and the possibilities in inconsistency of detail. Beardsley's marvelously controlled pen achieved beauty of detail and design and, as he insisted, growth in concept. The portrait of Réjane in *Fifty Drawings* is a likeness of the French actress, but it is also a study in variety of detail and direction. Perhaps Beardsley's reliance on detail, however, reached its zenith in the drawings for *The Rape of the Lock* or in the *Third Tableau of Das Rheingold*. In contrast is the remarkable lack of detail in his bookplate and in the *Fourth Tableau of Das Rheingold*. As Wilde wrote from Reading prison about Beardsley, "He brought a strangely new personality to English art, and was a master in his own way of fantastic grace and the charm of the unreal."[29] Beardsley may not have approved of *A Book of Fifty Drawings*, but it is nevertheless a monument to the iridescence and growth of an artist only a few months past his twenty-fourth birthday.

Indeed, Beardsley might well have felt artistically and personally fulfilled as Christmas and the end of the year came. The holiday season was a good one, too. He enjoyed examining the "ravishing toys" sent to children at the hotel. He liked his own gifts from Raffalovich, Max Beerbohm, Robert Ross and the "pile of little presents" which those same children put by Beardsley's plate on Christmas morning. Afterwards he delighted himself and the little "girls by bowing over their hands and kissing them as he thanked them."[30] Above all, whatever the pain and anguish of the past months, Beardsley could still look back on a year of miraculous achievement. Edmund Gosse congratulated him on his work and his spirit in a letter sent on December 29:

> How much beautiful work you have done in 1896! I quite marvel to think of your energy in wrestling so bravely with ill health. I see no trace of it in your beautiful drawings, so characteristic of your genius. You have put your stamp on the age. If you were to do no more your name could never be forgotten: you are part of the art history of the country.[31]

However much he may have treasured this tribute from a man whom Beardsley allowed to advise him and whom he addressed as "Maître," Beardsley also valued the salaciousness with which he could amuse Smithers and play the man of the world. Two days after receiving Gosse's letter, Beardsley wrote to Smithers telling how a lady had asked him to send her a copy of verses about any of his pictures. He said he had promptly wired her these lines:

> There was a young lady of Lima
> Whose life was as fast as a steamer.
>   She played dirty tricks
>   With a large crucifix
> Till the spunk trickled right down her femur.[32]

Still, Beardsley envied Raffalovich's opportunity "to hear the bells ring out and usher in the years."[33] He longed to go to London. But before he had composed the limerick for Smithers, Beardsley's "case had taken . . . a serious turn for the worse," he had to "lie low," to "keep on doing nothing," and to await his doctor's decision as to whether he was to go to "some more bracing place" or might be allowed to go to London.[34] Beardsley decided that his troubles were "principally nervous," and his depression was such that his doctor and consultants hesitated between Bournemouth and London. Of course Beardsley wanted their decision to send him to London, but instead they put "every obstacle" in his way so that by mid-January he was mildly paranoid. He felt "utterly helpless and deserted," at the mercy of his "surrounders." He declared that the way he had "been lumbered" into Boscombe and kept there was "simply disgraceful."[35] At last the doctors decided that on January 19 he was to go only a step away from Boscombe to Bournemouth.

Throughout his complaints and depression and weakness, Beardsley's interest in matters outside his illness never flagged. He might lament that he had "only sufficient brains to enjoy Eugène Sue's *Les Mystères de Paris*," but he asked Smithers to send him Voltaire in thirty volumes. Beardsley admired Smithers' production of the large-paper copies of *A Book of Fifty Drawings*, finding it better than the ordinary edition "a thousand times," and he thanked Beerbohm for a review of the album in *Tomorrow*. On January 16, in anticipation of his move, Beardsley arranged for H. G. Commin, a Bournemouth bookseller, to "warehouse" his books, some 230 volumes, and at the same time ordered "ordinary 3 fr 50" editions of *Madame Bovary* and *Les Liaisons Dangereuses*.

The next day Beardsley's illness recurred with such severity that he lay between life and death for a week. Near the end of January, Beardsley was carried downstairs in a chair and taken in a heated carriage from Pier View, Boscombe, to Muriel, a guest house on the Exeter Road in Bournemouth, and only on January 30 was he strong enough to "trail a pen." He could look around him, declare his quarters a success, and plan to retrieve his books from Commin's warehouse.

The two months he spent at Bournemouth were, in most ways, uneventful for Beardsley. Soon after his arrival at Muriel, he had thrust on him a new correspondence, one with Olive Custance. A well-born young woman, barely twenty-three, she enjoyed indulgence in a quixotic and pretentious romanticism, even to the extent of marrying Lord Alfred Douglas in 1902. That Olive Custance and Beardsley ever met is unlikely. She certainly knew about him, however, at least by late June 1894, when she had tea with John Lane and Richard Le Gallienne in Lane's rooms in The Albany. Her journal described her waiting shyly for Lane's appearance. She was "in pale pink with a large black straw hat trimmed with tulle and carnations"; and she "carried a sheaf of white arum lilies" on her arm. She recorded that Lane was shy, too, when he shook hands, but Le Gallienne was bold enough to look squarely at her and the moment he did she felt that she would love him and he, her.[36] Olive—or Opal, as she preferred to be called—had a tendency to fall in love without provocation. With Henry Harland, whom she was careful not to name in her journal, she exchanged passionate letters filled with melancholy self-analysis. And at the age of sixteen, she had come under the spell of John Gray, her "Prince of Poets," with whom she maintained a discreet exchange of sentiments for some years. Possibly she learned of Beardsley's illness from Gray or even from Raffalovich, Gray's lover. When she did, she began to write to Beardsley, very likely in an attempt to distract or comfort him with her poetic powers. Her talent in that direction was small but lyric. Olive's verses had appeared in *The Yellow Book* in 1896 and later, in 1897, Lane brought out her *Opals*, a volume of poetry. Her letters to Beardsley aroused little except irritation. He spoke of her once as "silly little O" and on February 11, 1897, he reported an eleven-page letter from her plus two pages of verse. "Ye gods!" he added. "If I were only Symons." Again in early March, Beardsley mentioned a "huge letter" from "Mdlle Custance." How much of his disdain for Olive Custance was real and how much was counterfeited for Smithers' benefit is impossible to say. He told Smithers that, in return for reading her letters, he expected her to buy his album in the large-paper edition. Nevertheless, he answered her letters, sometimes at length, and in September, with only a mild show of reluctance, he designed a bookplate for her.[37]

When the letters from Olive Custance began, Beardsley hardly had the strength to respond. Indeed, during his stay in Bournemouth his work was slight, owing to the fact that drawing tired him with the "mere physical exertion required" when he attempted "to bring anything to completion."[38] He made two drawings for Smithers' eleven-volume edition of Balzac's *Scènes de la vie Parisienne*. On February 11, he began an unsolicited frontispiece for Gautier's *Mademoiselle de Maupin*, a picture which he completed in color and sent to Smithers a month later. At the end of March, Beardsley determined to illustrate *Mademoiselle de Maupin*, "come what may," and began to work at the first of five more drawings. A "conte" called "The Celestial Lover" got as far as notes and a partially finished illustration in color. He finished *The Adulterer*, a drawing started in the previous August to illustrate a passage from Juvenal, and sold it to Pollitt for £10.

From Pollitt, Beardsley borrowed twenty sovereigns "on account of *Bathylle* and a coloured *Lysistrata*" to satisfy a "horrid writ" for a bill which he had owed long enough, Beardsley said, "to be forgotten by everyone concerned with it."[39] The bill was one which the tailor Doré had repeatedly tried to collect, without success. Beardsley could have paid it, and he should have. But even now, with the loan from Pollitt, Beardsley failed to pay, although he had complained that the writ had "fussed" him "beyond all words." And that was only one of his complaints. He was troubled, too, or so he said, by his enforced chastity, and he faithfully reported his *rêves moillés* to Smithers. Furthermore, because Dr. Harsant had all but promised that Beardsley could go to London when he left Bournemouth, he worried over finding rooms, asking both Smithers and Raffalovich to help. Beardsley was eager to have some sort of quarters settled before Mabel returned from her tour. Mabel's long absence in America was a deprivation and he frequently predicted her return as soon as she recognized the seriousness of his illness.

In early March, for the first time, Beardsley made clear his own recognition of it. Dr. Harsant had decided against London, much to Beardsley's disappointment. "I counted on it so much," he said to Raffalovich. Recalling his breakdown in Brussels of a year ago, Beardsley said that he supposed many people had not then expected him to live twelve months and added, "*I* should have been beside myself if I had thought that I should be in twelve months no better than I am now." With Smithers, Beardsley was more direct. "I may not have many months now to live," he wrote.[40] Still, he blamed his constant bleeding on the east wind and looked forward to improvement in a better climate, such as Menton's.

ii

In what Beardsley called his "ballsome existence," this welter of apprehension and unreality (the prospect of death can be nothing else), of frustration and the boredom of illness, and the state of being constantly "fussed," Beardsley reached as important a decision as he was to make. He accepted Catholicism. Mabel Beardsley had become a Catholic in March 1896. Except for the fact that he sent her a prayer book to mark the event, Mabel's conversion had no apparent influence on Beardsley. Instead, he was moved very gently to the Roman Catholic church by André Raffalovich, who was himself a convert. Ironically, Raffalovich, whose parents left Russia in order to be faithful to their own religion, Judaism, chose to become a vigorous proselyte in Catholicism. A legend of Raffalovich's conversion links it with John Gray's and the love affair between those two. This account tells that "the unregenerate couple set out together on a Mediterranean cruise in Raffalovich's yacht which was painted black and called 'Iniquity.' They returned pious Catholics."[41] The facts are totally different. After some variety of religious experience in Brittany, Gray arranged for instruction in the Church's doctrines, and in London on March 10, 1890, he was admitted to the Catholic church. What brought Raffalovich to conversion is unknown, but Florence Gribbell, his housekeeper-companion converted a year or two earlier, may have had a hand in it. In any case he was baptized at the church of the Jesuit Fathers, Farm Street, Mayfair, on February 3, 1896.[42] By late October of that year he was at work on Beardsley.

If the relationship between the two, Raffalovich and Beardsley, had changed at all since 1895 when Raffalovich probably helped Beardsley financially and showered him with invitations, then it had become more distant. Certainly Beardsley showed no particular sense of obligation, but as Ellen Beardsley said of her son, "He was always very courteous and had great dignity. No one ever took liberties with Aubrey."[43] While still at Epsom, he had accepted an invitation to visit Raffalovich at Weybridge, where he spent the summers, but Beardsley was forced by illness to move on to Boscombe without going to Weybridge. His letters to Raffalovich were perfunctory, often merely polite responses to the older man's comments on his reading and social occasions. More than once, in letters to Smithers, Beardsley made patronizing or disparaging references to "the Russian Prince." When there was a mix-up about the publication of one of John Gray's poems in *The Savoy*, Beardsley feared he had "put his foot in it" and urged Smithers "for *goodness sake*" to accept the poem.[44] Gray's verses did not appear, but in no time Raffalovich was designating the paternoster of his rosary as a prayer for Beardsley and inquiring about his "bookish wants." Gifts of chocolates and books, to which John Gray added his mite, began to flow. At the end of January, after his move to Bournemouth, Beardsley wrote a dutiful note of thanks for a gift of money. "Your sweet friendliness," he said, "helps me over such alarming difficulties."[45] In early November, while Beardsley was still at Boscombe, Raffalovich had sent a priest, Father Charles de Laposture, to call.

Beardsley's faith, however, could not be bought or seduced. When Raffalovich's butler, Joseph Tobler, succumbed to Catholicism in February, Beardsley declared himself envious of a young man "whose conduct of life puts no barriers in his way to the particular acceptance of what he believes in." But for himself, Beardsley was not convinced. Unlike Pascal, as Beardsley made clear, he was not ready to "sacrifice his gifts" or to deny his own "conduct of life." Still, he left the way open for Raffalovich. "Do not think, dear André," Beardsley wrote, "that your kind words fall on such barren ground. However I fear I am not a very fruitful soil; I only melt to harden again."[46]

Beardsley's mixed metaphor did not discourage Raffalovich. When Gray and he spent a few days in Bournemouth, he arranged for Father David Bearne to visit Beardsley. A convert and a writer of boys' books, Bearne was compatible with Beardsley. Their instant friendship was so apparent that "pillars of the Anglican faith" lectured Aubrey "à propos his communications with the kind fathers of the Sacred Heart."[47] Meanwhile Raffalovich had an opportunity for a grander gesture than he had made so far. As early as mid-February Beardsley talked with apprehension of his "exit from Bournemouth," although he reassured himself with the thought that no one would be "so hard as to expect more than 1d in the pound" from him. This was said to Smithers, and Beardsley often exaggerated his problems to Smithers; something might come from doing so. But Beardsley seemed honestly concerned. If money was not scarce and uncertain, his mother thought it was. Leaving him alone and "just a little tired," Ellen Beardsley had gone to London to investigate the possibilities of employment. After a talk with Raffalovich, her worries had vanished. She had decided against taking any work and had "settled to remain" with her son. In "brotherly affection," Raffalovich had proposed a regular monthly payment to the Beardsleys. Aubrey could only welcome such "wonderfully kind help . . . offered with so much intention and so much gentleness." He told his benefactor that in helping with "so much judgment," he was helping "doubly."[48]

At the same time, Beardsley was reading more and more saints' lives and seeing more and more of Father Bearne. It is not surprising that Smithers, after a visit to Beardsley in the last days of February, was "haunted . . . with visions of designing Jesuits."[49] And as Beardsley's health made no real improvement and the winds of March grew more shrill, and as Raffalovich began to justify the name of brother with which he began his "kind letters" and "dear Father Bearne" was increasingly "kind and patient," Beardsley began to cast out his doubts. At last he reached a decision. On March 30, 1897, he told Raffalovich, "Tomorrow, dear André, the kind name of brother you give me will have deeper significance."[50] On March 31, 1897, Father Bearne received Beardsley into the Church, an event which Beardsley called the "most important step" in his life.

Beardsley's relationship with Raffalovich can readily provoke doubts as to the sincerity of the conversion. As his illness grew more devastating and Raffalovich's gifts flowed in an ever larger stream, Beardsley's letters changed from perfunctory to platitudinous and at times downright unctuous. Arthur Symons found Beardsley's conversion credible only when he remembered the awe with which Beardsley had recounted a childhood dream. As they sat on their hotel balcony at Arques some eighteen months before his conversion, Beardsley told how, as a boy, he had waked at night and seen in the moonlight "a great crucifix, with a bleeding Christ, falling off the wall, where certainly there was not, and had never been, any crucifix."[51] Still more doubts can accumulate in light of his words to Pollitt, written less than a week before reception into the Church. In a letter of March 26, 1896, Beardsley wrote of having been "closeted for two mortal hours" with his "Father Confessor" and then added, "but my soul has long since ceased to beat."[52] But surely such a statement proves nothing. Blind belief is less important in a man with "positive intelligence" and the "imaginative sight of the very spirit of man as a thing of definite outline"—so Symons spoke of Beardsley—than the will to believe.[53] The novelist Ronald Firbank spent long hours on his knees in prayer, fearful that he was losing his faith.

Certainly his mother testified to Beardsley's sincerity. In 1904, after reading his letters to Raffalovich, Mrs. Beardsley said that she was "struck" with the simplicity of her son's references to his conversion. She wrote to Mabel,

> Knowing how truly religious & how devoted to his church Mr R. was, it is marvellous that the darling with his capability for fine writing and high sounding phrases, never once indulged it in speaking of holy things when he might in all sincerity have said so much.

She was relieved, Mrs. Beardsley said, that instead of exaggerating his religious feelings in those letters, he wrote in such a way that they fell "far short of what he really felt." She went on, "Shy as he was on the subject & little as he confided in me, he said more to me ab^t religion than is even hinted at" in the letters.[54]

By 1904, some inflation in Mrs. Beardsley's memories of her son is understandable. As she certainly knew, he was not always honest with Raffalovich, but Beardsley's honest evaluation of his faith is another matter. He was sometimes unduly impressed with the form and ritual of the Church. To fix himself in it at a time when he could hope only that the "end was less near" than it seemed was easy. "It is such a rest," he told John Gray, "to be folded after all my wandering."[55] But both sincerity and recognition of his own limitations are evident in Beardsley's letters to Raffalovich after receiving the sacrament. Because he was too ill to go out, the sacrament was brought to him on the morning of Friday, April 2. Later that same day, Beardsley told Raffalovich, "It was a moment of profound joy, of gratitude and emotion. I gave myself up entirely to feelings of happiness, and even the knowledge of my own unworthiness only seemed to add fuel to the flames that warmed and illuminated my heart." Then he added, "Oh, how earnestly I have prayed that the flame may never die out."[56]

CHAPTER VII

i

WELL before his conversion, Beardsley had Menton in mind as his next place of residence. Plans for him to leave Bournemouth on April 7, spend a night in London and then go straightaway to Menton were so definite that he was preparing for a "tender tearful meeting and farewell"[1] with Smithers when two days of "bleeding" followed by "slight returns" necessitated different arrangements. Beardsley stayed in London at least two days, long enough to see his own Dr. Thompson and determine on going no farther than Paris. His stay in London was eased by a "dear little flat" in the Hotel Windsor at Raffalovich's expense and the use of Raffalovich's carriage plus a gift of "pi books." When he left London, Raffalovich's personal physician, a Dr. Phillips, accompanied Mrs. Beardsley and Aubrey, watching over him all the way to the Hôtel Voltaire.

His mother, "utterly British," was unhappy but persevering in Paris, while Beardsley found it "the blessed place it ever was."[2] He paid his long overdue bill at the Hôtel St. Romain, and he sent his mother, as he was invariably to do on arrival in other places, to call on the parish priest and ask him to attend her son. He suddenly felt "as fit as a fighting cock" and for the first time in four months he walked the streets "as pertinaceously as a tart," he told Smithers.[3] Although Beardsley dared not climb stairs and had to be carried to temporary rooms on an upper floor of the hotel, he could go once more to a Duval or sit in a café to write his letters, and he strolled along the quays where the book and print shops were an "evergreen joy."[4]

Raffalovich put Beardsley in touch with both English and French people in Paris. Mrs. Ian Forbes-Robertson, sister-in-law of the actor, had him to lunch (river trout and strawberries) at Lapérouse, only a short walk from his hotel. William Heinemann was in Paris with his brother, and the novelist Rachilde—Mme. Vallette—came to call. At the end of April when Raffalovich, with Miss Gribbell and John Gray, stayed a few days in Paris, Beardsley went again to

Lapérouse with a party which included Rachilde and "some long haired monsters of the Quartier."[4] Were Mlle. Fanny and Alfred Jarry among them? Once, certainly, Beardsley lunched with them. Those two as well as Octave Uzanne, several priests, and Mme. Raffalovich were a few of the new friends Beardsley made, and he saw the old ones, Jacques-Emile Blanche and Henry Davray. And of course there were constant visitors to Paris, Will Rothenstein, for one, and Clyde Fitch, the American dramatist, for another.

During this stay in Paris, Beardsley even managed to produce two drawings. A cover design for a *bijou* edition of *The Rape of the Lock* was his first concern. He began it almost as soon as he reached Paris, but his rooms were not settled and there were so many people to see and so much to do that he could hardly get down to work, and then he caught the "most filthy cold." On April 7, after he had "thought and wrought" at length over the drawing, Beardsley sent the cover. He revived his interest in Ali Baba and drew a cover for it, too, but again this project lapsed. He promised Heinemann to make a picture for Vuiller's *History of Dancing*, carefully keeping it a secret from Smithers, who still paid Beardsley fairly regularly for exclusive rights. The picture he made for Heinemann was the charming *Arbuscula*, and although it was promised for June, it was not done until late August.

By late August, Beardsley had moved twice. From time to time in Paris, he had brief returns of bleeding and occasional exhaustion which put him to bed for a day or two. Paris was intended, anyway, as a way station; so in mid-May his mother and he spent a Saturday at St. Germain, inspecting it and engaging rooms at the Pavilion Louis XIV in the rue de Pontoise. Beardsley was ecstatic about his new prospects, a "pretty" hotel with a garden, the low cost, the nearby church, and the general convenience. "Everything one could possibly want—including coiffeur" seemed to be "in or near the rue de Pointoise," he told Raffalovich.[5] The plan was to move the following Friday, May 21. But Mrs. Beardsley had been none too well for some time. French food and French water did not agree with her. When preparations to move began, she was unable to "cope with eleven trunks," and Dr. Prendergast, an English doctor recommended by Raffalovich, forbade her to go. Someone's servant took care of the packing and, leaving his mother to follow, Beardsley went alone to St. Germain.

In a day or two, Mrs. Beardsley joined Aubrey for what proved to be a comparatively short stay. How Beardsley reacted to St. Germain is impossible to say. He maintained distinct roles, taking one attitude with Smithers and another with Raffalovich. To this "Dear Brother," between accounts of confessions and thanks for prayers, Beardsley wrote of "adorable weather," the town "too sweet for words," the ministrations of Père Henri, a "dear cheerful old man and the most friendly person imaginable."[6] To Smithers, Beardsley complained that the move and his mother's illness had "played the deuce" with him. He said that he lived "on thorns" because he was "in the mortal funk of the pauper's life—and death." He only wished he had done "even *one* piece" of work and raged that while his "present filthy life" went on, he could do nothing. But in the next breath he asked whether Smithers wanted erotic drawings.[7] To both men, however, Beardsley gave accounts of an ulcerated tongue, repeated hemorrhages, and a new physician, Dr. Lemarre, "learned, famous, and décoré." Lemarre declared that Beardsley could "scarcely be called a consumptive at all" and said that he was "quite curable." As a first step in that direction, Dr. Lemarre ordered Beardsley to walk in the forest near his hotel from four to six every morning. Beardsley compromised by keeping open his bedroom windows, which faced toward the forest. Mabel's expected arrival from America invigorated him, but she stayed only a short time and soon he was complaining of isolation, depression, and his "abject sort of life."[8] With his mother he began German lessons simply to have something to do. But nothing helped, not even the ministrations of Père Henri or an offer of more financial help from Raffalovich. Mrs. Beardsley had much to bear. At last in early July, the Beardsleys went to Paris to consult Dr. Prendergast and in keeping with his advice prepared to leave St. Germain.

By July 12, after an exhausting mix-up with trains, Mrs. Beardsley and Aubrey were settled into the Hôtel Sandwich at Dieppe. Of course, he was extremely pleased to be there, "leading almost precisely the same life" as he had two years before, "doing the same things at the same time."[9] That statement, like so many made to Raffalovich, was not entirely exact. Beardsley doubtless had the illusion of times past owing to the presence of so many old friends in Dieppe. Smithers came for a day or two almost every week. Robbie Ross came often, Vincent O'Sullivan and Billy Rothenstein were there. The Caracciolos were at the Villa Olga and Jacques-Emile Blanche was as usual at the Blanche villa for the summer. Blanche saw Beardsley sitting with Conder on the terrace of the casino. It was the bathing hour, and the casino orchestra was playing a waltz. Beardsley, who had escaped from his hotel without his mother's knowledge, "was coughing and muffled up, drinking a glass of milk and soda under a coloured umbrella on the terrace."[10] He had an old book which he was showing to Conder, and they were laughing gaily about it. Without doubt, Beardsley's laughter was a part of the past; it seldom sounded now. And the mischievous will to elude his mother was rare. At the end of July, when she talked of returning to Brighton owing to illness in her family, Aubrey was upset. "I should be a little nervous by myself," he confessed.[11] When Mrs. Beardsley decided she must go to Brighton, Aubrey was reassured by the fact that Mrs. Smithers happened to be in the same hotel.

Nevertheless, Beardsley was seriously troubled. Oscar Wilde had left Pentonville Prison on May 19, 1897, and later that day taken the night boat from Newhaven, arriving at 4:30 the next morning at Dieppe. There, using the name Sebastian Melmoth, he had registered at the Hôtel Sandwich, the same hotel to which Beardsley would come in July. On May 26, Wilde went with Robert Ross to the Hôtel de la Plage at Berneval-sur-Mer, a quiet village on the coast beyond Dieppe. In July and August, when the Beardsleys were in Dieppe, Wilde was still at Berneval and in and out of Dieppe constantly.

Friends of pre-prison days who encountered him now reacted in various ways. Blanche, while walking with Sickert, pretended not to see Wilde beckon from the Café Suisse. Vincent O'Sullivan, Rothenstein, and Conder not only did not ignore Wilde but they sat with him at the Café Suisse or the Café des Tribunaux and went as well to Berneval as his guests at dinner. Ernest Dowson, who was staying at Arques-la-Bataille until some time in August, developed a real liking for Wilde.

Mr. and Mrs. Smithers met Wilde for the first time that summer. Smithers saw in him an author whom no one else would publish and both Smitherses enjoyed Wilde's invitations. Mrs. Beardsley strongly disapproved of Wilde, and Aubrey's memories of him were hardly pleasant. When they happened to meet at the Hôtel Sandwich on July 24, however, Beardsley greeted Wilde cordially but left dangling his invitation to dinner. That Beardsley actually went to Berneval to dinner is most unlikely, but he certainly saw Wilde again and allowed him to influence the purchase of an elegant gray hat. At the same time, Aubrey was terrified lest Raffalovich learn about his having anything to do with Wilde. Raffalovich had recently increased his financial help; commencing on July 19, Beardsley received a gift of £10 in cash and £90 in a check each quarter. Because Raffalovich's donations were invariably designated as gifts, they demanded no repayment, and Beardsley had no intention of losing them because of Wilde. Beardsley knew only too well Raffalovich's hostility to Wilde, which had had public expression in Raffalovich's *L'Affaire Oscar*

Wilde. Beardsley knew that well, too. Raffalovich had read it aloud to him and given him a copy in 1895, the year of publication.

Now, with Wilde very visible in Dieppe and often at the Hôtel Sandwich to pick up mail and parcels sent him there, Beardsley decided that he must leave the hotel. Two days after his first encounter with Wilde, Beardsley told Raffalovich that he might leave it at once because "some rather unpleasant people" came to the hotel. Beardsley added, "For other reasons too I fear some undesirable complications may arise if I stay."[12] He made no reference to Wilde, but he had absolved himself, and Mrs. Beardsley rushed around looking for suitable quarters before she went to Brighton. She had no success and Aubrey stayed on at the Sandwich awaiting her return and a visit from Mabel after *Four Little Girls* closed at the Criterion.

The day after Mabel's arrival on August 22, the Beardsleys went from the Hôtel Sandwich to the grander Hôtel des Etrangers in the rue d'Aguado, facing the sea. Beardsley explained their change of address to his "Dearest Brother," Raffalovich, as owing to better food at the second hotel and remarked on how successfully they had moved, how much he had improved, and how much stronger he felt. But Mabel told Blanche that Beardsley was "feeling very tired" and, by doctor's orders, was staying in his room "on account of the nasty north wind."[13] In fact, Beardsley was so tired that he had to forgo meeting Edouard Dujardin and to let Mabel decide whether one of the ten color prints on satin of Aubrey's *Mademoiselle de Maupin* was an "indiscreet present" for Mlle. Olga Caracciolo or whether his *Virgin Mary* was more appropriate.

In the early part of his stay at Dieppe, Beardsley had been too weary, too weak, to work except at rare intervals. Then in August he told Pollitt, "*Mlle de Maupin* occupies my spirit enormously." In mid-August, Beardsley was talking in the future tense about a cover for O'Sullivan's *Houses of Sin,* and he posted it to Smithers in about a week. Also in mid-August, Beardsley told Uzanne about sketches for the Venetian scenes from *Casanova,* but they progressed no further. Only on September 2 could Beardsley describe as "beyond all words" the *Arbuscula,* promised to Heinemann two months earlier but finished in the last days of August. In early September, when Smithers showed him the manuscript of Wilde's *The Ballad of Reading Gaol,* Beardsley promised to make a frontispiece and a week later implied that he was at work on it. But neither Smithers nor Wilde had much faith in Beardsley's promise, made "in a manner," Smithers said, "which immediately convinced me he will never do it."[14] Of course, Beardsley had no intention of providing a drawing for anything by Wilde; but Beardsley was prevented from working by more than expediency. Once or twice in Blanche's studio, he had uselessly tried to draw; and one such effort had ended tragically, as Blanche recorded,

> [Beardsley] had taken a stick of charcoal and sketched on a pastel canvas a conductor, beating time, cutting off poppyheads, the heads of players in the orchestra. In a state of delusion he loudly asserted that this was to be his masterpiece; he nearly tore holes into the canvas and the easel tottered. Suddenly he sank back into an armchair and blood poured from his mouth. "This field of poppies is the field you have sown, it is like an orchestra in which the players take no notice of their conductor. Am I raving?"[15]

Part of a letter which Mabel sent to Blanche on September 2 supports his account. She wrote, "Aubrey is too fragile. Doctor Caron pronounces—but I'd rather not write the word."[16]

ii

Mrs. Beardsley was in a flurry of packing by that date, September 2. She was insistent on leaving Dieppe for Paris and from there going to some place, as yet undetermined, in the south. She knew only too well what Dr. Caron had pronounced about her son and, to add to her gloom, autumn rains had commenced in Dieppe. A few days later when the rain stopped the Beardsleys "stayed" their packing and their "flight to Paris." Aubrey informed Raffalovich and at the same time reported the opinion of two more doctors. Dr. Dupuy, a guest at the hotel, suggested a stay in Paris and a change in diet, more important, he said, than climate. Dr. Phillips, Raffalovich's doctor who had last seen Beardsley in April when they traveled together from London to Paris and who was now on holiday, declared that Beardsley showed "quite a marvellous improvement" and that, if he continued to be careful, he could recover and anticipate a "new life." Dr. Phillips also recommended Paris.

The doctors' prognosis meant nothing, but their recommendations answered the Beardsleys' wishes. Mrs. Beardsley wanted only to move on; each move seemed to allow her an escape from the implications of Aubrey's worsening condition, associated with the place she left. Furthermore, she had decided to find work for herself, coaching some "young fellow" in English; and if the French preferred

Sketch of Aubrey Beardsley by Walter Sickert *(Courtesy of the National Portrait Gallery)*

a "nursery governess," she had no objection to calling herself that. In pursuit of a job, she had asked for help from Douglas Ainslie, poet and translator, whom she knew through Mabel. Mrs. Beardsley thought Paris offered the widest possibilities unless she left her son, and that she refused to do. It was a necessity for her to be with him; the doctor had said "he must not be left," she told Ainslie.[17] As for Aubrey, fully aware of the "thin ice" he had "skated over since March 31," he was relieved to have to travel no farther than Paris.[18] So, on the evening of Tuesday, September 14, the Beardsleys arrived at the Hôtel Foyot, rue Tournon, Paris.

Except in the matter of location, little had changed for the Beardsleys. Mrs. Beardsley could get no job and she had to face the same problems and the ordeal of Paris, although according to Beardsley, Paris was "suiting" her much better this time. Beardsley was cheerful and lively for a few days. He grieved for Dieppe, "the most charming spot on earth,"[19] but Paris and its weather and his room at the Foyot were also charming for a few days. Then he caught cold and soon he began to suffer from neuralgia and despite the "marvellous summer weather" in Paris, he began to feel "quite incapable." Shortly before Raffalovich's second present of £100 arrived, Beardsley complained of being "stoné" and asked Smithers to send him 30s or a couple of pounds. In other words, the same problems persisted and Beardsley's solution to them went unchanged, wherever he might be. He wrote with fulsome thanks for his generosity to Raffalovich and told him about Dr. Dupuy's opinion, an advanced but "quite curable" illness and a long life ahead. He told his "dearest Brother" about the solace of confessing to Père Courbé, the pleasure of seeing Vincent O'Sullivan because he was a Catholic friend, the comfort derived from Raffalovich's prayers and the cheer, from his letters. At first Beardsley's letters to Smithers, too, were reasonably genial, but after little more than a month they changed. The tailor Doré, having had nothing from Beardsley, had got his Paris address from Smithers and again asked to be paid. Beardsley reproached Smithers, emphasizing the worry the tailor provoked. After instructing that most of his books be sold, he then wrote, "I am utterly wretched again nowadays with only the ghost of hope to keep me going." That was written on October 22. Three days later he declared that he was well and enjoying Paris, but on October 27, his entire letter was a complaint: "I am utterly cast down and wretched. I have asked my sister to come and see you and have a talk with you. I must leave Paris. Heaven only knows how things are to be managed."[20]

To separate the true Beardsley from the parts he had created for himself is difficult. Although he admitted to getting "dreadfully nervous, and stupidly worried about little things," Beardsley turned a hopeful side, bolstered by prayer and confession, to Raffalovich and a suffering, plaintive one to Smithers. The urgency for money was real to Beardsley. Those savings covered by his will were a private matter which obviously he was determined to keep private. But with Raffalovich's remittances and at least some payments from Smithers, the need was less pressing than Beardsley implied. Did he push his piety on the one hand, and his pain and distress on the other, a little too plaintively?

Of course his relationship with Smithers was complicated by matters having to do with his work. Certainly Beardsley had done little in Dieppe. Smithers had complained about him to Wilde in early September: "He has got tired already of *Mademoiselle de Maupin* and talks of Casanova instead. It seems hopeless to try and get any connected work out of him of any kind."[21] Beardsley's iridescent interests, his mercurial enthusiasms may have enlarged his stature, but they were beyond Smithers' patience. Needless to say, Beardsley's failure to perform at this time was owing partly to illness. He could not concentrate, and when he worked he was extremely slow. But ill or not, he disliked working to order, as he had demonstrated as long ago as the *Morte Darthur*. He put off doing promised work from loss of interest. He had, for example, owed a *Bathyllus* to Pollitt since March when Pollitt had advanced twenty sovereigns towards the tailor's dun. Yet Beardsley was still evading the obligation to make the picture in mid-September. He had hardly returned to Paris when he wrote to Pollitt, "*Bathylle* must and shall be done before long but just now life is atrociously knotted and I don't settle down readily to pencil and paper."[22] Beardsley also gladly interrupted work on a series to do a single picture. Later that month he spoke of the "wonderful" bookplate he had made for Olive Custance. Furthermore he always had "perfectly marvellous" schemes which he meant to complete in some future time. "The Rhinegold" was still in his thoughts that September, but it was never completed.

Beardsley's failure to complete *Mademoiselle de Maupin*, however, was owing not to his own inconsistency but to Smithers. For a time the friendship between the two men was strained, thanks to this book; and on Beardsley's part it never recaptured the same trust. But anyone as ill as he, is inclined to slough off emotion. And eventually they resolved their difficulties in such a way as to demonstrate consideration for each other and, as far as Smithers knew, understanding and generosity on the part of Beardsley. He had been seduced from *Mademoiselle de Maupin* by Casanova, but by the time he had finished reading "that great and appalling work *The Memoirs of Casanova*"[23] in early October, he no longer wanted to illustrate it. Instead, with the renewed vigor which currently characterized him, he was at work on *Mademoiselle de Maupin*, and on October 14 he sent Smithers three "full page pictures, illustrations for Part I of the Maupin." Smithers had suggested four for each part, but Beardsley objected. "Four drawings," he declared, "would establish a pretty stiff precedent. So let us say *three* for each part." He then listed the three which he proposed for the second part: "1. The party at Mad[me] Javannes 2. Rosette & the bear 3. Rosette & Albert."[24] Apparently, a week later Beardsley changed his mind, because he then sent *The Lady with the Monkey*, a picture which he called a "very good one." In a few days he referred to "four full page drawings for Part I" and said he had abandoned the idea of decorative initial letters.

Smithers, meanwhile, had been evasive about the book, and Beardsley was turning imperious. "The question of *Mlle de Maupin*," he wrote, "now becomes pressing. I shall soon be more than ready for you."[25] His mother encouraged Aubrey's attitude. She thought Smithers took advantage of her son. "Smithers treated him shamefully. He did not pay him and served him very badly," she said later.[26] Beardsley began to suspect Smithers of accepting his drawings under false pretenses and selling or otherwise using them for his own purposes. At that point, Beardsley sent Mabel to talk to Smithers. Aubrey began, too, to have doubts about the entire project. He told Smithers, "I am beginning to wonder whether the *Maupin* can be illustrated without being insufficient or indecent."[27] Still, Beardsley was disturbed by the uncertainties and difficulties of his position. What with his health, his problems with Doré caused most immediately by Smithers, and the suspicion that Smithers had betrayed him on a more serious and personal level, Beardsley was miserable. In a letter to Raffalovich dated October 31, Beardsley explained that he had not written sooner because he had "been so worried and upset" in the past week that he had been unable to write.

The truth was that Smithers did not have the money or the credit to produce *Mademoiselle de Maupin*. The fact that Beardsley wanted it printed in its original French instead of English made the book a commercial risk. Smithers at last admitted his position, and, although Beardsley vowed he would not "shelve" *Mademoiselle de Maupin*, he responded by writing a "less silly" letter "than usual." He advocated the sale of the *Maupin* drawings already in hand and asked Smithers to name some smaller work which could appear complete in the immediate future with "less outlay." Beardsley was eager to produce something very soon.[28] To Mabel, he indicated Smithers' circumstances and lamented the fact that his drawings might "hang about hidden to Doomsday." He only wished he dared offer his drawings to someone else. Since he could not go to London to straighten out his affairs, he determined to get a "set of pictures finished for some respectable English book" and keep them unknown to Smithers for the time being.[29]

Beardsley had suffered far more serious professional setbacks before. Yet this one seemed crucial because he knew that he might not have time to produce drawings for even a short book. Nevertheless he reassured Smithers with this letter of November 6:

> I ask for nothing better than to send you chef d'oeuvres, to have them published soon, printed well, and to *toucher* as often as can be a modest cheque or two. I will send you without fail (DV) within the next two months six drawings for some small and quite possible work.[30]

Whatever his doubts, Beardsley had behaved with good sense and seeming generosity. There was as well a sweet ("adorable," Beardsley would have said) consideration in his attitude toward Smithers. When Will Rothenstein came to Paris that autumn, he said he found Beardsley much changed both in character and outlook. Rothenstein went on,

> All artifice had gone; he was gentle and affectionate. . . . He had found peace . . .; but how rudderless he had been, how vain; and he spoke wistfully of what he would do if more time were allowed him; spoke with regret, too, of many drawings he had done, and of his anxiety to efface the traces of a self that was now no more.[31]

About November 11, when Smithers proposed, as a substitute for *Mademoiselle de Maupin*, Ali Baba, Beardsley agreed and even made a drawing for it. But he already had in view something else to illustrate, Ben Jonson's *Volpone*. By the time he left Paris on November 19, 1897, to go to Menton, he was "making things" for it. "Such a stunning book it will be," he told Pollitt.[32] By the time he had settled into the Hôtel Cosmopolitan at Menton and recovered from a difficult and exhausting train ride which had terrified him with a "sight" of his "own blood," Beardsley was "prepared to develop a new style."[33]

187

If, in Paris, as Beardsley had told Mabel, "nothing but work" amused, in Menton it was his obsession. He wrote about everything else to Raffalovich, telling him about "prospering in . . . wonderful sunshine," about Père Calixte, to whom Beardsley was to make his confessions, and about the "little town . . . so gay and amusing."[34] But to Mabel, and even more to Smithers, Beardsley wrote about his work and little else. "'Ninety-eight will either see my death or chefs d'oeuvre," he said, and added, "Be it the latter."[35] Although in late November *Ali Baba* was still under consideration and Beardsley thought of making a drawing of the forty thieves "all in a row," *Volpone* was his real concern. His aim was to produce something "grand and compelling." At first he was determined to have "strength of mind and opportunity" (by which he meant a January payment from Raffalovich) to finish all the drawings before sending them to Smithers. But Aubrey could not resist describing the first picture, *Volpone Adoring His Treasure*, as "one of the strongest things" he had done and confiding his hopes that those to follow would be "full of force both in conception and treatment."[36] And in no time Beardsley's plans for a small book grew to the elaborate concept outlined to Smithers in a letter of December 4. There Beardsley listed twenty-four drawings, all to be produced by line except the frontispiece, and a design for the cover. In a few days, he posted the design for the cover and one for a prospectus of *Volpone* as well as a "rough idea" for the wording of the prospectus which the publisher was to "improve, amplify, and glorify to any extent."[37] By December 11, an initial "to grace Act I" was "in train" and "adorable." Beardsley's only regret was that he could work no more than three or four hours a day, but he could "carry *Volpone* about" with him "from dawn to dawn, and dream of nothing else."[38]

Within a week, Smithers had shocked Beardsley out of his dream. The publisher was organizing a successor to *The Savoy* to be called "The Peacock." He wanted Beardsley as art editor. Beardsley agreed to make a cover and other drawings on one condition, "that is if it is *quite agreed that Oscar Wilde contributes nothing to the magazine anonymously, pseudonymously or otherwise.*"[39] Once again Wilde loomed as a threat to the gifts from Raffalovich. Beardsley saw in this projected magazine a threat to *Volpone* as well. He feared, he told Smithers, that with the work necessary to bring out a new periodical, *Volpone* would be pushed into the background. His letter, dated December 19, [1897], said about *Volpone*:

Ali Baba in the Wood (Courtesy of Fogg Art Museum, Harvard University and John L. Clark Esq., administrator of the Scofield Thayer Estate)

I beg of you not to allow it to be delayed; it will be an *important book* as you will see from the drawings I am sending you. Its marked departure as illustrative and decorative work from any other arty book published for many years *must create some attention*. I have definitely left behind me all my former methods.[40]

Although Beardsley later wanted "The Peacock" as a Catholic voice, and although eventually it came to nothing, discussion about the makeup of "The Peacock" went on with Beardsley firm in his conviction that they must "give birth to no more little back-boneless babies." On the "literary side" he advocated "the critical element" rather than "impressionistic criticism and poetry, and cheap short storyness." In other words, he disparaged the editorial policies of both Arthur Symons and Henry Harland. As for the "art side," Beardsley anticipated it as a reflection of his own development. His suggestion was that "The Peacock" attack *untiringly and unflinchingly* the Burne-Jones and Morrisian medieval business, and set up a wholesome seventeenth and eighteenth-century standard of what picture making should be."[41]

Plainly Beardsley saw the drawings for *Volpone* as the crown of his achievement. He had forsaken the influences from which his career derived. These pictures, which he feared were to be his last, were also to be his own, a product of what he had learned, shaped by his own intelligence and imagination and sense of beauty with a hand as skillful as ever.

Whether Smithers understood or not, his response to *Volpone* was almost as enthusiastic as Beardsley's. With no prompting, Smithers offered to reproduce in half-tone and thus allow for greater subtlety in Beardsley's drawings. The book was envisioned as a companion to *The Rape*, but Smithers decreed a larger book. At Beardsley's request Vincent O'Sullivan agreed to write a preface and Dowson was editing the text. Weekly payments to Beardsley were again in effect and, much to Beardsley's satisfaction, pictures began to go from Menton to London and proofs and blocks came back for his approval.

None of Beardsley's compulsion to produce one more set of drawings reached Raffalovich. Neither did Beardsley's discarding of his boyish jubilation. His letters to Raffalovich were still addressed to "Dearest Brother" and fulsomely grateful when £100 arrived on December 30. But they were more often superficial, and when they were not they were filled with kind comments on Menton's weather and Menton's "strong English contingent" or with pieties having to do with his own or Raffalovich's prayers and the priests who came to

Initial V for *Ben Jonson His Volpone: or The Foxe (Courtesy of Fogg Art Museum, Harvard University, Grenville L. Winthrop Bequest)*

visit. Raffalovich must have suspected the truth, because Mabel advised Beardsley to write about his work to Raffalovich. Beardsley's reply confessed that he did not like referring to his work in letters to Raffalovich. "He will only scold me," Beardsley went on, "but of course I must if it's really necessary. When I was in Paris I told him I drew a little."[42]

If that necessity existed, it was not fulfilled. Eight days after the letter to Mabel, that is on January 24, 1898, Beardsley wrote his usual amenities to Raffalovich. The only important statement was the opening one, which explained why he had not written sooner: "I have had to rest my arm a little owing to a rather painful attack of rheumatism."[43] Two days before, to Smithers, Aubrey had called it a "beastly attack." Neither statement was true. A "spell of wet weather" had brought on another attack of "congestion of the lungs," and Beardsley had to stay in bed. After January 26, he did not leave his room, and for at least a month he maintained his fiction of rheumatism. On February 21, he repeated it to Mabel. But the next day, to Pollitt, Beardsley made clear his reason for spending three weeks in bed; he told Pollitt about the illness, "It has left me an utter wreck and quite incapable of work. I am simply in an agony of mind over it." Indeed he was. During those weeks in bed, he had managed to do no more than write an imcomplete set of verses called "The Ivory Piece" and read O'Sullivan's "paper" on Ben Jonson, sent him on February 16 from Grantham, where O'Sullivan was visiting. Beardsley knew that his work was done. He stated his grief, intense and inevitable, in the simplest terms: "Such splendid things I had planned out, too."[44]

At the same time, Beardsley told Pollitt, "The dear saints are my only comfort, and give me patience." If they did—and he very much wanted them to—they were reached with difficulty. Beardsley's confessions were frequent and his devotional reading, already extensive, occupied more and more of his time. Now he often asked his mother to "read aloud a few sentences at a time & he meditated on them."[45] Once, after a long night of "anguish," his response to the new day was to ask his mother to recite the *Te Deum*. He kept by him his crucifix and rosary. Yet what he sought eluded him. "I believe," he told Raffalovich, "it is often mere physical exhaustion more than hardness of heart that leaves me so apathetic and extremely uninterested."[46] Beardsley was obviously one of those who, like Flannery O'Connor and Frederick Rolfe, had to struggle for faith every step of the way, but who knew that to be without it was impossible. By now, Beardsley had exchanged piety for devotion. Although he still clung to that sum of money willed to Mabel, he denied everything

192

else, even his work. On March 7, 1898, the day after an extremely severe hemorrhage, Beardsley wrote the oft-quoted letter to Smithers, "I implore you to destroy *all* copies of *Lysistrata* and bad drawings. Show this to Pollitt and conjure him to do same. By all that is holy *all* obscene drawings." To this he added, "In my death agony."[47]

Mabel, who was called to Menton at this time, found Aubrey more and more fervent. She also found him dying. On March 14, Beardsley was given the last rites. Early in the morning of March 16, 1898, under the influence of morphine to ease his breathing, Aubrey Beardsley died. He had told Mabel little more than two months before, "I know how trying it is to give up things."[48] It is to be hoped that the "replacement" he searched for with such diligence proved eternal.

Beardsley's "last sad rites" were held at Menton. After a requiem mass in the cathedral, a procession which included staff and guests from the hotel walked under a cloudless sky to the cemetery high on a hill, where Beardsley was laid to rest with "fragrant roses" in bloom nearby. On May 12 another requiem mass was held at the Jesuit Church, Farm Street, London, with "glorious music," concluding with Chopin's "Funeral March." His father's presence at either service is never mentioned. Two years later, R. Widmer, one of the staff of the hotel in Menton, sent Ellen Beardsley papers which she had inadvertently left behind. An accompanying letter ended with words about Aubrey Beardsley: "His sweetness and his modesty are unforgettable. It is a consolation to see him at rest in the midst of the flowers of our beautiful country."[49]

To lament Aubrey Beardsley's sleep among the flowers with the reflection that life is short and "the craft so long to lerne" is inevitable. To wonder what he might have accomplished had he had more than twenty-five years is irresistible. But such speculation is hardly relevant, and it is certainly futile. Indeed, except for those who loved him, the brevity of Beardsley's life is no cause for complaint. Like so many—Marlowe and Keats are two who come to mind—Aubrey Beardsley outstripped time with his achievement. A few years were enough for his reputation. It would have been only a slight exaggeration had he said, with Achilles, "Short is my date, but deathless my renown."

NOTES

Frequent abbreviations in the notes are ALS for autograph letter signed and TLS for typed letter signed. Names in parentheses are names of the owners of manuscript material cited.

CHAPTER I

1. Cf. Brigid Brophy, *Beardsley and His World*, London, 1976, pp. 11–19; Henry Maas, J. L. Duncan and W. G. Good, "Part I," in Aubrey Beardsley, *The Letters of*, eds. Henry Maas, J. L. Duncan and W. G. Good, Cranbury, New Jersey, 1970, p. 4.
2. Cf. Aubrey Beardsley (hereafter AB) to Vincent Beardsley, [Brighton, Christmas 1878]; AB to Mabel Beardsley, [Hurstpierpoint], October 15, [1879], [? February 27, 1880]; AB to Ellen Beardsley, Hurstpierpoint, [January–February 1880], [February 20, 1880], [ca. March 1880], [March 24, 1880]; AB to G. F. Scotson-Clark, [London, August 9, 1891], in *Letters*, pp. 6, 7, 10, 9, 11, 24.
3. Ellen Beardsley, "Recollections" [autograph record of a conversation with R. A. Walker at Lancaster Gate Terrace, December 23, 1920] (Princeton).
4. Ellen Beardsley, "Recollections"; see also Ellen Beardsley, ALS to Mabel Beardsley, Brighton, December 10, 1904 (Princeton).
5. Mabel Beardsley, "Aubrey Beardsley Aug 21st 1872 March 16 1898" (Princeton).
6. Ellen Beardsley, 'Recollections" (Princeton).
7. Ellen Beardsley, 'Recollections"; Mabel Beardsley, "Aubrey Beardsley" (Princeton).
8. Cf. AB to Ellen Beardsley, Hurstpierpoint, [January–February 1880], ca. July 1880; AB to Mabel Beardsley, Hurstpierpoint [? February 27, 1880], in *Letters*, pp. 9, 12, 10.
9. Cf. A. W. King, "The Art of Aubrey Beardsley With Some Personal Recollections of Him" (Princeton).

10. Mabel Beardsley, "Aubrey Beardsley" (Princeton).
11. Cf. Mabel Beardsley, "Aubrey Beardsley"; Ellen Beardsley, ALS to Mabel Beardsley, Brighton, December 10, [1904] (Princeton).
12. Cf. Mabel Beardsley, "Aubrey Beardsley" (Princeton); Brophy, pp. 30, 27–28.
13. Cf. AB to Lady Henrietta Pelham, [Epsom], February 1 [? 1883], in *Letters*, pp. 13–14; Mabel Beardsley, "Aubrey Beardsley" (Princeton).
14. Mabel Beardsley, "Aubrey Beardsley" (Princeton); cf. Brophy, p. 28.
15. Mabel Beardsley, "Aubrey Beardsley" (Princeton); cf. Brophy, pp. 31–34.
16. Cf. Robert Ross, *Aubrey Beardsley with . . . a Revised Iconography by Aymer Vallance*, London, 1921, p. 12.
17. G. F. Scotson-Clark, "Beardsley's School Days or Early Days Prior to 1893" (Princeton).
18. R. Thurston Hopkins, "Aubrey Beardsley's School Days," *The Bookman*, March 1972, pp. 305–306; cf. Malcolm Easton, *Aubrey and The Dying Lady*, Boston, 1972, pp. 2–3.
19. A. W. King, *An Aubrey Beardsley Lecture*, London, 1924, p. 24.
20. King, *Beardsley Lecture*, p. 25.
21. Hopkins, p. 306. Cf. King, "Beardsley"; Mabel Beardsley, ALS to Leonard Smithers, Hastings, October 3, n.y. (Princeton); Charles B. Cochran, *Secrets of a Showman*, London, 1925, pp. 4–5.
22. AB to King, London, [July 13, 1891], in *Letters*, pp. 22–23; King, "Beardsley" (Princeton).
23. AB to King, London, [July 13, 1891], in *Letters*, p. 23.
24. Cf. Hopkins, p. 305; King, "Beardsley" (Princeton); Cochran, p. 4.
25. Hopkins, p. 307; cf. Cochran, pp. 3–4.
26. Cochran, p. 4.
27. Cochran, p. 7.
28. Scotson-Clark (Princeton).
29. King, *Beardsley Lecture*, p. 27. Cf. Hopkins, pp. 305–307; Cochran, pp. 4–5, 7; Charles B. Cochran, "Aubrey Beardsley at School," *Poster and Art Collector*, August–September 1898, pp. 103, 104.
30. *Past and Present*, June 1885, pp. 45–46.
31. *Brighton Society*, July 9, 1887, and April 14, 1888.
32. *Past and Present*, June 1887, facing p. 48; cf. King, *Beardsley Lecture*, p. 26; Brophy, p. 36; Scotson-Clark (Princeton).

33. *Past and Present*, December 1900, pp. 92–93; cf. Cochran, *Secrets*, p. 4; above, p. 28.
34. Cf. Mabel Beardsley, "Aubrey Beardsley"; Scotson-Clark (Princeton); Brophy, pp. 37–38; Cochran, "Beardsley at School," pp. 102–103; Hopkins, p. 307; King, *Beardsley Lecture*, p. 28.

CHAPTER II

1. Cf. A. W. King, ALS to John Lane, Aysgarth, Yorkshire, December 4, 1920 (Princeton).
2. Cf. AB to A. W. King, London, [January 1889], in Aubrey Beardsley, *The Letters of*, eds. Henry Maas, J. L. Duncan and W. G. Good, Cranbury, New Jersey, 1970, pp. 15–16; Brigid Brophy, *Beardsley and His World*, London, 1976, pp. 43, 41; Malcolm Easton, *Aubrey and the Dying Lady*, Boston, 1972, p. 4; Brian Reade, *Beardsley*, London, 1967, p. 311, *n* 10; A. W. King, "The Art of Aubrey Beardsley with Some Personal Recollections of Him" (Princeton).
3. Cf. AB to King, London, [January 1889], in *Letters*, p. 16.
4. G. F. Scotson-Clark, "Beardsley's School Days or Early Days Prior to 1893" (Princeton); AB to King, London, [January 1889], in *Letters*, p. 16.
5. Cf. AB to Miss Felton, Brighton, [ca. 1887], in *Letters*, pp. 14–15.
6. Dulau & Co., Catalogue 165, *Books from the Library of John Lane and Other Books of the Eighteen-Nineties*, London, 1930, pp. 8–9 (George F. Sims); Mabel Beardsley, ALS to Leonard Smithers, Hastings, October 3, [1900] (Princeton).
7. In the collection of W. G. Good.
8. (Princeton).
9. AB to King, London, January 4, 1890, in *Letters*, p. 18.
10. Ellen Beardsley, ALS to Mabel Beardsley, Brighton, December 10, [1904] (Princeton); AB to King, London, January 4, 1890, in *Letters*, p. 18.
11. William Rothenstein, *Men and Memories Recollections of 1872–1900*, London, 1931, p. 185.
12. Cf. Holbrook Jackson, "Aubrey Beardsley," in *The Eighteen Nineties*, London, 1931, pp. 95, 97.
13. *Tit-Bits*, January 4, 1890, p. 203.
14. AB to King, London, [July 13, 1891], in *Letters*, p. 23.
15. AB to King, London, [July 13, 1891], in *Letters*, p. 21.

16. AB to King, London, [July 13, 1891], in *Letters*, p. 24; cf. above, p. 34.
17. Scotson-Clark (Princeton); Mabel Beardsley, "Aubrey Beardsley Aug 21st 1872 March 16 1898" (Princeton).
18. Reade, *Beardsley*, p. 312, *n* 17.
19. Cf. AB to G. F. Scotson-Clark, London, [July 1891], in *Letters*, pp. 19–20; see below, pp. 108–112.
20. Brophy, p. 41.
21. Cf. Scotson-Clark (Princeton).
22. See above, p. 32.
23. Stanley Weintraub, *Beardsley A Biography*, New York, 1967, p. 36.
24. Malcolm Easton, "Aubrey Beardsley and Julian Sampson an Unrecorded Friendship," *Apollo*, January 1967, pp. 66–67.
25. Cf. AB to Scotson-Clark, London, [July 1891], in *Letters*, pp. 19–20.
26. Mabel Beardsley, "Aubrey Beardsley" (Princeton).
27. Netta Syrett, *The Sheltering Tree*, London, 1939, pp. 68, 69.
28. AB to King, London, [July 13, 1891], in *Letters*, p. 23.
29. George Moore, "Hugh Monfert," in *Single Strictness*, New York, 1922, pp. 144–145.
30. Mabel Beardsley, "Aubrey Beardsley" (Princeton).
31. Mabel Beardsley stated that Oscar Wilde was not present. AB's account of the same incident spoke of "the Oscar Wildes" and has always been interpreted to include Oscar Wilde. Both accounts are suspect. For another version of Beardsley's first meeting with Wilde, see below, p. 82.
32. Mabel Beardsley, "Aubrey Beardsley" (Princeton); Rothenstein, pp. 257–258.
33. AB to King, London, [July 13, 1891], in *Letters*, p. 22.
34. Alfred Gurney, ALS to Ellen Beardsley, London, November 1891 (University College, London).
35. AB to Scotson-Clark, London, August 9, 1891; cf. AB to King, London, [August 10, 1891], in *Letters*, pp. 24, 26.
36. Scotson-Clark (Princeton); AB to King, London, October 13, 1891, in *Letters*, p. 30.
37. AB to Scotson-Clark, London, [July 1891]; cf. AB to King, London, [July 13, 1891], in *Letters*, pp. 23–24, 22.
38. AB to Scotson-Clark, London, August 9, 1891; cf. AB to King, London, [August 10, 1891]; AB to Scotson-Clark, London, [July 1891], in *Letters*, pp. 25, 24, 26.
39. Ellen Beardsley, ALS to Mabel Beardsley, Brighton, December 10, [1904]; Ellen Beardsley, "Recollections" [autograph record

of a conversation with R. A. Walker at Lancaster Gate Terrace, December 23, 1920], (Princeton). Cf. Easton, *Dying Lady*, pp. 113–114.

40. Cf. AB to King, London, [December 7, 1891], [July 1891], in *Letters*, pp. 31, 23.
41. Cf. AB to King, London, [August 10, 1891], [August 25, 1891], [December 7, 1891], [December 25, 1891], in *Letters*, pp. 26, 28, 30, 31; King, "Aubrey Beardsley" (Princeton); *The Bee*, November 1891, frontispiece.
42. Cf. AB to King, London, [January 5, 1892], in *Letters*, p. 32.
43. Elizabeth Robins Pennell, *Nights*, Philadelphia, 1916, p. 139.
44. Henry Harland, ALS to Edmund Clarence Stedman, London, December 24, 1890. Cf. Harland, ALS to Stedman, Upper Bangor, August 16, 1889; [Paris], November 18, [1892]; New York, July 13, 1889 (Columbia). See below, pp. 104–105.
45. Harland to Stedman, London, December 24, 1890 (Columbia).
46. AB to King, London, January 4, 1890, in *Letters*, p. 18; cf. above, p. 33.
47. Cf. Weintraub, p. 31; Aymer Vallance, "The Invention of Aubrey Beardsley," *Magazine of Art*, May 1898, pp. 362, 363; Robert Ross, *Aubrey Beardsley*, London, 1921, p. 20.
48. Vallance, p. 363.
49. Cf. Vallance, p. 363. The effort to interest William Morris in Beardsley has been mistakenly attributed to Oscar Wilde; cf. Oscar Wilde, *The Letters of*, ed. Rupert Hart-Davis, London, 1962, p. 290 *n* 3.
50. Ross, pp. 15–16. Cf. Rothenstein, p. 136; Katherine Lyon Mix, *A Study in Yellow*, Lawrence, Kansas, 1960, p. 44; Osbert Burdett, *The Beardsley Period*, New York, 1969, p. 71.
51. AB to King, London, [December 25, 1891]; AB to Robert Ross, London, [May 14, 1892]; AB to Scotson-Clark, London, [August 1891], in *Letters*, pp. 32, 33, 27.
52. AB to Scotson-Clark, London, [ca. February 15, 1893]; AB to E. J. Marshall, London, [Autumn 1892]; cf. AB to King, London, December 9, [1892] in *Letters*, pp. 43, 33–34, 37.
53. Cf. Ross, p. 44; Weintraub, p. 40.
54. AB to King, London, December 9, [1892], in *Letters*, p. 37; cf. W. G. Good, "Aubrey Beardsley A Reappraisal," *The Saturday Book*, ed. John Hadfield, Boston, 1965, p. 65.
55. AB to Scotson-Clark, London, [ca. February 15, 1892] in *Letters*, p. 43; Ross, pp. 38–39. Cf. Arthur Symons, *Aubrey Beardsley*, London, 1971, p. 14; Good, p. 74; King, "Aubrey Beardsley" (Princeton).

56. Cf. AB to Scotson-Clark, London, [ca. September 1891]; AB to Marshall, London, [Autumn 1892], in *Letters*, pp. 29, 35; Easton, *Dying Lady*, pp. 169–170.
57. Cf. Symons, pp. 13–14; Netta Syrett, *Strange Marriage*, New York, 1931, p. 93; Robert Speaight, *William Rothenstein*, London, 1962, p. 47.
58. Cf. Syrett, *Sheltering Tree*, p. 74.
59. Grant Richards, *Memories of a Misspent Youth*, London, 1932, p. 182; cf. Speaight, p. 38.
60. Rothenstein, p. 135; cf. Speaight, p. 35.
61. Rothenstein, p. 187.
62. AB to Scotson-Clark, London, [ca. February 15, 1893]; cf. AB to Marshall, London, [Autumn 1892]; AB to King, London, December 9, [1892], in *Letters*, pp. 43–44, 34, 37.
63. AB to Scotson-Clark, London, [ca. February 15, 1893], in *Letters*, p. 44.
64. Syrett, *Strange Marriage*, p. 93.
65. Weintraub, p. 37; Haldane Macfall, *Aubrey Beardsley*, London, 1928, p. 26; J. M. Dent, *The Memoirs of*, London, 1928, pp. 68–69.
66. AB to Scotson-Clark, London, [ca. February 15, 1893], in *Letters*, p. 44.
67. AB to Marshall, London, [Autumn 1892], in *Letters*, p. 34. The device is often given an erotic interpretation.
68. Cf. AB to Scotson-Clark, London, [ca. February 15, 1893], in *Letters*, p. 44. Dent dates his first meeting with Beardsley after returning from the United States, a journey which commenced in January 1893. Cf Dent, pp. 67, 59.
69. Weintraub, p. 39; see below, pp. 76–77.
70. AB to Scotson-Clark, London, [ca. February 15, 1893], in *Letters*, p. 44; Macfall, p. 31.
71. Lewis Hind, *Naphtali*, New York, 1926, p. 62; cf. Vallance, pp. 366–367; Ella Hepworth Dixon, *As I Knew Them*, London, 1930, p. 120.
72. Cf. Hind, p. 62; Macfall, pp. 34–35; Weintraub, pp. 41–42.
73. W. B. Yeats, "Introduction," in *Oxford Book of Modern Verse*, London, 1936, p. x; cf. Rupert Croft-Cooke, *Feasting With Panthers*, London, 1967, pp. 254–257.
74. Joseph Pennell, *Aubrey Beardsley and Other Men of the Nineties*, Philadelphia, 1924, pp. 21–23; D. S. MacColl, "Aubrey Beardsley," in *A Beardsley Miscellany*, ed. R. A. Walker, London, 1949, pp. 21–22.

75. Gertrude Atherton, *Adventures of a Novelist*, New York, 1932, p. 249; MacColl, p. 22.

76. Scotson-Clark (Princeton).

77. E. R. Pennell, *Nights*, p. 180; Edward Strangman, ALS to Ellen Beardsley, London, March 17, 1898 (Princeton); Ross, pp. 18–19; Jacques-Emile Blanche, ALS to Mabel Beardsley Wright, Offranville, August 17, 1912 (Princeton); Ellen Beardsley, "Recollections" (Princeton).

CHAPTER III

1. Oscar Wilde, *The Letters of*, ed. Rupert Hart-Davis, London, 1962, p. 348 *n* 3. See below, p. 82.

2. Cf. *The Studio*, April 1893, pp. 10, 15–19.

3. Cf. Joseph Pennell, "A New Illustrator: Aubrey Beardsley," *The Studio*, April 1893, pp. 14, 17–18.

4. Cf. AB, *A Book of Fifty Drawings*, London, 1896, p. [v]; AB to G. F. Scotson-Clark, London, [ca. February 15, 1893], in Aubrey Beardsley, *The Letters of*, eds. Henry Maas, J. L. Duncan and W. G. Good, Cranbury, New Jersey, 1970, p. 44.

5. AB to E. J. Marshall, London, [Autumn 1892], in *Letters*, p. 34.

6. AB to A. W. King, London, December 9, [1892], in *Letters*, p. 38.

7. AB to Marshall, London, [Autumn 1892], in *Letters*, p. 34.

8. Cf. Brian Reade, *Beardsley*, London, 1967, p. 314 *n* 37.

9. Cf. Frances Burney, *Evelina*, ed. Brimley Johnson, London, 1893; Reade, p. 314 *nn* 35 and 36.

10. Charles Lamb and Douglas Jerrold, *Bon-Mots of*, ed. Walter Jerrold, London, 1893, p. 39. See above, p. 22.

11. Sidney Smith and R. Brinsley Sheridan, *Bon-Mots of*, ed. Walter Jerrold, London, 1893, p. 58. See above, p. 63.

12. Smith and Sheridan, pp. 41, 177; Lamb and Jerrold, p. 13. Cf. Reade, p. 326 *n* 176.

13. Samuel Foote and Theodore Hooke, *Bon-Mots of*, ed. Walter Jerrold, London, 1894, p. 113; cf. Félicien Rops, *Dix Eaux-Fortes pour illustrer Les Diaboliques de J. Barbey d'Aurevilly*, Paris, n. d.

14. AB to Scotson-Clark, London, [ca. February 15, 1893], in *Letters*, p. 43.

15. Robert Ross, *Aubrey Beardsley*, London, 1921, p. 35. Cf. William

Rothenstein, *Men and Memories Recollections of 1872–1900*, London, 1931, p. 134; Aubrey Beardsley, *The Uncollected Works of*, London, 1925, Plates 61 and 62.

16. William Butler Yeats, *Memoirs*, ed. Denis Donoghue, New York, 1973, p. 92 *n* 2; Ellen Beardsley, "Recollections" [autograph record of a conversation with R. A. Walker at Lancaster Gate Terrace, December 23, 1920] (Princeton); Osbert Burdett, *The Beardsley Period*, New York, 1969, p. 37.

17. William Butler Yeats, "A Symbolic Artist and the Coming of Symbolic Art," *The Dome*, N. S., December 1898, p. 234.

18. A[lice] M[eynell], "Exhibitions," *The Pall Mall Gazette*, November 2, 1904, p. 10.

19. AB to Marshall, London, [Autumn 1892], in *Letters*, p. 34.

20. AB to Scotson-Clark, London, [ca. February 15, 1893], in *Letters*, p. 44.

21. Cf. *Lucian's True History*, tr. Francis Hickes, illustrated . . ., London, 1894, facing pp. 23 and 209.

22. Cf. *The Pall Mall Budget*, February 9, 1893, p. 154; C. Lewis Hind, "Introduction," in *The Uncollected Works of Aubrey Beardsley*, London, 1925, p. x.

23. Cf. *The Pall Mall Budget*, February 6, 1893, pp. 188, 190; February 23, 1893, p. 281.

24. AB to Scotson-Clark, London, [ca. February 15, 1893]; AB to King, London, December 9, [1892], in *Letters*, pp. 44–45, 38.

25. Cf. AB to T. Dove Keighley, London, [ca. March 1893], in *Letters*, p. 46.

26. Cf. Edgar Jepson, *Memories of a Victorian*, London, 1933, pp. 285, 255, 216.

27. AB to Keighley, Paris, May 18, 1893, in *Letters*, p. 49.

28. Elizabeth Robins Pennell, *Nights*, Philadelphia, 1916, pp. 260–261.

29. Joseph Pennell, *Aubrey Beardsley and Other Men of the Nineties*, Philadelphia, 1924, pp. 32–33.

30. Rothenstein, p. 134; cf. Katherine L. Mix, *A Study in Yellow*, Lawrence, Kansas, 1960, p. 30.

31. Mabel Beardsley, ALS to Douglas Ainslie, London, n. d. (Princeton). Cf. AB to William Rothenstein, London, [ca. November 1893], in *Letters*, p. 56; Rothenstein, p. 134.

32. Rothenstein, pp. 125, 131–134 *et passim*.

33. Cf. Robert Speaight, *William Rothenstein*, London, 1962, pp. 54–55; David Cecil, *Max*, Boston, 1965, pp. 65, 93, 95 *et passim*; Rothenstein, p. 144.

34. Cecil, p. 95.

35. Max Beerbohm to Douglas Cleverdon, [Rapallo], July 21, 1939, in *Max & Will*, ed. Mary M. Lago and Karl Beckson, Cambridge, Massachusetts, 1975, p. 154 *n* 2; cf. pp. 153–154.
36. Cf. Cecil, pp. 3–4.
37. Rothenstein, p. 186.
38. Rothenstein, p. 275.
39. Aymer Vallance, "The Invention of Aubrey Beardsley," *The Magazine of Art*, May 1898, p. 366.
40. AB to Robert Ross, London, [ca. August 1893], in *Letters*, p. 51.
41. Ellen Beardsley to Robert Ross, London, September 29, 1893, in *Robert Ross: Friend of Friends*, ed. Margery Ross, London, 1952, pp. 27–28.
42. Cf. J. W. Dent, *The Memoirs of*, London, 1928, pp. 69–70.
43. Ross, p. 32; Vallance, p. 36.
44. Cf. AB to Scotson-Clark, London, [ca. February 15, 1893], in *Letters*, p. 45.
45. Cf. AB to F. H. Evans, London, [ca. June 1893]; AB to Ross, London, [late August 1893], in *Letters*, pp. 50, 52.
46. George Moore to Jacques-Emile Blanche, Beeding, Sussex, December 13, [1887], in Jacques-Emile Blanche, *Portraits of a Lifetime*, New York, 1938, p. 293.
47. AB to Ross, London, [August 1893], in *Letters*, p. 51.
48. Cf. Arthur Symons, *Aubrey Beardsley*, London, 1971, pp. 18–20; Holbrook Jackson, "Aubrey Beardsley," in *The Eighteen Nineties*, London, 1931, pp. 94–95.
49. AB to Ross, London, November 1893, in *Letters*, p. 58.
50. See above, p. 26.
51. Cf. AB to Rothenstein, London, [September 1893], in *Letters*, pp. 54, 52 *n* 4; Max Beerbohm to Reggie Turner, London, [September 21, 1893], [September 22, 1893], in Max Beerbohm, *Letters to Reggie Turner*, ed. Rupert Hart-Davis, London, 1964, pp. 66, 69.
52. AB to King, London, [ca. November 27, 1893], in *Letters*, p. 57.
53. Cf. AB to Stone and Kimball, London, January 2, [1894]; AB to Ross, London, November [1893], in *Letters*, pp. 60, 58.
54. Elkin Mathews, ALS to Dr. T. N. Brushfield, London, February 7, 1895 (Reading).
55. Gertrude Atherton, *Adventures of a Novelist*, New York, 1932, p. 312; cf. Lionel Johnson, ALS to Louise Imogene Guiney, [London], August 8, 1897 (Princeton).
56. Frederick Rolfe, *Nicholas Crabbe*, New York, 1958, p. 23.
57. Oscar Wilde to John Lane, Babbacombe Cliff, [February 1893], in *Letters of*, pp. 327–328 and *n* 1.

58. Cf. Vallance, p. 366; John Lane, TLS to Ellen Beardsley, London, August 23, 1920 (Princeton); AB to King, London, December 9, [1892], in *Letters*, p. 38.

59. See above, p. 63.

60. AB to King, London, [July 13, 1891], in *Letters*, p. 22; cf. above, p. 40.

61. Cf. Rothenstein, pp. 187, 133–134, 173–174; Mabel Beardsley, "Aubrey Beardsley Aug 21st 1872 March 16 1898" (Princeton).

62. Beerbohm to Turner, London, [August 19, 1893], in *Letters to Reggie Turner*, pp. 52–53.

63. Beerbohm to Turner, London, [August 19, 1893], in *Letters to Reggie Turner*, p. 52; Beerbohm to William Rothenstein, London, [September 1893], in *Max & Will*, p. 21; Rothenstein, p. 174.

64. Brian Reade, *Aubrey Beardsley*, London, 1966, p. 6; cf. Alan Bird, *The Plays of Oscar Wilde*, London, 1977, p. 54 *et passim*.

65. AB to Ross, London, [late June 1893], in *Letters*, p. 50.

66. Cf. Reade, *Beardsley*, p. 337 *n* 286.

67. Cf. [Lewis Hind], "Bookman's Memories," *The Christian Science Monitor*, May 17, 1921, p. 3.

68. See above, pp. 66–67.

69. Cf. James G. Nelson, *The Early Nineties A View from the Bodley Head*, Cambridge, Massachusetts, 1971, pp. 242–243; Reade, *Beardsley*, p. 336 *n* 283; Epifanio San Juan, Jr., *The Art of Oscar Wilde*, Princeton, New Jersey, 1967, pp. 119–120; Jackson, "Aubrey Beardsley," p. 102.

70. AB to Rothenstein, London, [September 1893]; AB to Ross, London, [late August 1893], in *Letters*, pp. 54, 52.

71. AB to Ross, London, November [1893], in *Letters*, p. 58.

72. Cf. Wilde to Lane, London, [ca. December 1893], in *Letters of*, p. 348; Frances Winwar, *Oscar Wilde and the Yellow Nineties*, New York, 1940, p. 214; Rothenstein, p. 184; Mabel Beardsley, "Aubrey Beardsley"; cf. Reade, *Aubrey Beardsley*, p. 7.

73. Oscar Wilde to Lord Alfred Douglas, Reading, [January–March 1897], in *Letters of*, p. 432.

74. *Idem*.

75. AB to Ross, London, November [1893]; cf. AB to John Lane, London, November 4, [1893], in *Letters*, pp. 58, 56.

76. Cf. AB to Ross, London, November [1893], in *Letters*, p. 58.

77. AB to King, London, [September 27, 1893]; AB to Rothenstein, London, [September 1893], in *Letters*, pp. 55, 54.

78. Cf. Stanley Weintraub, *Beardsley A Biography*, New York, 1967, p. 70.

79. A. W. King, "The Art of Aubrey Beardsley with Some Personal Recollections of Him" (Princeton); "New Publication," *The Studio*, February 15, 1894, p. 184; cf. Nelson, p. 242; Rothenstein, p. 136.

CHAPTER IV

1. Cf. Alexander Michaelson [pseudonym of André Raffalovich], "Aubrey Beardsley," *Blackfriars*, October 1928, p. 610.
2. Cf. William Rothenstein, *Men and Memories Recollections of 1872–1900*, London, 1931, p. 181.
3. Brian Reade, *Beardsley*, London, 1967, p. 343 *n* 333.
4. AB to Robert Ross, London, November [1893], in *Aubrey Beardsley, The Letters of*, eds. Henry Maas, J. L. Duncan and W. G. Good, Cranbury, New Jersey, 1970, p. 58.
5. Katherine L. Mix, *A Study in Yellow*, Lawrence, Kansas, 1960, p. 68.
6. Mabel Beardsley, "Aubrey Beardsley Aug 21st 1872 March 16 1898" (Princeton); Mix, p. 168.
7. Cf. *Robert Ross Friend of Friends*, ed. Margery Ross, London, 1952, pp. 34–35.
8. Cf. Mix, pp. 64–67; James G. Nelson, *The Early Nineties A View from the Bodley Head*, Cambridge, Massachusetts, 1971, pp. 298–299; D. S. MacColl, "Sketch of Aubrey Beardsley," in *A Beardsley Miscellany*, ed. R. A. Walker, London, 1949, p. 23; *et al.*
9. Henry James, "Preface," *The Novels and Tales*, 26 vols., New York, 1922, XIV, v–vi.
10. Evelyn Sharp, ["The Yellow Book Crowd"], *Manchester Guardian*, January 19, 1924, p. 7; Henry Harland, ALS to Edmund Stedman, [Paris], May 22, 1893; November 18, [1892] (Columbia).
11. Mix, p. 69.
12. Max Beerbohm to Reggie Turner, London, [January 1, 1894], in *Max Beerbohm, Letters to Reggie Turner*, ed. Rupert Hart-Davis, London, 1964, p. 88; AB to Ross, London, [ca. January 3, 1894], in *Letters*, p. 61.
13. AB to Ada Leverson, London, [? January 4, 1894]; AB to Ross, London, [ca. January 3, 1894], in *Letters*, pp. 62, 61; AB to Oscar Wilde, n. p., 1894 in Dulau & Co. Catalogue 165, *Books from the Library of John Lane and Other Books of the Eighteen-*

Nineties, London, 1930, p. 95 (George F. Sims); Mix, p. 70; Arthur Waugh, *One Man's Road*, London, 1931, p. 250.

14. James, "Preface," p. v.
15. James, "Preface," p. vi; cf. H. Montgomery Hyde, *Henry James at Home*, New York, 1969, p. 53.
16. AB to Wilde, n. p., 1894 in Dulau Catalogue 165, p. 95 (George F. Sims); cf. AB to Ross, London, [ca. January 3, 1894], [January 1894], in *Letters*, pp. 61, 62.
17. Reade, *Beardsley*, p. 344 *n* 343.
18. AB to John Lane, London, [March 1894], in *Letters*, pp. 65–66.
19. Beerbohm, *Letters to Reggie Turner*, p. 92.
20. John Lane, "Publisher's Note," in Aubrey Beardsley, *Under the Hill*, London, 1904, p. viii.
21. Oscar Wilde to Mrs. Patrick Campbell, London, [February 1894], in Oscar Wilde, *The Letters of*, ed. Rupert Hart-Davis, London, 1962, p. 353.
22. "What the Yellow Book Is to Be," *The Sketch*, April 11, 1894, pp. 557–558.
23. Elkin Mathews, ALS to Dr. T. N. Brushfield, London, February 7, 1895 (Reading); Elizabeth Robins Pennell, *Nights*, Philadelphia, 1916, pp. 186–187.
24. Netta Syrett, *Strange Marriage*, New York, 1931, p. 255.
25. Oscar Wilde to Lord Alfred Douglas, London, [ca. April 16, 1894], in *Letters of*, p. 354; cf. Violet Wyndham, *The Sphinx and Her Circle*, London, 1963, p. 44.
26. Quoted by Hyde in *James at Home*, p. 53.
27. The *Weekly Irish Times*, April 28, 1894, p. 4.
28. The *World*, April 25, 1894, p. 26.
29. London *Times*, April 20, 1894, p. 3. *The Pall Mall Budget's* comment has not been located but is derived from Stanley Weintraub, *Beardsley*, New York, 1967, p. 107. Cf. *The Daily Chronicle*, April 16, 1894, p. 3.
30. *The Yellow Book*, July 1894, pp. 281–284.
31. AB to editor of *The Daily Chronicle*, March 1, 1894, in *Letters*, p. 65; cf. *Daily Chronicle*, March 1, 1894, p. 3; March 2, 1894, p. 3.
32. In *Letters*, pp. 68, 67; cf. *Pall Mall Budget*, May 3, 1894, p. 20; *Daily Chronicle*, April 16, 1894, p.3; April 17, 1894, p. 3.
33. Rothenstein, p. 187.
34. William Butler Yeats, *Memoirs*, ed. Denis Donoghue, New York, 1973, p. 90.
35. Michaelson, "Aubrey Beardsley," p. 610.
36. Syrett, *Strange Marriage*, p. 93.

37. Wyndham, p. 72.
38. Cf. Gertrude Atherton, *Adventures of a Novelist*, New York, 1932, pp. 248–249; Rothenstein, p. 213; Mix, p. 31.
39. Arthur Symons, *Aubrey Beardsley*, London, 1971, p. 12; cf. Robert Ross, *Aubrey Beardsley*, 1921, p. 30.
40. Cf. Ella D'Arcy, "Yellow Book Celebrities" (Martyr Worthy Collection); Sharp, p. 7.
41. Mabel Beardsley, "Aubrey Beardsley" (Princeton).
42. Cf. G. F. Scotson-Clark, "Beardsley's School Days or Early Days Prior to 1893" (Princeton); AB to G. F. Scotson-Clark, London [ca. February 15, 1893], in *Letters*, p. 45.
43. Cf. Frank Harris, *My Life and Loves* . . ., 2 vols., London, 1961, I, p. 15; Malcolm Easton, *Aubrey and the Dying Lady*, Boston, 1972, pp. 250–251; *The Yellow Book*, January 1895, Pl. 367; Reade, *Beardsley*, p. 347 *n* 366.
44. Alexander Michaelson [André Raffalovich], "Aubrey Beardsley's Sister," *Blackfriars*, November 1928, p. 669; Scotson-Clark (Princeton); cf. below, p. 109.
45. Cf. Michaelson, "Beardsley's Sister," p. 671; Easton, pp. 182–183, 175–178.
46. Cf. Yeats, *Memoirs*, pp. 94 *n* 1, 92; Henry Maas, J. L. Duncan, and W. G. Good, "Part II 1893–1895," in *Letters of Aubrey Beardsley*, Cranbury, New Jersey, 1970, p. 42 *n* 1; W. G. Good, "Aubrey Beardsley A Reappraisal," in *The Saturday Book*, ed. John Hadfield, Boston, 1965, p. 71; Easton, pp. 76–77.
47. AB to F. H. Evans, London, [June 27, 1894], in *Letters*, pp. 71–72; Mabel Beardsley, "Aubrey Beardsley" (Princeton).
48. The manuscript is the property of the Philip H. & A. S. W. Rosenbach Foundation, Philadelphia. The manuscript bears the title "Under the Hill." An expurgated version of the first day and early morning of the second was published with that title in the first two numbers of *The Savoy*, 1896 (see below, pp. 138, 158), and republished by John Lane in 1904. An inaccurate version of the entire manuscript was published privately with the title *The Story of Venus and Tannhäuser* in 1907. Subsequent publications have been no more exact. Quotations here are from the manuscript.
49. In *Letters*, p. 53.
50. Cf. AB to Evans, Malvern [November 1894] in *Letters*, p. 79.
51. Aymer Vallance, "The Invention of Aubrey Beardsley," *The Magazine of Art*, May 1898, p. 368.
52. Cf. Ellen Beardsley, "Recollections" [autograph record of a

conversation with R. A. Walker at Lancaster Gate Terrace, December 23, 1920] (Princeton).

53. July 1894, pp. 53–55; cf. AB to Maurice Baring, London, [April 1894], in *Letters*, p. 67 *n* 2.
54. Henry Harland to John Lane, London, various dates in Dulau & Co. Catalogue 165, p. 97 (George F. Sims).
55. Cf. [John Lane], "Notes" (Princeton).
56. AB to Evans, London, [June 27, 1894], in *Letters*, p. 72.
57. AB to Evans, Haslemere, Surrey, [August 20, 1894], in *Letters*, p. 73; cf. AB, ALS to Mrs. Williams, London, n. d. (Princeton).
58. See above, p. 105.
59. Cf. Ellen Beardsley to Robert Ross, London, September 5, [1894], in *Robert Ross*, p. 26.
60. Cf. AB to Evans, London,, [June 27, 1894], [early October 1894], in *Letters*, pp. 72, 75; above, p. 72; AB, ALS to Edmund Gosse, London, September 5, [1894] (Kenneth A. Lohf).
61. Cf. AB to T. Fisher Unwin, London, [ca. November 12, 1894]; AB to Evans, London, [early October 1894], [November 1894], in *Letters*, pp. 78, 75, 79.
62. In *Letters*, pp. 78–79.
63. Edmund Gosse, ALS to unnamed correspondent, London, June 19, 1902 (Princeton); cf. AB to Gosse, London, February 20, [1895], in *Letters*, p. 64 and *n* 2. Beardsley's letter in *Letters* is mistakenly dated 1894.
64. Ada Leverson, "Reminiscences by" in Violet Wyndham, *The Sphinx and Her Circle*, London, 1963, pp. 109–115; cf. H. Montgomery Hyde, *Oscar Wilde*, New York, 1975, p. 222.
65. Cf. AB to C. D. R. Williamson, London, [ca. March 1895]; AB to Leverson, London, [April], in *Letters*, pp. 81, 82; Brandon Thomas, ALS to Mabel Beardsley, London, September 16, 1903 (Princeton); AB, ALS to Ada Leverson, London, n. d. (Kenneth A. Lohf).
66. Cf. Reade, *Beardsley*, pp. 348 *nn* 371–374, 351 *n* 394.
67. (Princeton).
68. Cf. Ella D'Arcy to John Lane, London, April 20, [1895], in Karl Beckson, "Ella D'Arcy, Aubrey Beardsley, and the Crisis at 'The Yellow Book': A New Letter," *Notes and Queries*, August 1979, pp. 331–333. At least one copy of the first state of the fifth number of *The Yellow Book* survived, once the property of Edmund Gosse and now at Princeton University. Cf. E[d-mund] G[osse], "The Suppressed Yellow Book" (Princeton); Lane, "Notes" (Princeton); William Watson, "Hymn to the Sea," *The Yellow Book*, April 1895, [11]–13.

CHAPTER V

1. AB to Ada Leverson, London, [April 1895], in Aubrey Beardsley, *The Letters of*, eds. Henry Maas, J. L. Duncan and W. G. Good, Cranbury, New Jersey, 1970, p. 82. (The reference is to two letters.)
2. Cf. Henry Harland to Edmund Gosse, Paris, [May 5, 1895], in *Transatlantic Dialogue*, eds. Paul F. Mattheisen and Michael Millgate, Austin, Texas, 1965, p. 231.
3. *Idem*; cf. Karl Beckson, *Henry Harland His Life and Work*, London, 1978, pp. 80–81.
4. Harland to Gosse, Paris [May 5, 1895], in *Transatlantic Dialogue*, p. 231; Arthur Waugh, *One Man's Road*, London, 1931, p. 251; Katherine L. Mix, *A Study in Yellow*, Lawrence, Kansas, 1960, p. 145. Cf. Beckson, pp. 22–24; Henry Harland, ALS to S. S. McClure, New York, November 25, 1885; Henry Harland, ALS to Edmund C. Stedman, New York, November 26, [1885], (Columbia).
5. AB to William Rothenstein, London, [September 1893] in *Letters*, p. 54; AB to John Lane, Dieppe, [ca. July 1895], in Dulau & Co. Catalogue 165, *Books from the Library of John Lane and Other Books of the Eighteen-Nineties*, London, 1930, p. 100 (George F. Sims); AB to Frederic Chapman, London, [April–May 1895], in *Letters*, p. 83 *n* 4.
6. Cf. AB to André Raffalovich, London, May 11, 1895, in *Letters*, p. 84.
7. Harland to Gosse, Paris, [May 5, 1895], in *Transatlantic Dialogue*, p. 231.
8. Cf. Brocard Sewell, *Footnote to the Nineties*, London, 1968, pp. 18, 24–27 *et passim*; Ella Hepworth Dixon, *As I Knew Them*, London, 1930, p. 133.
9. Alexander Michaelson [André Raffalovich], "Oscar Wilde," *Blackfriars*, November 1927, pp. 697–698, 701.
10. Alexander Michaelson [André Raffalovich], "Aubrey Beardsley," *Blackfriars*, October 1928, p. 609.
11. Michaelson, "Beardsley," pp. 609–610.
12. Michaelson, "Beardsley," p. 610; Alexander Michaelson [André Raffalovich], "Aubrey Beardsley's Sister," *Blackfriars*, November 1928, p. 671; cf. Beckson, p. 81.
13. Cf. AB to Raffalovich, London, [ca. May 1895], [December 1895], May 15, 1895, in *Letters*, pp. 84, 109, 85 *et passim*.
14. Cf. Brian Reade, *Beardsley*, London, 1967, p. 350 *n* 386; AB to Raffalovich, London, [ca. May 29, 1895], [May 25, 1895], [ca.

May 16, 1895], [December 1895], in *Letters*, pp. 103, 86, 87, 89 *et passim*.

15. Michaelson, "Beardsley," p. 610.
16. Cf. Maynard Solomon, *Beethoven*, New York, 1977, pp. 20–24; Sigmund Freud, "Family Romances" in *Collected Papers*, ed. James Strachey, 5 vols., New York, 1959, V, 74–76.
17. AB to Clara Savile Clarke, London, [ca. July 1895]; AB to Raffalovich, London, [June 2, 1895], in *Letters*, pp. 93 *n* 2, 90.
18. Cf. Reade, *Beardsley*, pp. 341–342 *nn* 323–324. The canvas is the property of the Tate Gallery.
19. William Rothenstein, *Men and Memories Recollections of 1872–1900*, London, 1931, p. 186.
20. *The Savoy*, January 1896, pp. [64]–66.
21. Cf. Arthur Symons, "Bohemian Chelsea" in *Mes Souvenirs*, Chapelle-Réanville, [1929]; Nancy Cunard, *These Were The Hours*, ed. Hugh Ford, Carbondale, Illinois, 1969, pp. 71–72; William Butler Yeats, *Memoirs*, ed. Denis Donoghue, New York, 1973, pp., 97–98, 87; Michael Levy, *The Case of Walter Pater*, London, 1978, pp. 170, 171, 186.
22. Arthur Symons, *Aubrey Beardsley*, London, 1966, p. 7; cf. Mabel Beardsley, "Aubrey Beardsley Aug 21st 1872 March 16th 1898" (Princeton).
23. Arthur Symons to Herbert Horne, [London, August, 23, 1893], in Ian Fletcher, "Symons and Beardsley," *Times Literary Supplement*, August 18, 1966, p. 743; conversation with Brian Reade. Cf. Symons, *Beardsley*, p. 7.
24. Symons, *Beardsley*, p. 7.
25. AB to Raffalovich, [London], June 14, 1895, in *Letters*, p. 91.
26. Symons, *Beardsley*, p. 7.
27. Cf. Ellen Beardsley, "Recollections" [autograph record of a conversation with R. A. Walker at Lancaster Gate Terrace, December 23, 1920], (Princeton); Rothenstein, p. 245; Robert Speaight, *William Rothenstein*, London, 1962, p. 94; Yeats, *Memoirs*, p. 94 *et al*.
28. George F. Sims, "Leonard Smithers," *The London Magazine*, September 1956, pp. 33–34, 40; cf. Malcolm Pinhorn, "The Career and Ancestry of Leonard Smithers," *Blackmansbury*, August 1964, p. 5.
29. Rothenstein, p. 244; Max Beerbohm and Robert Ross quoted in Oscar Wilde, *The Letters of*, ed. Rupert Hart-Davis, London, 1962, p. 627 *n* 2; Charles Cochran, *Secrets of a Showman*, London, 1925, p. 88; Yeats, *Memoirs*, p. 91. Cf. Speaight, pp. 94–95; Sims, pp. 33, 39; Jack Smithers, *The Early Life and Vicissitudes of*, London, 1939, p. 30.

30. Oscar Wilde to Reggie Turner, [Dieppe], August 10, 1897; Oscar Wilde to Robert Ross, Posillipo, [October 7 and 8, 1897], in *Letters of*, pp. 630–631, 654.
31. [Aleister Crowley], *Aceldama*, London, 1898, p. 25; Arthur Symons, "Dieppe 1895," *The Savoy*, January 1896, p. 101; see above, pp. 111–112.
32. In *Letters*, p. 97.
33. Symons, *Beardsley*, p. 7; AB to Rothenstein, Dieppe, [ca. July 1895], in *Letters*, p. 94 *n* 1.
34. Symons, "Dieppe," p. 101.
35. AB to Rothenstein, Dieppe, [August 1895], in *Letters*, pp. 93–94. The editors of Beardsley's *Letters* date this letter "[circa July 1895]."
36. Symons, *Beardsley*, p. 8.
37. In Rothenstein, p. 249; cf. Symons, *Beardsley*, pp. 10, 11. Symons states that AB was at work on "The Three Musicians."
38. Cf. Jacques-Emile Blanche, *Portraits of a Lifetime*, New York, 1938, pp. 93–94, 51–52; Symons, *Beardsley*, p. 8.
39. Cf. Charles Conder to William Rothenstein, Dieppe, n. d., in Rothenstein, p. 250; Symons, *Beardsley*, pp. 7–8.
40. AB to Leonard Smithers, London, [? August 19, 1895], in *Letters*, pp. 97–98.
41. Cf. AB to Ada Leverson, London, [1895], in Paul C. Richards, Catalogue 96. See below, pp. 157–158.
42. Cf. AB to Rothenstein, London, [late August 1895]; AB to Smithers, London, [? late August 1895], in *Letters*, pp. 99, 98.
43. AB to H. C. J. Pollitt, London, [October 1895], in *Letters*, p. 102.
44. AB, holograph receipt signed Ed Bella, [London], August 13, 1895 (Princeton). The receipt for this apparently unknown drawing reads, "Received of Aubrey Beardsley a coloured drawing to be used as cover for number of 'La Plume.'"
45. (Princeton); see also AB to Raffalovich, Boscombe, [November 28, 1896], in *Letters*, p. 217.
46. Conversation with W. G. Good; cf. AB to Raffalovich, [May 28, 1895], [June 2, 1895], June 5, 1895, in *Letters*, pp. 88, 90.
47. AB to Lane, Dieppe, [late September 1895], in Dulau Catalogue 165, p. 100 (George F. Sims); AB to Smithers, Dieppe, [late September 1895], in *Letters*, p. 99. A part of a sentence in the letter to Lane appears in *Letters*, p. 94, where it is dated "[circa July 1895]"; internal evidence in the complete letter indicates that the date given here is the correct one.
48. Cf. AB to Pollitt, London, [October 1895]; AB to Smithers, Dieppe, [late September 1895], in *Letters*, pp. 102, 101.
49. AB to Smithers, London, [ca. November 10, 1895], in *Letters*, p.

104. Cf. Reade, *Beardsley*, p. 351 *nn* 394–395.

50. Cf. Grant Richards, *Author Hunting*, London, 1960, pp. 34–35 *n* 1; Reade, *Beardsley*, p. 354 *n* 414; Edgar Jepson, *Memories of a Victorian*, London, 1933, pp. 286–287; Ernest Dowson to Arthur Moore, [Paris, ca. December 13, 1895], [ca. January 12, 1896], in Ernest Dowson, *The Letters of*, eds. Desmond Flower and Henry Maas, Cranbury, New Jersey, 1967, pp. 331, 339.

51. "An Apostle of the Grotesque," *The Sketch*, April 10, 1895, p. 562; Jack Smithers, pp. 28, 39; Rothenstein, p. 245.

52. Timothy D'Arch Smith, *Love in Earnest*, London, 1970, p. 96; cf. above, p. 142; below, p. 162.

53. Cf. AB to A. W. King, London, [December 9, 1895]; AB to Smithers, London, [November 1895], [November 7, 1895], in *Letters*, pp. 107, 106, 105, 103 *et passim*.

54. Dowson to Moore, Paris, [December 22 and 27, 1895], in *Letters of*, p. 336.

55. Cf. Symons' autograph corrections on a *Savoy* prospectus with the Pierrot cover; Leonard Smithers, ALS to Edgar Jepson, London, November 8, 1895 (Benkovitz).

56. *The Star*, January 20, 1896, p. 1; *Punch*, January 25, 1896, p. 46; *The Sunday Times*, January 26, 1896, p. 6.

57. Yeats, *Memoirs*, p. 91; *The National Observer*, November 9, 1895, p. 725.

58. AB to William Heinemann, London, [January 1896], in *Letters*, p. 111.

59. AB to Raffalovich, London, [December 1895–January 1896], in *Letters*, p. 110; Henry Maas, J. L. Duncan and W. G. Good, "Part III 1895–1896," in *Letters of Aubrey Beardsley*, Cranbury, New Jersey, 1970, p. 96; Symons, *Beardsley*, pp. 29–30; Edmund Gosse, ALS to [? John Lane], London, June 19, 1902 (Princeton).

60. Dowson to Henry Davray, Pont-Aven [ca. March 13, 1896]; cf. Dowson to Samuel Smith, [Pont-Aven, ca. March 24, 1896], in *Letters of*, pp. 345, 351; AB to Raffalovich, London, [? January 26, 1896], in *Letters*, p. 114.

61. Cf. Reade, *Beardsley*, p. 352, *nn* 404–413; A. W. King, "The Art of Aubrey Beardsley with Some Personal Recollections of Him" (Princeton); Edmund Gosse, ALS to AB, London, May 16, 1896 (Princeton); Joseph Pennell, *Aubrey Beardsley and Other Men of the Nineties*, Philadelphia, 1924, p. 42; AB to Mabel Beardsley, Paris, [ca. March 12, 1896]; AB to Smithers, Paris, [ca. March 10, 1896], [ca. March 9, 1896], [? March 7, 1896], [February–March 1896], in *Letters*, pp. 118, 117, 115–116;

Dowson to Moore, Pont-Aven, [ca. February 20, 1896]; Dowson to Herbert Horne, Pont-Aven, March 19, 1896 in *Letters of*, pp. 343, 347.

62. Cf. AB to Smithers, Brussels, [ca. March 24, 1896], [March 26, 1896], [ca. April 10, 1896]; AB to Mabel Beardsley, Paris, [ca. March 12, 1896], in *Letters*, pp. 119, 120, 124, 118; Dowson to Davray, Pont-Aven, [ca. April 24, 1896], in *Letters of*, p. 355.

CHAPTER VI

1. AB to Leonard Smithers, Brussels, [ca. April 10, 1896]; cf. AB to Smithers, Brussels, [April 8, 1896], [April 20, 1896], [April 26, 1896], [April 28, 1896], in Aubrey Beardsley, *The Letters of*, eds. Henry Maas, J. L. Duncan and W. G. Good, Cranbury, New Jersey, 1970, pp. 124, 123, 125, 126, 127 *et passim*.

2. Cf. AB to Smithers, Brussels, [April 28, 1896], [April 10, 1896], [April 8, 1896], [April 6, 1896], in *Letters*, pp. 127, 124, 123, 122.

3. In *Letters*, p. 124.

4. Cf. AB to Smithers, Brussels, [ca. April 20, 1896], [April 26, 1896], [May 2, 1896], [March 24, 1896], [April 1, 1896], [April 8, 1896], in *Letters*, pp. 125, 126, 129, 119, 121, 123 *et passim*.

5. Cf. AB to Smithers, Brussels, [May 3, 1896], [May 2, 1896], [April 28, 1896], in *Letters*, pp. 130, 129, 127.

6. Edmund Gosse, ALS to AB, London, May 16, 1896 (Princeton); AB to André Raffalovich, London, [May 5,1896]; cf. AB to Robert Ross, London, [May 6, 1896], in *Letters*, pp. 130, 131–132.

7. Ernest Dowson to Leonard Smithers, Pont-Aven, [ca. May 25, 1896], in Ernest Dowson, *The Letters of*, eds. Desmond Flower and Henry Maas, Cranbury, New Jersey, 1967, p. 363; cf. AB to John Gray, London, May 1896, in *Letters*, p. 133.

8. AB to H. C. J. Pollitt, Crowborough, [June 7, 1896], in *Letters*, p. 136.

9. Brian Reade, *Beardsley*, London, 1967, p. 360 *nn* 460–466.

10. Cf. AB to Smithers, Epsom, [June 29, 1896], in *Letters*, p. 139.

11. AB to Smithers, Epsom, [July 3, 1896], [ca. July 10, 1896], [June 30, 1896]; AB to Raffalovich, Epsom, [July 15, 1896], in *Letters*, pp. 140, 141, 143, 139 *n* 2, 144.

12. CF. AB to Smithers, [Epsom, ca. July 11, 1896], in *Letters*, p. 143.

13. Cf. below, p. 185; AB, "Last Will and Testament" [holograph], Epsom, July 17, 1896 (Reading).

14. AB to Smithers, [Epsom, July 29, 1896], in *Letters*, p. 147.
15. AB to Smithers, Boscombe, [ca. September 20, 1896], in *Letters*, p. 168.
16. AB to Smithers, Boscombe, [September 17, 1896], [August 14, 1896], in *Letters*, pp. 166, 151.
17. AB to Smithers, Boscombe, [August 18, 1896], in *Letters*, p. 152.
18. J. M. Dent, ALS to Ellen Beardsley, London, September 21, [1896] (Princeton); AB to Smithers, Boscombe, [October 4, 1896]; cf. AB to F. H. Evans, Boscombe, [October 4, 1896], in *Letters*, pp. 177, 178.
19. AB to Smithers, Boscombe, [September 11, 1896]; cf. AB to Smithers, Boscombe, [ca. August 27, 1896], [August 18, 1896], [September 4, 1896], [ca. September 8, 1896], [September 17, 1896], [August 21, 1896], in *Letters*, pp. 156, 152, 159, 161, 166, 154.
20. AB to Smithers, Boscombe, [September 26, 1896], in *Letters*, p. 171.
21. AB to Smithers, [Boscombe, ca. August 31, 1896], in *Letters*, p. 157.
22. AB to Ross, Boscombe, [November 1896], in *Letters*, p. 212.
23. AB to Smithers, Boscombe, [December 13, 1896], in *Letters*, p. 226; Ellen Beardsley to Robert Ross, Boscombe, December 10, 1896, in Aubrey Beardsley, *The Letters of*, eds. Henry Maas, J. L. Duncan and W. G. Good, Cranbury, New Jersey, 1970, p. 224 *n* 1.
24. AB to Raffalovich, Boscombe, December 20, 1896, in *Letters*, p. 228.
25. AB to Smithers, Boscombe, [September 18, 1896], in *Letters*, p. 167.
26. AB to Smithers, Boscombe, [October 7, 1896], in *Letters*, p. 181.
27. AB to Smithers, Boscombe, [ca. November 6, 1896], in *Letters*, p. 198.
28. AB to Raffalovich, Boscombe, [ca. December 22, 1896], in *Letters*, p. 229.
29. Oscar Wilde to More Adey, Reading, [September 25, 1896], in Oscar Wilde, *The Letters of*, ed. Rupert Hart-Davis, London, 1962, p. 410.
30. Ellen Beardsley, "Recollections" [autograph record of a conversation with R. A. Walker at Lancaster Gate Terrace, December 23, 1920] (Princeton).
31. (Princeton).
32. In *Letters*, p. 236.

33. AB to Raffalovich, Boscombe, [ca. December 22, 1896], in *Letters*, p. 230.
34. AB to Max Beerbohm, Boscombe, [ca. December 27, 1896], in *Letters*, p. 235.
35. AB to Smithers, [Boscombe, January 13, 1897], in *Letters*, p. 242.
36. Olive Custance, Holograph Diaries, May 30, 1894–February 17, 1899 (Berg).
37. AB to Smithers, Bournemouth, February 11, 1897; Boscombe, [January 7, 1897]; cf. AB to Smithers, Paris, [September 23, 1897]; Bournemouth, [March 5, 1897], in *Letters*, pp. 250, 240, 371, 267.
38. AB to Raffalovich, Bournemouth, [March 26, 1897], in *Letters*, p. 285.
39. AB to Pollitt, Bournemouth, [March 24, 1897], in *Letters*, p. 284.
40. AB to Smithers, Bournemouth, [March 7, 1897]; AB to Raffalovich, Bournemouth, [March 24, 1897], [March 7, 1897], in *Letters*, pp. 269, 283, 268.
41. Hugh Trevor-Roper, *Hermit of Peking*, New York, 1977, p. 296 *n*.
42. Cf. Brocard Sewell, *Footnote to the Nineties*, London, 1963, pp. 38, 5, 7.
43. Ellen Beardsley, "Recollections" (Princeton).
44. AB to Smithers, Boscombe, [September 24, 1896], in *Letters*, p. 170.
45. AB to Raffalovich, Bournemouth, [January 30, 1897], in *Letters*, p. 244.
46. AB to Raffalovich, Bournemouth, [? February 11, 1897], in *Letters*, pp. 249–250.
47. AB to Raffalovich, Bournemouth, [February 25, 1897], in *Letters*, p. 259.
48. AB to Raffalovich, Bournemouth, [February 28, 1897], [February 26, 1897]; AB to Smithers, Bournemouth, [February 22, 1897], in *Letters*, pp. 260–261, 259, 255.
49. AB to Smithers, Bournemouth, [March 3, 1897], in *Letters*, p. 264.
50. AB to Raffalovich, Bournemouth, [March 30, 1897], in *Letters*, p. 287.
51. Arthur Symons, *Aubrey Beardsley*, London, 1971, p. 11.
52. In *Letters*, p. 286.
53. Symons, *Beardsley*, p. 11.
54. Ellen Beardsley, ALS to Mabel Beardsley, Brighton, December 10, [1904] (Princeton).
55. AB to John Gray, Bournemouth, [April 3, 1897]; cf. AB to

Raffalovich, Bournemouth, [March 30, 1897], in *Letters*, pp. 293, 287.

56. In *Letters*, p. 291.

CHAPTER VII

1. AB to Leonard Smithers, Bournemouth, [April 3 and 4, 1897], in Aubrey Beardsley, *The Letters of*, eds. Henry Maas, J. L. Duncan and W. G. Good, Cranbury, New Jersey, 1970, p. 293.
2. AB to Mabel Beardsley, Paris, [April 10, 1897], in *Letters*, p. 297.
3. AB to Smithers, Paris, [April 10, 1897], in *Letters*, p. 298.
4. AB to Mabel Beardsley, Paris, [April 26, 1897], in *Letters*, p. 308.
5. AB to André Raffalovich, Paris, [May 15, 1897], in *Letters*, p. 318.
6. AB to Raffalovich, St. Germain, [May 25, 1897], in *Letters*, p. 325.
7. AB to Smithers, St. Germain, [May 31, 1897], in *Letters*, p. 328.
8. AB to Smithers, St. Germain, [June 11, 1897], in *Letters*, pp. 334–335.
9. AB to Raffalovich, Dieppe, [July 13, 1897], in *Letters*, p. 346.
10. Jacques-Emile Blanche, *Portraits of a Lifetime*, New York, 1938, p. 91.
11. AB to Raffalovich, Dieppe, July 26, [1897], in *Letters*, p. 351.
12. AB to Raffalovich, Dieppe, July 26, [1897], in *Letters*, pp. 351–352.
13. Mabel Beardsley to Jacques-Emile Blanche, Dieppe, August 22, [1897], in Jacques-Emile Blanche, *Portraits of a Lifetime*, New York, 1938, pp. 95–96. Blanche dated the letter 1895, an obvious impossibility.
14. Leonard Smithers to Oscar Wilde, n. p., September 2, 1897, in Aubrey Beardsley, *The Letters of*, Eds. Henry Maas, J. L. Duncan and W. G. Good, Cranbury, New Jersey, 1970, p. 366 *n* 1.
15. Blanche, p. 97.
16. Blanche, p. 96.
17. Ellen Beardsley, ALS to Douglas Ainslie, Dieppe, September 11, [1897] (Princeton).
18. AB to Raffalovich, Paris, [September 15, 1897], in *Letters*, p. 368.
19. AB to H. C. J. Pollitt, Paris, [September 16, 1897], in *Letters*, p. 369.

20. In *Letters*, pp. 382, 380; cf. p. 381.
21. Smithers to Wilde, n. p., September 2, 1897, in Beardsley, *Letters*, p. 366 *n* 1.
22. AB to Pollitt, Paris, [September 16,1897], in *Letters*, p. 370; see above, pp. 171–172.
23. AB to Raffalovich, Paris, October 3, 1897, in *Letters*, p. 376.
24. AB, ALS to Leonard Smithers, Paris, October 14, [1897] (Martyr Worthy Collection). Cf. *Letters*, p. 379, where part of this letter is printed with the supposititious date "[circa October 18, 1897]".
25. AB to Smithers, Paris, [? October 25, 1897], in *Letters*, p. 382.
26. Ellen Beardsley, "Recollections" [autograph record of a conversation with R. A. Walker at Lancaster Gate Terrace, December 23, 1920] (Princeton).
27. AB to Smithers, Paris, October 28, [1897], in *Letters*, p. 382.
28. AB to Smithers, Paris, November 2, 1897, in *Letters*, pp. 384–385.
29. AB to Mabel Beardsley, Paris,, [ca. November 10, 1897], in *Letters*, p. 389.
30. In *Letters*, p. 388.
31. William Rothenstein, *Men and Memories Recollections of 1872–1900*, London, 1931, p. 317.
32. AB to Pollitt, Paris, [November 18, 1897], in *Letters*, p. 392.
33. AB to Smithers, [Menton, ca. November 1897]; cf. AB to Pollitt, Menton, [November 22, 1897], in *Letters*, pp. 397, 396.
34. AB to Raffalovich, Menton, November 29, [1897], in *Letters*, p. 398.
35. AB to Smithers, Menton, [December 3, 1897], in *Letters*, p. 400.
36. AB to Smithers, Menton, Nogember 29, [1897], in *Letters*, p. 399.
37. AB to Smithers, Menton, [ca. December 9, 1897]; cf. AB to Smithers, Menton, December 8, [1897], in *Letters*, pp. 404, 403. Several rough drafts of the prospectus in holograph are dated January 1898 (Princeton).
38. AB to Pollitt, Menton, December 11, [1897], in *Letters*, p. 405.
39. AB to Smithers, Menton, December 19, [1897], in *Letters*, p. 409.
40. In *Letters*, p. 409.
41. AB to Smithers, Menton, December 26, [1897], in *Letters*, p. 413.
42. AB to Mabel Beardsley, Menton, January 16, [1898], in *Letters*, p. 426.
43. In *Letters*, p. 428.
44. AB to Pollitt, Menton, [February 22, 1898], in *Letters*, p. 436. Cf. [AB], "The Ivory Piece," [holograph MS] (Princeton).

45. Ellen Beardsley to Mabel Beardsley, Brighton, December 10, [1904] (Princeton).
46. AB to Raffalovich, Menton, February 27, [1898], in *Letters*, p. 438.
47. In *Letters*, p. 439.
48. AB to Mabel Beardsley, Menton, January 10, 1898, in *Letters*, p. 421.
49. R. Widmer, ALS to Ellen Beardsley, Menton, April 9, 1900 (Princeton). This letter is written in French.

INDEX

art works (*cont.*)
Sentimental Education, A, 95
Siegfried, 53, 63
Slippers of Cinderella, The, 115
Tannhäuser, 36
Toilet of Salome, The, 84
Tristan and Isolde, 160
Triumph of Joan of Arc, The, 47
Virgin Mary, 181
Volpone Adoring His Treasure, 188
Wagnerites, The, 72, 116
Woman in White, The, 161
literary works:
"Art of the Hoarding, The," 112
"Ballad of a Barber, The," 141,
157–158, 159, 160
"Brown Study, A," 34, 35
"Celestial Lover, The," 171
"Comedy of the Rhinegold, The," 166, 185
"Ivory Piece, The," 192
"Jolly Masher, The," 31
"Lights Are Shining . . . , The," 42
"Race for Wealth, A," 34
"Ride on an Omnibus, A," 27
"Story of a Confession Album, A," 34
"Three Musicians, The," 132, 138, 148
Under the Hill, 138, 148, 151, 157–158,
159, 160–161, 166; see also Venus and
Tannhäuser
"Valiant, The," 27
Venus and Tannhäuser, 106, 108, 111,
112, 115, 136, 137, 138, 141, 142,
158, 168
"Very Free (Library) Reading with
Apologies to W. S. Gilbert, A," 27
Beardsley, Ellen Agnus Pitt (Mrs. Vincent),
17, 18, 19, 21, 22, 23, 37, 41, 42, 53,
60, 64, 66, 73, 76, 91, 115, 141, 158,
161, 162, 164, 166, 173, 174, 175,
177, 178–179, 180, 181, 182, 184,
186, 193
Beardsley, Mabel, 15, 17, 18, 19, 22, 23, 25,
27, 31, 34, 38, 40, 41, 42, 46, 51, 54,
60, 64, 66, 68, 73, 82, 84, 91, 102,
104, 105, 106, 108, 118, 120, 123,
126, 127, 128, 131, 133, 141, 152,
153, 157, 158, 159, 161, 164, 172,
181, 182, 184, 186, 188, 192, 193
Beardsley, Vincent Paul, 17, 18, 19, 22, 37,
51, 54, 64, 73, 115, 131, 141
Beardsleys, The, 15, 97, *et passim*
Bearne, Father David, 174
Becket, 68
Bee, The, 43
Beerbohm, Julius, 76
Beerbohm, Max, 16, 73, 74, 76, 78, 83, 91,
92, 95–96, 97, 98, 100, 102, 104, 116,

118, 134, 138, 148, 150, 169, 170
Beethoven, Ludwig van, 131
Bell, R. Anning, 96
Bergson, Henri, 126
Bernard, Claude, 126
Bernhardt, Sarah, 35, 126
Besant, Walter, 45
Betty, Mrs. Kemyss, 23
"Bilious Boot, The," 98
Blackburn, Vernon, 57
Blackburn Technical Institute, 43
Blake, William, 36
Blanche, Jacques-Emile, 60, 137, 138, 150,
152, 178, 179, 180, 181, 182
Bodley Head, The, 90, 97, 102, 122, 123,
125, 142
Bon-Mots, 65, 66, 67, 84, 168
Bonnard, Pierre, 89
Book of Bargains, A (O'Sullivan), 166
Book of Love, The, 73
Bosie, see Douglas, Lord Alfred
Boudin, Philomène, 79
Bourchier, Arthur, 166
Brangwyn, 63
Brighton Grammar School, 23, 24, 25, 27,
28, 31, 50
Brighton Grammar School Old Boys Associa-
tion, 34
Brighton Society, 27
British Barbarians, The (Allen), 142
British Broadcasting Company, 74
Brough, "Lal," 26
Brown, Ford Madox, 35, 38
Brown, Frederick, 41, 42, 43, 68, 91
Bruntons, The, 128
Bryces, The Annan, 128
Burne-Jones, Sir Edward, 16, 35–36, 38, 40,
41, 42, 43, 46, 48, 50, 51, 53, 54, 57,
60, 61, 63, 168, 190
Burne-Jones, Mrs. (Lady), 40
Butcher, Miss, 98
Byng, H. S., 150

Café Royal, 16, 70, 74, 102
Caird, Mona, 45
Calixte, Père, 188
Cambridge A.B.C., 112
Cambridge Theatre of Varieties, The, 31, 35
Cameron, H. H., 164
Campbell, Mrs. Patrick, 15, 16, 96, 98, 100
Caracciolo, Duchesse, 137
Caracciolo, Olga Alberta, 137, 181
Caracciolos, The, 179
Caran d'Ache, 89
Carlyle, Thomas, 19
"Carmen CI" (Catullus), 166
Caron, Dr., 182

220

221

223